The Cockney Who Sold the Alps

Albert Smith and the Ascent of Mont Blanc

ALAN MCNEE

Victorian Secrets 2015

Published by Victorian Secrets Limited
32 Hanover Terrace
Brighton BN2 9SN

www.victoriansecrets.co.uk

The Cockney Who Sold the Alps: Albert Smith and the Ascent of Mont Blanc
First published 2015

Composition and design by Catherine Pope
Cover image shows the Mer de Glace. Original image held by the Library of
Congress, Washington DC.

A catalogue record for this book is available from the British Library.

ISBN 978-1-906469-52-8

For Jack McNee
1930-2009

CONTENTS

INTRODUCTION

---•◆•---

All the world knows Mr. Albert Smith. Charles Dickens, 1857

Albert Smith is the most famous Victorian nobody has ever heard of. During his lifetime, he was a household name – arguably one of the most famous people in Victorian Britain. Today Smith is almost entirely forgotten. Even the physical evidence of his existence is scarce.

Walking along the south side of Piccadilly on virtually any afternoon or evening during the 1850s, the passer-by would have had to squeeze past a crush of carriages and pedestrians outside the Egyptian Hall, an ornate building that stood diagonally opposite the Burlington Arcade. The Egyptian Hall had already been one of the most popular venues in London, hosting a range of exotic exhibitions and performances, before it became the site of Albert Smith's greatest triumph. Smith gave 2,000 performances there of his *Ascent of Mont Blanc* show, creating a sensation comparable in scale and influence to the Great Exhibition of 1851. The Hall was demolished in the early twentieth century, and nowadays the passer-by would be unlikely to notice the building called Egyptian House that stands on its site, home to an unremarkable group of tenants: hedge funds, professional services firms, and upmarket property letting agencies.[1] The only vaguely exotic inhabitant in the present century is the London bureau of the Egyptian State Tourist Office, presumably renting space there because of the building's name.

Less than a mile to the north-east of the former Egyptian Hall stands 14 Percy Street, just off Tottenham Court Road. A blue heritage plaque commemorates the poet Coventry Patmore (best known for his sentimental paean to Victorian womanhood, *The Angel in the House*) who lived here for a year in the 1860s. Another blue plaque honours the actor Charles Laughton, who lived next door at number 15 from 1928 to 1931. No plaque marks the fact that Albert Smith called 14 Percy Street home throughout the 1840s, and also lived at number 12 for two years in the 1850s. Nor is there any memorial to Smith in his birthplace, the town of Chertsey in Surrey. In Brompton Cemetery, the great Victorian graveyard in west London where Smith was buried, his grave lies untended and overgrown, barely visible from the path a few feet away.

Smith's novels, journalism, and travel writing are now virtually unread, and few people have heard of his Egyptian Hall show, or the other performances that built his reputation. This obscurity set in remarkably quickly after his death in

1860; by 1891 his friend Edmund Yates had declined a proposal from the publisher George Bentley to write his biography, on the grounds that few people had any interest in Smith.[2]

Smith's reputation may have waned fast, but what a reputation it had been. Doctor, journalist, comic performer, raconteur, novelist, traveller, showman, playwright, and inveterate self-publicist, Albert Smith's multifarious talents were outstripped only by his boundless self-belief and his huge personality. Smith was an early contributor to *Punch* and to numerous other periodicals, and a writer of successful plays and pantomimes. As well as being a best-selling writer of fiction, who achieved the rare feat of making a comfortable living by his pen, he was also a prolific journalist who broke with the convention of anonymity by insisting on signing all his articles. He numbered Dickens, Thackeray, William Howard Russell, Edwin Landseer, and Phineas T. Barnum among his social circle, and in later life he mixed with royalty. He was a minor player in controversies of the age such as the Garrick Club scandal and the row over Dickens's affair with Ellen Ternan. By his early thirties he had been robbed by highwaymen in Italy, narrowly escaped death in a hot air ballooning accident, and dodged arrest in Paris during the June Days Uprising of 1848. He became one of the original members of the Alpine Club, adapted Dickens's work for the stage, and married into the renowned Keeley acting dynasty. When George Eliot published her first fiction, *Scenes of Clerical Life*, in book form in 1858, she asked her publishers to send complimentary copies to a select group that included Dickens, Thackeray, Tennyson, Jane Carlyle, James Anthony Froude... and Albert Smith.[3]

The more one digs into Smith's extraordinary life, the more his connections to the major figures and developments of the Victorian age emerge, and the more Queen Victoria's description of him in her diary as 'inimitable' rings true. Not everyone admired Smith. Douglas Jerrold, one of Smith's colleagues on *Punch*, remarked that Smith's habit of signing his articles with the initials A.S. represented only two-thirds of the truth.[4] Jerrold echoed the opinions of many who found Smith bumptious and vulgar, and were irritated by his tireless self-promotion and thrusting ambition. But many others in the restless, entrepreneurial world of Victorian Britain saw in Smith the model of the self-made man: energetic, imaginative, and a bold risk-taker who extracted the maximum benefit from his considerable God-given talents.

If Smith had never gone near Mont Blanc, his life would have been remarkable enough. But, as his first biographer wrote of him, 'If existence may be expressed in terms of music, then his life was a melody to which the great white mountain added a counterpoint, swelling until it became the dominant theme.'[5] Smith climbed Mont Blanc in 1851, fulfilling a long-held ambition. The following year he staged his show about the ascent at the Egyptian Hall and, in the words of *The Times*, 'Mont Blanc mania' ensued. Smith's Mont Blanc show had a profound impact on British attitudes to the Alps, and helped to bring about the growth of mass participation in mountain tourism.

Smith was by no means the first person to climb Mont Blanc. However the highest mountain in the Alps, at 4,810m (15,781ft), had been ascended fewer than forty times since the first successful attempt in 1786. That represented an average of less than one ascent each year, and the feat was still rare enough that it was heralded by cannons fired in celebration when climbers returned safely to the valley. In the five years after Smith's ascent, the mountain was climbed eighty-eight times, a rise in frequency that can be attributed largely to the publicity he created.[6]

'Probably no event in England has awakened so keen an interest in the Alps as the entertainment which the late Albert Smith gave in the Egyptian Hall', wrote the mountaineers C. D. Cunningham and W. De W. Abney in the late 1880s, and in the decade after Smith's death it was widely acknowledged that he had been deeply influential in the growth of Alpine mountaineering and tourism.[7] Smith came along at just the right historical moment, when peace on Continental Europe, the growth of the railway network, and rising middle-class affluence were all making foreign travel a realistic option for the kind of people who comprised his audience at the Egyptian Hall. For decades before Smith, the Alps (and mountains in general) had been wrapped up in the images and assumptions of Romantic literature, and for centuries before that they had simply been blank spaces on the map, objects of dread and even disgust. After Smith, the Alps – and later the domestic mountain landscapes of Britain – would become the venue for a new form of active physical engagement, a trend that would eventually give rise to the multi-million pound outdoor clothing and activities industry of the present day. Albert Smith was by no means the only cause of this change in perspective, but he was certainly an important catalyst for it.

Albert Smith's story, then, is not simply a cautionary tale about the fleeting nature of fame and celebrity – although the contrast between his present-day obscurity and the fame of his lifetime means it could serve as such a tale. It is also a story about social class, about the role of visual display and exhibition culture, and about the opening up of the Alps as what one later writer would call a 'playground' for the aspiring middle classes of Victorian Britain.[8] By selling his audience an image of the Alps that it found appealing, aspirational, and potentially accessible, and by couching this appeal in the right combination of showmanship and educational content, Smith reinvented the Alps for a new generation of visitors.

1: GARDENS OF EARTHLY DELIGHTS

*A man gets no attention paid to him in society if he only talks about
Derwentwater or Snowdon, whereas he commands an audience directly if he
alludes to Zurich or Vesuvius.* Albert Smith, *Gavarni in London* (1849)

Early on the morning of 5 March, 1856, a couple of months short of his forti-
eth birthday, Albert Smith was woken by his brother Arthur with the news that
Covent Garden Theatre had been destroyed by fire. Ever the sceptic, his first reaction was 'O! nonsense', but when he heard the same news relayed by the milkman
and then by the parlour maid of the house next door, Smith jumped out of bed
and left his Percy Street home for Covent Garden, just over half a mile away.
Arriving on the scene, Smith used 'the doubtful advantage of being "known to
the police"' to shoulder his way through to the front of the crowd and past the
barricades, to see the smouldering ruins of the theatre close up.

Writing about it shortly afterwards in *Household Words*, the two-penny weekly
magazine edited by his friend Charles Dickens, Smith would display his talents as
a reporter with a vivid and economical portrait of what he witnessed:

> Some huge, bare, blackened walls, with square perforations, from which the fire-
> men, with their hatchets, were crashing the remaining glass and window frames
> for the hose to enter; a roofless portico, still plastered with tawdry posting bills;
> a few charred and shortened beams seen through the window-holes, still blazing,
> and every now and then coming down with a great fall upon the embers below;
> and everywhere within the boundary walls a haze of smoke and flashes, and
> flying tons of water coming from unseen supplies, and spluttering, hissing, and
> crackling against the smoking ruins from all directions – this was all that occu-
> pied the spot where Covent Garden theatre stood not half a dozen hours before.[1]

Smith acquired a log of burnt oak from the ruins, and later used it to bind a
privately printed version of his account, for circulation among friends.[2] As well as
demonstrating Smith's considerable journalistic skills, this account also illustrates
his innate feel for the muddled, impressionistic way that childhood memories are
retained in adulthood. Musing on the time he had spent at Covent Garden over
the years, Smith recalled his earliest impressions of the theatre, the first he ever
attended. He was uncertain what age he would have been, but he was sufficiently
young that his parents put him to bed during the day so he would be able to
stay awake that evening. He saw *King Lear* and *Cherry and Fair Star* (the latter

a popular melodrama which was still being performed at other London theatres until at least the late 1860s), but all he could really remember of the evening was that he was taken to the theatre's saloon bar during the interval between plays 'for a glass of wine and water and a macaroon', and that 'there was a large ship with spangled sails, which, I have always had an impression, sailed around the pit; but this must have been a confusion of ideas resulting from the utter bewilderment in which I passed the evening'.[3]

Smith's evocation of the confused, muddled sensory impressions of childhood mingle with an implicit awareness that something significant had taken place on this occasion. However accurate or otherwise his memories of the event, Smith's childhood visit to Covent Garden had clearly imprinted something on his sensibility. As we will see, other early experiences reinforced this effect. Looking back, it seems almost predestined that young Albert would grow up to become a showman.

* * *

Albert Richard Smith was born in Chertsey, Surrey, on 24 May 1816 to Richard and Maria Smith.

A contemporary account, written just two years before Albert's birth, describes Chertsey as 'consisting of one long street running from East to West'. In this bucolic market town, cows still swim across the river from the meadow at Laleham to pasture and 'the curfew-bell is tolled [...] from Michaelmas to Lady-day, at eight o'clock in the evening'.[4] Albert Smith himself was reported to have said of his birthplace that it had 'outlived its antiquity', but this picture of a sleepy backwater left behind by the tide of events belies the fact that Chertsey was also a staging post on the journey from London to Windsor, and would remain an important coaching town until the railway arrived there in 1848.[5] The Smith family home at 13 Windsor Street, directly opposite St. Peter's Church, stood close to the junction of roads leading to London, Guildford, and Windsor, and just a little further down the street was the Swan Hotel, a 'Royal Post House' where carriages to and from Windsor Castle changed horses on their way to Claremont.[6]

Dickens visited the town, and used it as the setting for part of *Oliver Twist* (1838). The attempted burglary during which Oliver is shot and wounded is set in Chertsey, and Oliver subsequently stays at the Maylies' house there while recovering from his injuries.[7] The controversial Whig politician Charles James Fox (1749-1806) had spent his final days at the nearby St. Anne's Hill home of his wife, the former courtesan Elizabeth Armistead. Elizabeth herself lived on at St. Anne's Hill until her death at the age of 91, her dubious origins and scandalous career 'on the town' in the previous century evidently forgotten or at least tactfully ignored by her Victorian neighbours, who organized a cortège of forty Chertsey tradesman to pay their respects at her funeral procession in 1842.[8]

Albert's father was the town's doctor, known as 'Doctor Dicky', and was described by a local historian, writing in the early twentieth century from anecdotal accounts, as 'a little gentleman of pleasant though brusque manner, and with a heart brimful of kindly sympathy and genuine goodness'.[9] The social position of doctors was changing at this time, with the increased professionalization that would see them firmly entrenched in the middle classes later in the century. All the evidence about Smith's family background suggests Richard Smith had already benefitted from this shift, and that he was considered a solid, respected member of the community; significantly, he was a country doctor with his own private practice rather than a barber-surgeon, the latter position still carrying connotations of the old naval 'sawbones'. This was the period in which the medical profession was increasingly regulated and organized; the year before Albert's birth, 1815, had seen the passing of the Apothecaries' Act, requiring licencing by exam of all medical practitioners, and a series of other developments in the period from around 1780 onwards had begun the transformation of medicine into a profession that extolled the scientific method and commanded status and respect.[10] The life of a medical student (which Albert would later experience in London and Paris) may still have been as dissolute as that of Benjamin Allen and Bob Sawyer in *The Pickwick Papers* (1836-37), drinking neat brandy and guzzling oysters with their feet up on the table.[11] For a well-established country practitioner like Richard Smith, however, the profession was rather more sedate and certainly more remunerative, and the Smiths appear to have lived in modest but comfortable circumstances.

Nonetheless, when Albert later began to mix in social circles such as the Garrick Club in London, his relatively modest social origins would be the cause of snobbery among some contemporaries. In this respect, he had more in common with Dickens, whose social origins were of course much humbler, than with born 'gentlemen' such as William Makepeace Thackeray. Not that Smith ever seemed particularly bothered by such questions – one of the more endearing aspects of his personality was the degree to which he seems to have been entirely oblivious to the disapproval he caused in some quarters. Writing about the notion of 'good blood' – in other words, breeding – he would cheerfully describe himself as 'a scion of the most common-place, confused, and unsatisfactory stock in the world'.[12] Whatever airs and graces he would be accused of giving himself later in life, Albert never claimed to have had anything other than a solidly ordinary background.

Smith would initially follow his father into the medical profession, and the two briefly practised together at Chertsey, but he moved to London at the first possible opportunity and soon abandoned medicine for journalism. He nevertheless seems to have retained a degree of affection for his home town, and would continue to draw on his knowledge of Chertsey and its environs in his writing. In his first novel, *The Adventures of Mr. Ledbury and His Friend Jack Johnson* (1844), for instance, Smith has the eponymous Johnson and his cousin Morris flee from the authorities on a punt down the Thames, which comes to grief on a weir at Penton Hook, near Laleham.[13] Smith kept a house in Chertsey until late in his life, and would often take parties of friends there for the weekend. *The Times* correspondent William Howard Russell, renowned for his dispatches from the Crimean War, recorded in his diary how Smith would have a marquee erected on the lawn there on Sundays, serving up 'oysters, lobster salad, cold fowl, lamb and peas – till it was time to rush for the last train to Waterloo'.[14] According to one account, Dickens would sometimes visit for fishing expeditions to the nearby Mixtenham Meadows.[15]

At the age of ten, Smith was sent off to the Merchant Taylors' School – at that time located in Suffolk Lane in the City of London. For such a prolific writer, he has left relatively few explicitly autobiographical recollections of his schooldays, although as we will see he drew on his miserable experience at Merchant Taylors' for his second novel. In his non-fiction writing, however, he does record one event that was to have a lasting impact on him. At the age of twelve, young Albert was taken to the Vauxhall Pleasure Gardens.

The Royal Gardens, Vauxhall, as they officially became known in 1822, had been in existence since at least the early 1660s, but were at the height of their fame and popularity in the early nineteenth century. Comprising twelve acres to the south of Lambeth, near the site of present-day Vauxhall station, the Gardens at this time would have included such attractions as the Heptaplasiesoptron, a series of glass plates on which 'manifold reflections were produced of revolving pillars, palm-trees, twining serpents, coloured lamps and a fountain', and a 'building of wood and canvas representing a Hermit's Cottage', complete with resident hermit, 'pursuing his studies by the aid of a lamp, a blazing fire and a brightly shining moon'.[16] Although the Gardens started to decline in popularity not long after Smith's boyhood visit, eventually closing permanently in 1859, Vauxhall at this time was still a dramatic, even hypnotic spectacle for a young boy. Live music, fireworks, refreshments, illuminated fountains, tightrope walkers, lion tamers, and balloon ascents, not to mention prostitutes and pickpockets, combined to make up a dazzling, multi-sensory experience that far surpassed the humdrum reality of everyday life. Years later, told that the Gardens were to close, Smith would grieve for the disreputable fun of those heady days:

> And they coolly talked of building houses – common, uninteresting houses! –
> on the very ground that the rockets had gone up from, and occasionally, come

down again through the sky-lights of the neighbouring dwellings, bursting and shedding their coloured stars upon the staircases in a most diverting manner, and allowing the inhabitants a private exhibition to themselves.[17]

Smith recalled being taken to Vauxhall at the age of twelve, 'to celebrate my having moved head-boy from the division form into the fourth, at Merchant Tailor's [*sic*] School'.[18] 'The entire evening was to me one scene of continuous enchantment', he wrote:

> The Battle of Waterloo was being represented on the firework-ground, and I could not divest myself of the idea that it was a real engagement I was witness-ing, as the sharpshooters fired from behind the trees, the artillery-waggon blew up, and the struggle and conflagration took place at Hougomont. When I stood years afterwards on the real battle-field I was disappointed in its effect. I thought it ought to have been a great deal more like Vauxhall.[19]

Smith's childhood memories and his adult reaction to Vauxhall's closure both exhibit features that would recur in his writing all through his career: the contrast between the bright spectacle of the dramatic public display and the drab reality of the quotidian; the gap between expectation and reality, particularly the reality of visiting foreign countries. 'Before people see a person or a place', he wrote in 1847, 'they always form an idea to themselves of what he or it is like, and they are always decidedly wrong in their notions', and this dictum could almost serve as a manifesto for much of Smith's travel writing.[20] Again and again he would return to this theme of the disappointment felt when a much-anticipated site or experi-ence – his first glimpse of Venice, his first encounter with the Turkish ambassador, his first stroll down the Champs-Elysées – turned out to be less impressive when encountered for the first time.

> Thus, before we saw the Turkish ambassador, we imagined somebody between Bluebeard and the old gentleman who sells the pastilles in the Lowther Arcade: we had pictured Venice as a floating city of moonlight, and masked balls, and gaudy gondolas, with every window in it lighted up as for a *fête*, and sounds of music from every palace: we painted the Champs-Elysées as a lovely verdant expanse, watered by blue and sparkling rivers, whose flower-enamelled banks scented the clean air. Instead we found the Turkish Ambassador was like an ordinary foreign gentleman; we discovered Venice to be a gloomy, tumble-down likeness of Pall-mall and the Piazza, Covent Garden; out at sea, with all the pal-aces made into hotels, and as dark as pitch at night; and we perceived that the Champs-Elysées was without a blade of grass – that the only water was in those incomprehensible pit-holes, which everybody in the dark always tumbles into; and that you were half stifled with dust and the smell of asphalt, from one end to the other.[21]

Smith's descriptions of all sorts of foreign locations were characterized by this combination of disappointment and debunking. Indeed, his first encounters with Vauxhall, and later with Mont Blanc, were among relatively few experiences he did not claim to be disappointed by.[22] Even though his earliest notions of Vauxhall had been 'formed of an old coloured print which decorated a bed-room at home, and represented the Gardens as they were in the time of hoops and high head-dresses, bag-wigs and swords', he was actually enchanted rather than disappointed by his subsequent experience of visiting the gardens.[23] What he did take from the experience, though, was a preference for the exotic and the spectacular to the mundane business of reality.

Recalling a dancing show he witnessed being set up in advance of its performance, Smith recalled his childhood sense of the disjunction between the glamour of the performance and the dispiriting seediness of the off-stage performers:

> Could it be possible that those dirty people in shirt-sleeves, who were drawing out the long poles from their flat wagon, were the same who would appear on its platform the next day, in flesh-coloured tights and velvet jackets? Was it really the case that the woman in the dingy common shawl, and without a bonnet, returning from the baker's with a stale half-quartern under her arm, would dance outside tomorrow in spangled muslin and satin shoes? It was possible, we knew, and yet we scarcely believed it.[24]

What Smith loved was drama, performance, colour, the grand gesture and the enchanting anecdote. If that sometimes meant exaggerating the facts to make a story more entertaining, he had few scruples about doing so. 'There are many dreary things in the world besides death, debtors' prisons, and theatres by daylight', he wrote. 'A "genteel" dinner-party of rural aristocracy is amazingly slow, and so is a wet Sunday at Worthing.'[25] Smith made it his life's work to avoid 'theatres by daylight' – the dreary, humdrum reality that intruded when daylight was allowed in and the magic drained away. His unstated mission was to make the world more spectacular and entertaining, less dreary and disappointing, and he used showmanship and hyperbole to achieve this.

Yet at the same time, he had a competing and seemingly contrary urge to debunk, to deflate, and to render the exotic in familiar terms. Describing the road to some waterfalls on Penang, in Malaysia, Smith would write that it 'reminded me of the Mortlake entrance to Richmond Park', while Macau made him feel as if 'a fifth-rate bit of Portugal had been caught up by a waterspout and dropped down here by mistake'.[26] As one of his early editors put it, 'It was a great part of his fun to laugh at romance, to explode fables, to expose shams, and to take the jocularly sensible view of the subject.'[27]

As we will see, this irreverence for the conventions of travel writing would lead to Smith being considered rather a 'cockney' writer by some critics; he was often accused by later generations of travellers of having set in motion a process of 'cocknification' of the Alps, as if with his Mont Blanc show he had single-handedly lowered the social tone of resorts such as Chamonix. But the tension between Smith's robust, John Bullish comments on foreign places and people ('reports of Continental disturbances should never keep any one at home', he commented airily in *The Story of Mont Blanc*) and his contradictory desire to create awe-inspiring entertainment from his own travels is one of the features that keeps his work interesting and readable today, and it would prove to be a significant factor in the success of his Mont Blanc show at the Egyptian Hall.[28] Smith wrote tellingly in his account of the Mont Blanc ascent about this tension, with a shrewd assessment of how quickly the public appetite for stories of adventure and spectacular mountain scenery might wane if not whetted by skilful showmanship:

> The first view I had of the Mont Banc range burst on me suddenly, through the mist – that wondrous, breath-checking *coupe d'oeil*, which we all must rave about when we have seen it for the first time – which we so sneer at others for doing when it has become familiar to us.[29]

If his first experience of Vauxhall Pleasure Gardens taught the young Albert Smith the power of colour, spectacle, and drama, he also soon learned that these things had to be carefully managed to maintain the illusion. It was a lesson that would serve him well in his later career.

Vauxhall, then, was to have a profound impact on Smith's life and work. But Smith did not have to travel all the way to London to experience a world of glamour, spectacle, and adventure. Another early influence was to be found back in Chertsey, where Smith shared a home with his younger brother Arthur and his sisters Laura Maria and Rose.

The adult Smith would recall how in those days 'children's books were rare presents, and were so prized, and read, and read again, until the very position of the paragraphs was known by heart'.[30] Of the few books available to him as a child, three stood out – the ones that dealt with Mont Blanc.

Smith would terrify Laura Maria, five years his junior, by creating a panorama from the 'most sensational views' from John Auldjo's illustrated 1828 account of climbing Mont Blanc. The year before Auldjo's book was published, the ten-year-old Smith had been given a copy of *The Peasants of Chamouni*, recounting the ill-fated 1820 attempt on Mont Blanc by Joseph Hamel. The two books are very different in content and tone, but together they provided a powerful early stimulus. Not only did they plant the seed of his desire to climb Mont Blanc but they also taught him the power of visual display.

Auldjo's book includes a list of illustrations of 'perilous positions', with titles such as 'Scaling a Wall of Ice', 'A Dangerous Part of the Glacier', and 'Bridge of Snow where the Party Breakfasted', the latter showing a group of figures sitting on an ice-bridge across a gaping chasm, calmly eating a picnic breakfast. The drama of the illustrations is matched by the tone of Auldjo's narrative, as in this account of a particularly hair-raising moment on the ascent:

> I stopped for an instant and looked down into the abyss beneath me: the blood curdled in my veins, for never did I behold anything so terrific, as the view disclosed by the rapid glance into that deep icy pit, intensely blue at the upper part, but gradually fading into a vapoury indistinctness of colour, which created the idea of fathomless depth, and, if precipitated into it, a hopeless fall of endless descent.[31]

These descriptions captured the young Albert's imagination so effectively that he 'got up a small moving panorama of the horrors pertaining to Mont Blanc from Mr. Auldjo's narrative', which was so effective that his sister 'would become quite pale with fright'. Auldjo's introduction to his account of climbing the mountain is instructive in that it seems to presage the pragmatic, unromantic approach that Smith would later make his own. Auldjo begins his account of glimpsing Mont Blanc for the first time with a fairly conventional prose style that gestures towards the cult of the Romantic Sublime, still a powerful influence in the early nineteenth century: 'The mind, at first lost in astonishment, and gradually recovering from its effects, dwells with admiration on the magnificent scene.' However, he then goes on to write:

> The beholder then feels an earnest desire to reach the summit, which his eye can hardly distinguish from the light clouds that often flit around it; while the knowledge that the enterprise, though equally difficult and dangerous, is still practicable, increases the anxiety to achieve it.[32]

This is broadly the motivation that Smith himself would later claim for climbing Mont Blanc – neither Romantic search for the Sublime nor scientific enquiry but simply unapologetic thrill-seeking and challenge. If Auldjo's ethos was still relatively unusual in the 1820s, it would later become the dominant mode of writing and speaking about mountain climbing – and Smith would be one of the figures who effected that change.

Young Albert's other book, *The Peasants of Chamouni*, uses the framing device of an English mother being asked by her children about life in Switzerland ('Oh, mamma', exclaimed Lucy, 'do give us some account of Switzerland; I always fancy that it is a charming country'). The prose style is stilted even by the standards of early nineteenth-century children's literature: 'The sources of the Rhine and the Rhone are among the Alps, are they not, mama?' inquired Edward. 'Yes, you are right,' said his mother. 'I will now give you a slight description of the romantic views and situations which abound in those mountains.'[33] However, the tone of high-minded instruction soon segues into the rather more exciting tale of the 1820 Hamel expedition to Mont Blanc, in which three members of the party were killed by an avalanche.[34] This account included many features that would later appear in Smith's own writing and shows about Mont Blanc, and more generally about his Alpine travels: the trials of pre-locomotive travel; the nature of the St. Bernard dogs from the hospice of the Great Saint Bernard Pass; the dangers of avalanches, crevasses, and ice bridges; a description of a bivouac on the rocks of the Grands Mulets. 'Oh, how shocking', exclaimed the children in the book as their mother recounted the details of how an avalanche buried the three guides, and the dangerous descent that followed for the surviving climbers.

The Peasants of Chamouni concludes with this reassuring homily: 'May you learn from this melancholy occurrence, that sublunary happiness, however promising its appearance, is no security for the future.'[35] Albert, however, took a rather different lesson from his reading, namely that it was possible to scare the living daylights out of his younger sister with tales of mountain adventure and misadventure.

Some time later – precisely when is not clear – a friend gave Smith a copy of Horace Bénédict de Saussure's *Voyages dans les Alpes*. Saussure, a Genevan aristocrat with a passion for science, had spent ten years from 1774 travelling through the Alps and studying their geology and natural history. He had effectively sponsored the first ascent of Mont Blanc in 1786 by offering a cash prize to anyone who could reach the summit, and made the ascent himself in 1787.[36] The *Voyages* was his magnum opus, a four-volume work published between 1787 and 1796. Very different in tone from the other two works that had captured the young Albert's imagination, it nonetheless provided further fuel for his growing obsession with Mont Blanc.[37] The nearest thing to a mountain Albert had experienced in his Chertsey childhood, he would later recall, was St. Anne's Hill – a modest 250-feet elevation from which it was sometimes possible to see the capital on a clear day. Yet through his childhood reading, Smith not only developed a taste for the idea of mountain travel. He also gained an innate feeling for the magisterial power that a panoramic view could provide. It was this instinct that would eventually inspire his greatest triumph.

2: 'THE NICEST PLACE IN EUROPE'

If there is anything more delightful than travelling with plenty of money,
it is certainly making a journey of pleasure with very little. Albert Smith,
'Recollections of a Cheap Tour', *Bentley's Miscellany*, 1848

Smith left the Merchant Taylors' School in 1831, at the age of fifteen. The official School Register simply lists him as having attended between 1826 and 1831, with a brief summary of his subsequent career – and he published relatively few recollections of his time there, compared to his extensive accounts of his time as a medical student in Paris.[1]

However, when Smith published his second novel, *Fortunes of the Scattergood Family* (1845), it included a deeply unflattering portrait of life at Merchant Taylors', and he made no attempt to disguise the school's identity. His close friend Edmund Yates wrote that Smith based the story of young Fred Scattergood's horrific bullying by teachers and fellow pupils on his own experiences at Merchant Taylors', and that like his fictional protagonist, Smith had run away from the school.

Smith's suffering would not have been particularly unusual at the time; Fred's ordeal in *Scattergood* bears comparison with, for instance, the recollections of Anthony Trollope, born a year earlier than Smith, whose harrowing experiences at Winchester school were taking place at almost exactly the same time as Smith was attending Merchant Taylors'.[2] It is notable, however, that Smith only alluded to this brutalizing experience within the confines of a novel. His references to Merchant Taylors' in his non-fiction work were generally relatively breezy. He mentioned, for example, in an 1848 piece on 'Lord Mayor's Day' that his earliest recollections of this annual event were connected to the school, which gave the boys a holiday to attend the show.[3] He recalled having 'great fights with Mercer's and St. Paul's', other schools in the City of London, and 'pitched battles in Little St. Thomas Apostle and Great-Knight-Rider-street'.[4] In his account of the Covent Garden fire he also recalled being 'head over heels in schoolboy love with Fanny Kemble, and saving four weeks' allowance to see her in Juliet; and, after watching the robbery of the Bath mail, and hearing "Hurrah for the Road" in *Paul Clifford*'.[5] The first of these visits to the theatre would have been when he was a thirteen-year-old student at Merchant Taylors', although the production of Edward Bulwer-Lytton's *Paul Clifford* was not until 1835, by which time Smith was a medical student.[6]

Otherwise, Smith's references to schooldays are mainly confined to rather ambivalent comments about his classical education. Strolling around Athens in 1849, he was struck by the way ordinary shop signs used Greek characters 'hitherto only associated with my Merchant Tailors' [sic] School knowledge of the Diatessaron, Isocrates, and the Iliad, but now used to betoken the store of the baker, the coffee-house keeper, and the bookseller'.[7] Elsewhere, Smith seems to have been less grateful for his rigorous schooling in classics. In a comic article about the habits of 'The London Medical Student', he suggested that students would later look back upon time wasted at medical school 'in the same spirit that every boy, when he grows up and begins to mix with the world, deeply regrets the time he has wasted on his Latin and Greek, and wishes he could change his knowledge of these two languages for German and French'.[8] As we will see in Chapter 6, it would only be in the fictional world of Fred Scattergood that Smith would deal with the darker side of his schooldays.

Leaving school in 1831, Smith seemed destined to follow his father into medicine. His precise activities over the next four years are unclear, and it seems most likely that he spent some time gaining practical experience at his father's Chertsey practice until in 1835 he enrolled as a surgeon pupil at Middlesex Hospital, then located in Marylebone Fields in central London. The Hospital's Medical School 'for the teaching of Anatomy and Physiology, Chemistry, Physics and Biology' had just opened in October of that year, although teaching on the wards had taken place since the hospital opened almost a century earlier.[9] Three years living the wild life of a London medical student would give him plenty of material for his later books as well as some more sobering experiences, including, he claimed, witnessing a public execution from a vantage point on the roof of Newgate prison.[10] But Smith also found time during this period to write his first published work, a pamphlet criticizing the pseudo-science of phrenology, the mistaken but then influential belief that the size and shape of the skull could give useful information about human character and the workings of the brain. Smith's tract, printed for him in 1837 by Chertsey stationer Robert Wetton, rejoiced in the full title, *A Few Arguments against Phrenology; principally with regard to the Question, "Whether the external Form of the Head corresponds to the Surface of the Brain"*. As might be expected, it did not cause a huge stir in the publishing world, but it was reviewed in John Timbs's popular two-penny weekly *The Mirror of Literature, Amusement, and Instruction*, where Smith was described as 'a rising student in one of our metropolitan hospitals', and his arguments against phrenology as 'pertinent and well-pointed'.[11] The *Phrenological Journal*, presumably not the most objective reviewer, gave Smith's pamphlet a cooler welcome, noting that, 'The writer announces himself as a student of medicine; and we should be inclined to guess that he is in the *beginning* of his medical studies.' It went on to advise Smith 'not again to write about Phrenology until he has made himself more fully acquainted than he now is, with its evidences and bearings. Having his professional studies to attend to, at present, we can scarcely expect a sufficiency of knowledge to be acquired for some few years.'[12]

In fact, Smith qualified as a surgeon and joined the Royal College of Surgeons in 1838, the same year this review appeared. He appears to have been as undaunted by this criticism as he would prove to be by all subsequent attacks, and quickly began to combine his medical career with more forays into journalism. Long after he had quit medicine, Smith would trade on his time as a medical student in his journalism and novels, usually to comic effect. His sketches of medical students generally involve them getting up to no good – for example, hatching a plan to bring in bags of cats and let them loose in the dissecting room along with dogs, cockerels, hens, rats, and ferrets: 'How gratifying to every philanthropist must be these proofs of the elasticity of mind peculiar to a Medical Student!', Smith remarks with mock sententiousness. 'Surrounded by scenes of the most impressive and deplorable nature, in constant association with death and contact with disease, his noble spirit, in the ardour of his search after professional information, still retains its buoyancy and freshness.'[13] He contributed a series of articles to the *Medical Times* on 'The Confessions of Jasper Buddle, a Dissecting Room Porter' (using the pseudomym 'Rocket'), and his earliest work for *Punch* would also deal with the experience of medical training. In 'The Physiology of the London Medical Student', published in the very first number of *Punch* in 1841, and in 'Curiosities of Medical Experience', published the following year, Smith celebrated the disreputable behaviour of the students but also gave some hints as to why he had come to regard even the precarious trade of hack journalism as a more attractive career than medicine. 'Next to imprisonment for debt there are few positions in life more cheerfully exhilarating than that of house-surgeon to a hospital', he wrote, before enumerating with heavy sarcasm the various 'attractions' of such a role:

> Constantly surrounded by scenes of the most pleasant and mirth-inspiring description; breathing the purest atmosphere in the world; reveling at lunch upon hospital cheese, which is a relish apparently prepared, with the nicest culinary art, from bees-wax, yellow soap, and doubtful eggs; faring sumptuously every day withal at the board-room dinner-table, in company with the matron, house-apothecary, secretary, and other choice spirits, who delight in the sunshine of humour or wit; and never depressed by the wearisome monotony of lying in bed all night long, his existence is, indeed, enviable.[14]

After qualifying, Smith moved to Paris to carry out further training at the Hôtel-Dieu – the city's oldest hospital, located close to Notre-Dame – and later at another hospital in Clamart, to the south west of Paris. He chose to live cheaply in the Quartier Latin, that 'dense congeries of narrow, dirty, tortuous streets, that cling and twist round the Sorbonne and Pantheon like mudworms round a pebble at low water'.[15] If life as a London medical student had been mildly dissolute, Smith's time in the Quartier Latin, the centre of Bohemian Paris, was positively riotous. He would later recall returning to his lodgings on the Rue St. Jacques at daybreak, arm in arm with his companions, singing songs heard earlier at the Opéra Comique, and how he had 'worn a *débardeur's* dress for a whole week to-gether, and whirled and galloped to the music of Musard and Magnus in the *salle* of the Rue Vivienne'.[16] He even admitted to having been locked up for the night in the *violon* (prison cell) below the staircase of the Opéra Comique, after some over-exuberant and presumably drink-fuelled dancing in the aisles of the theatre. He 'appeared before the police the next morning in our glazed hat, blue shirt, and black velvet trowsers, to make what excuse we best might for having, under the very shadow of the *garde municipale,* with their tiger-skin helmets, given ourselves up '*un p'tit pas trop fort*' to the *abandon* of the dance, in defiance of the placard which informed us that our style was '*défendu par les autorités*'.[17]

Smith clearly developed a flirtatious relationship with various *grisettes*, the young working-class Parisian women who were often sentimentalized in literature of this period, and he would write about this group affectionately in later years.[18] How far some of these flirtations went is hard to say, given the relatively circum-spect tone of writing about sexual relationships at this time, but Smith's eye for the opposite sex is fairly clear when he writes of a 'fine specimen of the Parisian *grisette* – small, but perfect in figure, with chestnut hair lying in smooth bands upon her fresh cheeks, and dark eyes that almost spoke, so eloquent was their expression'.[19] Reading between the lines of some of his accounts, Smith seems to have been the sort of man who tried his luck whenever he could, especially while travelling abroad. On his visit to Istanbul (then Constantinople) in 1849, he was evidently rebuffed by local women on more than one occasion, and complained that 'every attempt I made at philandering with the belles of Stamboul, and once or twice under unusual advantages, turned out to be a total, not to say contempt-ible, failure'.[20] The word 'philandering' may have had a more innocent meaning than it would now suggest – simply meaning an innocent flirtation – but the tone is sufficiently louche to suggest that Smith had more serious intentions.

Whatever sexual adventures he may have enjoyed in Paris, Smith finished his time there with plenty of extra medical experience (the Hôtel-Dieu was a popular venue for training doctors as it tended to receive patients with unusual ailments, and because then, as now, it was the main accident and emergency hospital for Paris), fluency in idiomatic French, and a growing body of published journalism. He began sending back 'Sketches of Paris' for the *Mirror of Literature, Amusement, and Instruction*, the same publication that had previously reviewed his work on phrenology. Articles in the *Mirror* were unsigned, as was the general rule in periodical journalism at this time, so it is impossible to be certain which were Smith's contributions, but short items on the French police, education system, and the Palais Royal all appeared in 1838 and seem likely to have been his work.[21] But his Paris sojourn had also given him the opportunity to travel more widely in France and beyond. Most significantly, it allowed him his first sight of the Alps.

Smith set off from Paris with a fellow medical student on 21 September 1838. They had the equivalent of twelve pounds each, carried in five-franc pieces stuffed inside a leather belt, and were carrying old army knapsacks and wearing hobnailed boots (purchased for three francs and five-and-a-half francs respectively, as Smith carefully informed his readers). Smith also carried a set of pistols, which a border guard on the French-Italian frontier later threatened to confiscate, before being placated with the gift of a pocket-knife. Their journey from Paris to Geneva by *diligence* – a large stage coach, typically drawn by four horses and with two or three separate compartments, that plied fixed routes in France – would take them high up into the Jura mountains, and involved three days of hard travelling.[22]

Smith's account of this journey was written in what would become his trademark style – practical, debunking, acutely aware of costs and full of tips and wrinkles for saving money, and keen to make the reader aware of his own shrewdness. 'I am not going to enter into any long descriptions of scenery or places in this diary', he reassured his readers. 'Much of the ground has been gone over by competent writers […] I am only going to show […] how we were very merry and saw a great deal for next to nothing at all.'[23] Smith never let slip an opportunity to point out how he had gained the upper hand in his dealings with hoteliers, coachmen, and fellow travellers. When the *diligence* stopped for lunch on the first day's journey, Smith shopped for bargains in the town of Melun (now a suburb of southern Paris, but then a town about 25 miles from the capital) spending less than ten sous on some pears and a 'brick' of bread two feet in length, and was gratified to note that his fellow passengers had paid three francs each for their set lunch. Arriving at Sens that evening, having travelled 75 miles south from Paris in a day, the other passengers paid four francs to eat at the town's main hotel. Smith had befriended the postilion, who told him about a *cabaret* (a simple tavern rather than a place of entertainment) where he and his friend ate 'hot roast veal, omelette, bread, butter, salad, wine, and brandy, for twenty-four sous each'. And so it went on. Smith's 'Cheap Tour' in places reads like a litany of boasts about how he had been quicker-witted and sharper-elbowed than the next man or woman.

Whether he is inviting the *conducteur* and driver of the coach to dinner, in order to eat at his leisure and be assured of finding the cheapest place in town to do so, or sitting on the cheaper seats outside the *diligence* to ensure he has a good view of the Alps, Smith presents himself as shrewd and worldly. Arriving in Geneva after three days of hard travelling, he calculates that he and his companion have spent the equivalent of just two pounds, twelve and sixpence each – about a quarter of what the journey would have cost if they had 'lived conventionally'.

Some of this was simple practicality on the part of a young man travelling abroad with limited funds: 'as medical students we were compelled to manage our means', he pointed out. But from this and subsequent accounts – not to mention the recollections of Smith's contemporaries – it is clear that he was careful with money as a point of principle. Indeed, he seems to have actively relished living cheaply, and he always enjoyed an altercation over prices ('Had a good row about the bill', he recorded cheerfully in his diary after leaving a Singapore hotel in the late 1850s.)[24] Smith's dictum that 'if there is anything more delightful than travelling with plenty of money, it is certainly making a journey of pleasure with very little – provided always that health and spirits are good, and that one can find a companion similarly circumstanced' was one that he would stick to even after his Mont Blanc show made him a wealthy man.

But Smith's approach to travelling was not determined solely by parsimony. Even on these early travels he displayed a keen sense of curiosity, and was baffled – as he would be later in life during his journeys to the Middle East, North Africa, and Asia – by the determinedly incurious nature of some of his fellow travellers, particularly his own countrymen. Running on ahead of the *diligence* at Montereau, a town in north-central France near the junction of the Seine and Yonne rivers, Smith and his companion came across some criminals tied up on a platform in the market square, their names and crimes written on placards above them. 'None of the other passengers saw this exhibition', he noted: 'indeed it was curious to notice that two English people in the *coupé* drew down the blinds on account of the sun, and when they did not do this they were asleep'. Smith would later bemoan this same dour lack of interest in their surroundings in British expatriates in Hong Kong and mainland China, and in the Anglo-Indians he met on his journey back from east Asia. Many of his fellow passengers on the voyage out 'had lived for years in China, but could tell me absolutely nothing about it', he noted in his diary in 1859. 'Their minds had become reduced to what they worked in – the 'godowns' or stores.'[25] Nor was he attracted to roughing it just for the sake of discomfort. He certainly displayed no nostalgia later in life for the age of travel by *diligence*. 'It was a blessed thing when the stage coaches were run off the roads by the winged engine of the rail', he declared. 'We all of us remember the misery of a journey on a coach ten or fifteen years ago', describing the whole experience as being 'as bad and dreary and miserable as it could well be'.[26] Smith was perfectly happy to accept modern comforts and improved modes of travel, provided he didn't have to pay too much for them, and he was rarely if ever nostalgic for the 'good old days'.

Approaching Geneva on 24 September, Smith got out to walk ahead of the slow-moving *diligence* as it trundled down the hard cobbled road from Les Rousses, high in the Jura. Turning a corner, he caught sight of Lake Geneva, 'beautifully blue, with the Alps on the other side, their summits only showing above the clouds; and the country like a coloured map at our feet'. The passengers inside the coach saw nothing of this, Smith noted with satisfaction, as one window was hard up against the mountainside and the other was facing a steep precipice. Nor did they share the 'glorious sight' of sunset on Mont Blanc that evening, as they were all at the *table d'hôte* dinner at the expensive Hôtel des Bergues. Smith, of course, had pumped the *conducteur* for local knowledge and found a 'clean second-rate inn' where he had eaten cheaply before going out to watch the sunset. The following day, Smith set off on foot for Chamonix. He managed to hitch a ride on a lumber-wagon some of the way, and stopped at Arpenaz, home of the celebrated waterfalls that gush almost 1,200 feet directly out of a hole in the cliffs. Here Smith and his companion were approached by a local entrepreneur who offered to fire a cannon to produce an echo – a common attraction for Alpine tourists since the eighteenth century – but decided it was too expensive. Instead they 'waited until a car full of travellers who were not far behind us came up, who directly ordered this exhibition, by which we were the gainers, as there was no charge for listening'. At their next stop they joined forces with two other travellers, an Edinburgh physician and a Frenchman who was 'going all over Europe with two shirts and a pocket-comb', and Smith came across his first Swiss boy, who was 'very dirty and lubberly, had a large goitre, and was half-witted'.[27] As with so many details of his travels, Smith filed away the Frenchman in his memory – he would later resurface in *Ledbury* in the guise of Mr. Crinks, travelling around Europe with 'two shirts, four socks and a toothbrush. Find two shirts quite enough, one down and t'other come on.'[28]

Continuing on to the baths at St. Gervais, Smith met Victor Tairraz, owner of the Hôtel de Londres at Chamonix. Thirteen years later, other members of the Tairraz family would be among the guides who would take Smith to the summit of Mont Blanc, but for now Albert was more concerned with finding cheap lodgings. Victor Tairraz agreed to let them stay cheaply on the top floor of the hotel, and a delighted Smith reciprocated by remaining loyal to the Hôtel de Londres for life, staying there during all his subsequent visits to Chamonix.

By the time of Smith's visit, Chamonix was already an important Alpine resort. Nowadays a busy town of around 10,000 inhabitants, its population swollen in winter by skiers and in summer by hikers, climbers, and mountain bikers, Chamonix is located in south-eastern France, very close to the border with Switzerland. Variously spelt Chamouny or Chamouni at the time of Smith's visit, it was then part of the Kingdom of Sardinia, returning to France in 1860, when the new *département* of Haut-Savoie was created. A remote and obscure Alpine village until the middle of the previous century, it had become popular with British travellers since the 1741 visit of William Windham and Richard Pococke, who had coined the name 'Mer de Glace' for the famous glacier.[29] Chamonix had subsequently benefitted from the fascination with mountain scenery engendered by Romantic literature in the late eighteenth and early nineteenth century, and the first tourist hotel, significantly named the Hôtel d'Angleterre, opened in 1770. By the time Smith arrived in 1838, John Murray's *Handbook for Travellers to Switzerland* (which covered the Alpine regions of other states as well) was describing it as 'a large and important community, which displays almost the bustle of an English watering-place in the most retired, heretofore, of the alpine valleys'.[30]

Smith was enchanted by Chamonix as soon as he arrived. This was partly because an Englishman whose birthday it was invited him to share a bottle of champagne. But something more profound happened to Smith in Chamonix, as if the childhood influences of Auldjo and the other accounts of Alpine travel that had captivated him were suddenly able to reassert their influence. The tone of his narrative changes when he arrives in the Alps. The debunking and practicality do not entirely disappear – he did, after all, describe the famed Mer de Glace as looking like a ploughed field – but what he himself calls 'my own practical eyes' suddenly seem to recognize the magic in the scenes before them. The man who has spent the journey so far mocking the conventions of Romantic travel writing (vineyards, for instance, 'are great things for untravelled poets to sing of, but sadly monotonous in a landscape') now writes, 'Every step I took that day on the road was as on a journey to fairy-land.' His prose style shifts a gear, as if even practical, sceptical Smith has to reach for the language of Romanticism to express what he feels in the Alps:

> And when passing the last steep, as the valley of Chamouni opens far away to the left, the glittering rocky advanced post of the Glacier des Bossons came sparkling from the curve, I scarcely dared to look at it. Conscious that it was before me, some strange impulse turned my eyes towards any other objects – unimportant rocks and trees, or cattle on the high pasturage – as though I feared to look at it.

Chamonix was, he wrote simply in his diary, 'the nicest place in Europe'.[31] Throughout his life Smith would return to Chamonix, and when the town was ravaged by fire in July 1855 he would offer to receive subscriptions for a relief fund, contributing twenty pounds himself.[32] In the seven or eight years after his first visit, Smith returned to Chamonix as often as possible, generally in the autumn when he could spare a few weeks. 'Gradually the guides came to look upon me as an *habitué* of the valley', he boasted; 'indeed I almost regard Chamouni now as a second home'. It was, he wrote, his 'first love', and even after visiting 'the more vivid attractions of Paris, Naples, and the brilliant East', he always found himself drawn back to it.

Years afterwards, writing his account of his 1851 Mont Blanc ascent, Smith would recall the sleepless night of excitement he spent at the Hôtel de Londres, waiting to see his first glimpse of the 'Monarch of the Mountains' the following morning. After the first 'wondrous breath-checking *coupe d'oeil*' described in Chapter 1, 'the whole of that sojourn at Chamouni passed like a dream'. For once, Smith forgot his instinct for penny-pinching and his urge to debunk and deflate. Albert was smitten.

3: 'THE PANORAMANIA'

'I recall these first efforts of a showman – for such they really were – with great pleasure'. Albert Smith, *The Story of Mont Blanc*

Mont Blanc may have captured his imagination, but Smith did not suddenly change his approach to travelling upon arrival at Chamonix. A robust, no-nonsense style continued to characterize his travel writing, as this admonition to readers who might want to follow in his footsteps suggests:

Pedestrians must not expect to find everything *couleur de rose*. Trivial annoyances of every description will be constantly starting up, but if temper is lost, they become ten times worse: a firm resolve should be taken to laugh at everything, with the certainty that however vexatious the occurrence may be at the time, it will only serve to talk about the more merrily when you get home again.[1]

Nonetheless, something had changed for Smith in Chamonix. His childhood fascination with Mont Blanc had been rekindled, and he formulated a plan to reach the summit – still an unusual and potentially dangerous undertaking at this stage. Each morning Smith would look out of his bedroom window up in the top garret of the Hôtel de Londres and gaze at the mountain. Each sunset he would wander out into the fields behind the town to 'see the rosy light creep up it, higher and higher, until it stood once more – cold, clear, mocking the darkening peaks below it – against the sky'. He had spent hours reading accounts of the ascent and studying models and maps of the route, and hoped that another traveller would attempt the climb during his stay there, allowing Smith to tag along as a porter. He could not afford to hire the guides required to set off for the summit; Chamonix had established the Compagnie des Guides in 1821, in the wake of the Hamel tragedy, and one of the rules of the municipality was that visitors could not attempt to climb Mont Blanc without a local guide.

Smith was out of luck on this first visit, and in any case was probably unrealistic in expecting anyone to take a fellow tourist along as a porter instead of hiring one of the experienced and acclimatized Chamoniards. Although he would return to Chamonix regularly over the next seven or eight years – as well as travelling extensively in other parts of Europe – it would not be until 1851 that he would eventually get the opportunity to reach the summit. The day after he left Chamonix, Mont Blanc was climbed by Comtesse Henriette d'Angeville, only the second woman to reach the summit.[2] By then, though, Albert was on his way back to Paris, and thence to Britain.

Smith spent a couple of years in medical practice with his father back in Chertsey. These Chertsey years were busy but rather dull, and – according to his own account – one evening he found himself impelled to look out the old panorama he had used to entertain his sister.[3] In 1827 Chertsey had acquired its own Literary and Philosophical Society, based on Guildford Street just around the corner from the Smith family home. Smith copied his old pictures on a larger scale, about three feet high, 'with such daring lights, and shadows, and streaks of sunset, that I have since trembled at my temerity as I looked at them'.[4] He rigged up a mechanism with a local carpenter to roll the images on a rotating spool, and used this simple home-made panorama as the basis for an illustrated lecture on his travels, which he described as his 'Alps in a box'.[5] His show was 'considered quite a "hit"', Smith recalled, although he was candid about the fact that it benefitted from the relatively uninspiring nature of other presentations to the Literary and Philosophical Society: 'the people had seen incandescent charcoal burnt in bottles of oxygen, and heard the physiology of the eye explained by diagrams, until any novelty was sure to succeed'. Building on his success at Chertsey, Smith toured with his show during the next two or three years, visiting similar institutions in Richmond, Brentford, Guildford, Staines ('There are certainly places in Great Britain more frivolous and dissipated than Staines', he would later remark in *Ledbury*), Hammersmith, Southwark – a tour that he would remember as the 'first efforts of a showman'.[6] He and his brother Arthur (who would become stage manager for Smith's much larger and more professional Mont Blanc show at the Egyptian Hall in the 1850s, and would also manage Charles Dickens's lecture tours) would drive to each place in a four-wheeled chaise, and would find themselves waiting before the performance in the institution's committee room – 'a sort of condemned cell, in which the final ten minutes before appearing on the platform were spent, with its melancholy decanter of water and tumbler before the lecture, and plate of mixed biscuits and bottle of Marsala afterwards'. It was a low-key, provincial start to his career, but it was show business of a sort and Smith would look back upon that period of his life with affection. He would also draw on these years for various incidents in his novels. The portrait in *Ledbury* of the 'Clumpley Literary and Scientific Institution', at which there were 'experiments with the gases, and chemical transformations; tricks with the air-pump, and dissolving views; electro-type, and galvanic batteries – in fact, all sorts of entertaining sights', clearly draws upon these years.[7] So does the introduction of a Literary and Philosophical institution known as 'The Parthenon' in *Christopher Tadpole*, and its eponymous hero's short-lived career as a traveller lecturer. The speakers who visit

The Parthenon in *Tadpole* even wait 'in a little room like a condemned cell', just like Albert and Arthur.[8]

Smith's modest experiments in creating moving panoramas reflected the importance of this medium in the wider world of Victorian entertainment. The moving panorama had been around for decades, growing out of the static versions of the late eighteenth century. From the time of the artist Robert Barker's very first panorama in 1789, depicting a 360-degree view of Edinburgh's Calton Hill, spectators 'visiting these all-embracing pictures could imagine that they were actually there, experiencing exciting views of the fleet at anchor at Spithead, or far-away cities like London, Paris or Constantinople'.[9] The format quickly became popular, not just in Britain but on Continental Europe and America, crossing the Atlantic after the landscape painter Thomas Cole saw panoramas while visiting London in 1829. Cole returned to America and began to paint huge panoramic landscapes.[10] Giant panoramic scenes also toured the major cities of Germany and the Netherlands.

In 1792, Barker constructed a Rotunda – a gigantic brick cylinder – in Leicester Square to exhibit his panoramas. Significantly, Mont Blanc was the subject of panoramas at the Leicester Square Rotunda from 1826, indicating the degree to which Smith was tapping into an interest that already existed, although the 'Monarch of the Mountains' shared the billing with views of Rome, Benares, Kabul, Damascus, and Pompei.[11] Smith himself would later coin the term 'Panoramania' to poke fun at the phenomenon, suggesting that the desire for new subjects to display in panoramic form had become so voracious that 'the world will be unable, within a year or two, to furnish new subjects'. With his trademark bathetic humour he predicted that subjects such as 'Night on the Hyde-Park Prairie' and 'The Tottenham-court road by sunrise', or a representation of 'Mr. Straggles and his party when they made out the north-west passage from Temple-bar to Piccadilly' would soon replace the views of naval battles, Alpine landscapes, and Gothic ruins that had been the traditional subject of panoramas.[12]

Well before Smith wrote this, the basic panorama format had diversified into a host of spin-off technologies, and by the early nineteenth century 'dioramas, cosmoramas, cycloramas, myrioramas and a host of other 'oramas' were being presented to an eager public.[13] The most important and successful of these was the diorama, which 'consisted of an enormous canvas, 20 feet high and several hundred long wound round a concealed spool hidden behind the proscenium'.[14] Dioramas are defined by Ralph Hyde, probably the leading authority on the history of panoramic painting, as 'large realistic paintings which seemed miraculously to change their appearance'.[15] The diorama as it is usually understood in the nineteenth century really began with Louis Daguerre, best known as the inventor of the daguerreotype, the earliest version of the photographic process.[16] Daguerre opened a very successful diorama in Paris in 1822, and quickly turned his attention to London, where his Regents Park Diorama opened in 1823. Audiences first saw a depiction of the ruins of Holyrood Chapel in Edinburgh, after which 'a low, subterranean rumbling led to the whole auditorium being slowly swung around to face another tableau, a mountain landscape in the Alps'.[17]

As Hyde points out, some aspects of the diorama were already familiar to audiences in 1820s Britain; moving pictures operated by clockwork had been around since the time of Samuel Pepys; transparencies had been used at Vauxhall Gardens and on stage at Drury Lane, and innovative lighting effects had been used in such stage spectaculars as Philippe Jacques de Loutherbourg's 1781 'Eidophusikon' in Leicester Square.[18] Daguerre's show, however, brought a new level of both excitement and verisimilitude to the entertainment business. The diorama could represent the passing of time and the seasons through different kinds of weather, 'from the hazy morning to the clear night, and from the calm beauty of a summer's day to the brooding and stormy sky'.[19] If the panorama had worked to bring the spectator right into the middle of the picture being exhibited, simultaneously creating a heightened sensation of reality and yet an awareness of the artificial process by which that sensation was being constructed, the diorama took this paradoxical reality effect still further. 'Contemporary audiences', report Daguerre's biographers Helmut and Alison Gernsheim, 'invariably expressed the greatest astonishment and delight at the unbelievable illusion of reality that was created by the subtle changing effects no less than by the more spectacular transformation scenes'.[20]

The diorama format became hugely popular in the wake of Daguerre's show, but another similar but distinct technology came into being almost simultaneously – the moving panorama. It was this format that Smith would later adopt and adapt at the Egyptian Hall, supplementing the moving images with his own unique talents as a narrator. Moving panoramas proceeded horizontally across a proscenium stage, being wound from a hidden spool at one end of the stage to a second spool at the other end.[21] They were first used onstage at the Theatre Royal, Drury Lane in 1800, when the Christmas pantomime incorporated a series of views of 'the most magnificent buildings in London'.[22] By the 1820s the moving panorama had been used to depict everything from river voyages, aeronautical adventures, the search for the North-West passage, and a reconstruction of the Battle of Waterloo. By the 1840s, the initial surge of excitement over moving panoramas was on the wane, but the fortunes of the format were revived by two different moving panoramas of the Mississippi, the first by John Banvard and the second by 'Professor' Risley and John R. Smith.[23] Banvard, who exhibited his

'Mississippi' in the Egyptian Hall from December 1848 and subsequently took it on tour around Britain for two years, is perhaps the most important and direct predecessor to Albert Smith. Like Smith, he accompanied his visual material with a lecture, which as well as being 'descriptive and statistical [...] was laced with jokes and poetry, all delivered with an attractive Yankee twang'.[24] Leaving aside the Yankee twang (Smith's own tones were variously described as 'strident and high-pitched'; a 'high treble'; an 'unpleasant falsetto'; and 'high and flutey'), this could serve as a description of Smith's own Egyptian Hall shows.[25]

By the time Banvard and Smith were exhibiting at the Egyptian Hall, it had become one of the main venues for moving panoramas, despite its relatively conventional theatrical design. Earlier panoramas, notably the Regent's Park Colosseum, built in 1827, had used a specially designed rotunda format to exhibit panoramic views through 360 degrees. The Egyptian Hall had no rotunda, relying instead on rollers to move the panoramic scenes, horizontally in the case of Banvard's Mississippi panorama and vertically in Smith's show. The panorama had moved away from being a specialized format requiring a purpose-built structure to exhibit – by the mid-century, many shows involved some kind of panoramic element, and audiences could no longer be thrilled and satisfied simply by the novelty of a panoramic view. Nonetheless, panoramas, dioramas, and moving panoramas all remained potent forces for providing what Martin Meisel calls a public spectacle in which 'the appetite for truth and fact shared the stage with the appetite for wonder'.[26] This appetite of the Victorian public for the combination of entertainment and instruction was the context in which Smith's early days touring regional literary and philosophical institutions took place, and it was a very similar context in which he would launch his Egyptian Hall shows – indeed, Smith's first Mont Blanc show at the Egyptian Hall took place just after the ultimate demonstration of this combination, the Great Exhibition of 1851.

Smith himself generally took a dim view of the mingling of education with entertainment. His early lectures to accompany his 'Alps in a box' shows certainly purported to be educative, with material about the various theories of glacier motion and the history of attempts on Mont Blanc. But his later, far more successful Egyptian Hall shows tended to eschew earnest educative material in favour of amusing anecdotes, comic songs, and fast-paced narration. As early as 1843, Smith was demonstrating his suspicion of attempts to use entertainment as a way of promoting useful knowledge – or at least of the danger of entertainment being wholly supplanted by education. 'Our increased education is gradually driving out of our hearts what little inclination to honest mirth the altered times have left us', he complained, in an article in his first published collection, *Comic Sketches from the Wassail Bowl*. 'Science', Smith declared, 'has so startled our ancient pastimes, that few have had the good fortune to withstand her march, and assert their ancient powers of attraction for the citizens of London.' If the old, traditional entertainments are to survive, he predicted, it will be 'in some altered and deeply philosophical form', so that, for example, 'the garlands would revolve around the Maypole by voltaic electricity; and the "miracles, mysteries, and moralities" performed on a cart during the season of Lent, would be supplanted by travelling lectures from scientific institutions, in perambulating vans driven by steam'.[27] The time is fast approaching, he warns,

> when our very nurseries will be the schools for science; when our children's first books will be treatises on deeply scientific subjects; and when even their playthings will partake of the change. The Dutch toys will be thrown aside for the Daguerrotype; the doll's house will be a model of the Adelaide Gallery; and the nursery carpets and morning dresses will be burnt full of holes by the acid from the doll's galvanic trough or hydrogen apparatus.[28]

Smith's suspicion of earnest attempts to smuggle education and improvement into what he believed should have been pure entertainment were very much in character. One of his earliest articles for *Punch* magazine was a satirical piece called 'Transactions of the Geological Society of Hookham-cum-Snivey', in which he mocks a group of amateur provincial geologists who excavate a public sewer and proceed to earnestly analyse the contents.[29] As with many early contributions to *Punch* by Smith and others, the humour of this piece has not aged well and now seems laboured, but the tone is consistent with Smith's distrust of anything too 'improving'.

Smith was by no means opposed to acquiring knowledge or education – his journalism and travel writing demonstrate a lively, enquiring mind that was always interested in the industry, customs, language, and cuisine of the countries he visited. But in his own entertainments, education would always play second fiddle to amusement. So, for example, in his Mont Blanc show he tended to relegate detailed information about the countries depicted to the printed publicity material such as handbooks that he used to help publicize the entertainment. An 1856 handbook to 'Mr. Albert Smith's Ascent of Mont Blanc', priced at sixpence, noted that,

> It has been the Author's intention to render this Handbook a slight improvement upon the majority of pamphlets sold at exhibitions and entertainments. It is meant less as a companion in the room than as a reference after "Mont Blanc" has been visited, supplying a great deal of information, which, necessary to the proper understanding the subject, would be somewhat tedious in the lecture room.[30]

In other words, there was a place for information and education, but that place was on the printed page, not in the Egyptian Hall.

Yet Smith was undoubtedly a beneficiary of the very tendency to value educative and informative content that he so often deprecated. The 'Ascent of Mont Blanc', and Smith's earlier show, 'The Overland Mail', existed and thrived in the context of mid-century 'exhibition culture'. As we shall see when we examine the show more closely, one of Smith's achievements was to create a sense of omniscience, authority, and authenticity on stage. It could be argued that one of the common themes in the exhibitions of the mid-century, whether Banvard's all-encompassing view of the Mississippi, Smith's Mont Blanc show, the Great Exhibition at the Crystal Palace, or the numerous other shows and exhibitions that took place in London and throughout the country, was an attempt to impose order and control over an irregular and disorderly world. The art historian Malcolm Andrews points out that the whole panoply of panorama and diorama technology 'worked hard to complete [...] an illusion of authenticity', quoting the example of Daguerre's 1832 *View of Mont Blanc from the Valley of Chamonix,* which had involved importing from Chamonix 'a complete chalet and its outhouses. A live goat was tethered in a shed, and the sounds of alpenhorn and singing accompanied the spectacle.'[31] This degree of striving for verisimilitude, suggests Andrews, 'is more than simply a transcription of the original: it is partly a transplanting of the original [...] To add to a landscape painting three-dimensionality, sound and movement blurs the distinction between artefact and nature.'[32] This comment could just as easily be applied to Smith's show twenty years later, in which an authentic Swiss chalet, chamois and St. Bernard dogs were introduced to heighten the sense of authenticity.

This attempt at outdoing the original, and taming the power of nature with the tools of science and knowledge, would also be displayed in Hyde Park, where the Great Exhibition attempted to create what historian Paul Young calls a spectacle of 'revelatory scope'.[33] In the same year, 1851, the geographer James Wyld's Great Globe was displayed in Leicester Square. Comprising a giant globe, around sixty feet in diameter, which audiences could enter to view a scale model of the earth, Wyld's Globe was 'an ingenious geography lesson; the surface of the world in relief was shown *inside* the huge structure, viewed from a series of iron steps and galleries'.[34] Young suggests, however, that the Globe's attempt at comprehensiveness in displaying the entire world to a London audience was ultimately a failure in comparison to the greater comprehensiveness and 'systematic world picture' represented by the Great Exhibition.[35]

Smith's shows did not explicitly claim quite this level of totalizing vision, but for all Smith's disclaimers of instructional aims, his show, too, was a spectacle of 'revelatory scope'. 'The Ascent of Mont Blanc' would emerge against this background of visual and exhibition culture, and engage with its panoramic predecessors to create not just an illusion, but a kind of reality effect – a spectacle in which both audience and entertainer colluded in the pretense that they were witnessing and participating in an ascent of Mont Blanc, a voyage to Boulogne, or a river trip down the Rhine. Like his young sister, Smith's audiences would enjoy a frisson of excitement generated by the terrifying spectacle of glaciers and precipices.

All that was to come later, however. For now, Smith had a more pressing ambition. It was increasingly obvious that this ambitious and energetic young man would not be satisfied with his father's life as a country surgeon. Even while practicing medicine in Chertsey and travelling with his moving panorama of Mont Blanc, Smith also found time to build up a growing portfolio of articles. His ticket to London would come not from stage showmanship but from journalism. Smith began publishing work in the *Literary World,* another publication edited by John Timbs, in the late 1830s while still living in Chertsey. He also had articles published in a relatively short-lived publication called *Cosmorama*, edited by Ebenezer Landells, who would go on to become one of the founders of *Punch*.[36] Smith's 'Sketches of Evening Parties' in the *Literary World* were followed by his account of 'The Passage of the Great St. Bernard', in which he described visiting and crossing the famous pass that connects the Swiss canton of Valais with Aosta in Italy. He also wrote up a local Chertsey legend about the 'curfew bell' of Chertsey Abbey. Smith's version of the Blanche Heriot tale was published in the local *Almanac* in 1840, with his stage adaptation opening at the Surrey Theatre two years later.[37] By the time that production opened, the next stage in Smith's life had begun. In 1841, he finally moved to London.

4: FUGITIVE PIECES

We adore the streets. Albert Smith, 'Physiology of the London Idler', *Punch*

If Smith's years at school in London had been miserable, his second period of living in the capital was to prove much happier and more productive. Although he also continued to travel abroad regularly and to write about his journeys, London life provided most of the material for what his fellow *Punch* contributor George Hodder called his 'fugitive pieces' – the short, ephemeral journalism at which Smith excelled, and the first medium in which he achieved renown.[1]

Smith's first London home was at 14 Percy Street, off Tottenham Court Road, an area which the London historian Jerry White points out was marked by its social mix of 'artists, music teachers, and professionals'.[2] Smith would later describe Percy Street as one that leads 'from a great thoroughfare to next to none at all, and so is tolerably quiet in itself, although close to a running stream of population'.[3] This running stream was to provide ample material for a writer with Smith's combination of curiosity, observation, and appetite for hard work. Although he began his residence here by screwing a brass plate to the door announcing himself as a 'surgeon-dentist', Smith soon became more absorbed in the life of the streets around him, and in documenting that life. It is not entirely clear how long his medical practice continued, or even if it was ever a viable business, but soon after moving to Percy Street he was making most if not all of his living from journalism. 'It is a pleasant thing connected with medical examinations', Smith would later write in *Ledbury*, apropos of the medical student Mr. Prodgers, 'that nearly all the subjects which they can embrace may be discarded from the mind the instant the ordeal is over, without the least detriment to any future professional career'.[4] Even allowing for a novelist's licence and the medical professional's bravado, Smith does seem to have made a very deliberate decision that it was time to turn his back on medicine. Throughout his novels he continued to demonstrate a quiet pride in the medical profession, but it was clear that he had now chosen the life of a writer, not a doctor.

A few of Smith's contemporaries left recollections of the writer in what the novelist and dramatist Edmund Yates called his 'sanctum'. Yates describes visiting Smith and finding him 'as usual, in his foreign blue blouse, pottering about in his sanctum in Percy Street, than which there never was such another room for the collection of extraordinary valueless curiosities, prints, pictures, plaster-casts, and quasi-artistic rubbish of every possible description, thickly overlaid with dust'.[5] Another friend, the journalist George Augustus Sala, described Smith's study as being like a curiosity shop, 'although the "curios" were not highly remarkable from the standpoint of high art, and were not very antique'. The room was littered with fancy dress costumes, including the *débardeur's* costume that Smith had enjoyed wearing in Paris, cakes of Viennese soap in the shape of fruit, miniature Swiss chalets, a medical student's skeleton, and – a feature which virtually every visitor to Smith's home remarked on – a small working model of a guillotine 'which had had the place of honour assigned to it on the mantelpiece of the stuffy back room where Albert in his French *ouvrier's* blouse usually wrote his copy'.[6]

It was from this unprepossessing headquarters that Smith would produce an astonishing breadth of writing over the next few years. His journalist's eye alighted on everything, from Christmas pantomimes to the pleasures of whitebait suppers, street musicians to crossing sweepers, Punch and Judy shows to the antics of medical students. He wrote about excursions to Ascot, the changing fashions of various London districts, the Greenwich Fair, a visit to the Chinese junk *Keying* when it arrived in Britain in 1848, and the comings and goings of visitors to the Lowther Arcade, the popular shopping gallery on the Strand. 'We adore the streets', Smith wrote in 1842.

> We know there are thousands of our fellow-men who regard them merely as the spaces included by two boundary lines of bricks and mortar for the purposes of transition from one spot to another. But we look upon them as cheap exhibitions – al fresco national galleries of the most interesting kind, furnishing ever-varying pictures of character or incident.[7]

The theatre of the streets was Smith's most frequent topic, but he could just as easily turn his hand to evenings at the opera, the social niceties of dinner parties, and of course to travel writing. Although he would most closely be identified with journalism about London over the next decade – writing not only for the newly created *Punch* but also for a range of periodicals such as *Blackwood's Edinburgh Magazine*, and for annuals including *The Keepsake* and *The Book of Beauty* – his first big break as a journalist came with an 1841 article published in *Bentley's Miscellany*, in which he described his experience of being held up by bandits while travelling between Venice and Florence in the summer of 1840.[8]

Smith had just spent a week in Venice, 'that amphibious city of human beavers', and was keen to move on; but, as he pointed out, 'travelling in the Lombardo-Venetian kingdom is very different from driving a cab with your carpet-bag to Euston Square, or Nine Elms', and all the scheduled transport was booked up. He and his travelling companion managed to find a traveller from Hamburg who was similarly anxious to leave, and they agreed to share the cost of a posting carriage three ways.[9] Stopping at the first post-house on their journey, Smith noted the interest with which some of the locals were inspecting the travellers' baggage, and later concluded that the hold-up was pre-planned, and that the postillion ('an ill-looking hound' whose 'features bore the stamp of cunning and villainy') was probably an inside accomplice. They continued on their way at about ten in the evening, and Smith's fellow passengers were soon asleep, leaving him 'listening to the monotonous '*hi!*' of the postillion, and the eternal jangling of the bells on the bridles', when the coach came to a sudden halt. Looking out the front window, Smith saw a party of six or seven men 'ranged in a semicircle across the road, pointing their guns at the carriage, and gradually closing around us'.

What happened next was swift, violent, and must have been genuinely frightening – even for a traveller as unflappable as Smith, who had the presence of mind to slip seven English sovereigns he was carrying in his pocket into his mouth, and then hide another in his shoe. 'I had barely concealed this last', wrote Smith, 'when the curtains were torn violently down, and the muzzles of six guns made their appearance in a most unpleasant propinquity to our heads, followed by half a dozen of the most ill-favoured visages I had ever seen.'

As well as fully cocked guns, 'the ruffians were likewise armed with pistols in their girdles, and long poniard-knives that dangled from their necks and gleamed romantically in the moonbeams'. Being Smith, he was instantly reminded of the production of *Paul Clifford* he had seen at Covent Garden many years earlier, in which the Bath mail-coach was robbed on stage.[10] This reverie was abruptly shattered when the ringleader of the bandits, an 'immense ruffian of six feet two', grabbed Smith by the collar and pulled him bodily out of the carriage, throwing him to the ground, whereupon 'a general rifling immediately commenced'.

Smith handed over the money in his pockets, and had his knife and pencil-case taken from him, but managed to persuade the bandits that his pocket-book contained his passport and was allowed to keep it; 'a circumstance I hailed with much satisfaction, since in one of its compartments was a letter of credit upon Rothschild for one hundred pounds, which I saved'. Everyone's braces and handkerchiefs were stolen, and Smith's scarf, fastened round his neck with two gold pins and a chain, was cut away. 'My readers may be assured that the feel of the cold steel against my neck was anything but pleasant,' he noted. The bandits found Smith's leather belt stuffed with notes and coins, and were threatening to cut off the finger of a German traveller who couldn't remove his ring when Smith remembered that he, too, had a ring that could not easily be removed. As the German struggled to get off his ring Smith 'managed to slip the ring round until the signet was turned towards the palm, and thus escaped their notice.'

Finally the robbers shoved their victims back into the carriage and rode off.

Albert Smith. Reproduced by permission of Bill Douglas Cinema Museum, University of Exeter.

The only things Smith had managed to save were the sovereigns he had put into his mouth and shoe, his pocket-book, and some miniature gondolas, souvenirs of his time in Venice, which were in the same pocket as his handkerchief. 'As we were starting again they threw into the carriage my old straw boating-hat which I had worn all the way from Chertsey', he recalled. The carriage resumed its journey to the next post house at Rovigo, a town about 50 miles from Venice, where the *carabinieri* were called.

A Prussian nobleman, the Baron de Hartmann, whom Smith had met in Venice (and who arrived at Rovigo on the scheduled *diligence*, thus avoiding the robbery), lent Smith and the other robbed passengers sufficient money to continue their travels and pay their bills, observing that 'the word of an Englishman was sufficient' security to lend him money. Smith was able to travel back to Britain, finding to his satisfaction that 'our adventure made us the heroes of all the *table d'hôtes* between Florence and Geneva, and we frequently heard our own story recounted, with many amusing exaggerations'.

Some people were sceptical about Smith's own version of the story, not for the last time in his career. He acknowledges as much in *Bentley's*, admitting that several people have already claimed he made the whole episode up, but insists in a postscript to the article that he was contacted several months after the event by the Home Office, asking him to make a deposition before a magistrate at the request of the Austrian Ambassador regarding a highway robbery in Lombardy. And while Smith mostly made light of the danger he had been exposed to, it is clear that when he wrote, 'If we had offered the least resistance, we should have been killed', he was in deadly earnest.

This is not to say that Smith didn't embellish some details. He would have been well aware that his readership still largely viewed *banditti* through the romantic prism created by the seventeenth-century Neapolitan artist Salvator Rosa, whose paintings had been collected by the aristocratic arbiters of taste in eighteenth-century England and had subsequently influenced the writings of Horace Walpole and William Gilpin as well as the painting of J.M.W. Turner.[11] Although Smith begins his article by debunking this romanticized view of *banditti*, warning his readers not to believe that 'brigands are dressed in spangled green velvet tunics, with ribands bound round their calves, and watches and medals hung about them after the manner of Mr. Wallack', he knew that the idea of being robbed by bandits was still considered sufficiently romantic to give his readers a vicarious thrill.[12] He certainly thought it was a good enough story to use again, employing it in his 1848 novel *The Struggles and Adventures of Christopher Tadpole*, where Mrs. Hamper is robbed and kidnapped by brigands.[13]

'A Rencontre with the Brigands' exhibits some of the best qualities of Smith's writing. It is economical, fast-paced, and compelling, and avoids the over-writing and loquacity that plagues some of his novels, in particular. It was a useful calling card for the twenty-five-year-old Smith, and he had chosen a good time to become a full-time writer. Just as his father had practised medicine at the right time to benefit from a shift in its status, Albert came along at just the historical moment when the profession of 'writer' was being established, and when it was more feasible than ever before for those writers with sufficient talent and energy to make a living from their work. Among the most important causes of this change was a big increase in the number of outlets for prose. The market for both fiction and periodicals had expanded greatly during the 1830s, in the wake of the success of the so-called 'silver fork' novels of the 1820s, and the new six-shilling reprints of novels offered by publisher Richard Bentley.[14] The outstanding popularity of Dickens's *The Pickwick Papers* in the mid-thirties had helped, too, with publishers more willing to take a risk on publishing new fiction in monthly instalments. This, in turn, expanded the potential readership for fiction while allowing both authors and publishers a steady income stream over the typical twenty to twenty-one month period of serialization. Meanwhile, the number of magazines and their total circulation was growing dramatically, as the repeal of taxes on paper and newspapers from the 1830s through to the 1860s allowed publishers to charge lower prices.[15]

These developments and others made it feasible for Smith to support himself as a professional writer. The novelist and historian Walter Besant estimated that by 1836 there were about 4,000 people living 'by literary work' in London, of whom 700 were journalists.[16] Nonetheless, for the average hack writer life remained precarious: the newspaper editor James Grant wrote in 1841 that out of perhaps 10,000 people who had tried to make a living from writing over the past two decades, 'it would be hard to name twenty individuals, or one of every five hundred, who have been able to convert their literary talents into the means for procuring for themselves a permanent and ample living'.[17] These odds did not improve much during the time that Smith was pursuing his own literary career, but the indomitable Albert was destined to beat them.

One of the new publications that emerged in response to these changes was *Punch*, launched by Henry Mayhew and Ebenezer Landells in July, 1841 as *Punch, or the London Charivari*.[18] It would soon become 'not merely the most successful Victorian comic periodical, but – measured by circulation, influence, and longevity – one of the most successful magazines that has ever existed'.[19] At its inception in 1841, though, it was a brash young upstart with a very specific sensibility, fusing the long tradition of satire and caricature in British publishing with a broadly radical, anti-Establishment stance and Puckish wit and irreverence. As Brian Maidment points out, the first few volumes of *Punch* – in other words, those that Smith contributed to – were characterized by 'their bohemian/radical politics, their visual experimentation, their preoccupation with Regency carica- ture tropes, especially the grotesque human body, and their roots in the collective bonhomie of a male coterie'.[20] The radical politics and the aspect of an all-male 'literary brotherhood' would prove to be important in Smith's eventual rejection by what Patrick Leary calls the 'self-described "literary brotherhood"' of 'the most exclusive literary men's club in London'.[21] Smith's own politics were reflexively conservative, and while he was eminently 'clubbable' the charges of 'cockney' vul- garity that would be levelled against him throughout his career seem to have been an element in his fall from grace at *Punch*.

All that was to come later, however. In 1841, Mayhew and his co-editor Mark Lemon seem to have been impressed by the young writer's credentials, and in par- ticular by his work on Landell's earlier publication *Cosmorama*.[22] Smith's first piece for *Punch* was 'Transactions of the Geological Society of Hookham-cum-Snivey', swiftly followed by his articles on life as a medical student: 'The Physiology of the London Medical Student' and 'Curiosities of Medical Experience' (see Chapter 2). Smith became a regular contributor to *Punch* over the next three years, while also branching out into writing plays, comic song, and translations. Between

1841 and early 1844 his main work was for *Punch*, and the magazine's ledgers show him being paid for dozens of articles over this period, varying from a few lines through to longer pieces serialized over several issues.[23] His series on the 'Physiology of London Evening Parties' is an example of the latter, stretching over twelve parts. Smith signed these articles under the pen name 'Rocket' for the first couple of instalments, before either he or his editors decided to drop this. The articles describe the lengthy and elaborate preparations for an evening party, in terms which Smith would later repeat in novels including *Ledbury* – he even introduces a character called Mr Ledbury, a rather gauche young gentleman who doesn't know how to talk to women at parties. Over the course of the series, he enumerates various social types, such as 'The Uninteresting Young Lady' ('should you dance with her, you would find it a most pumping uphill task to establish a conversation'), 'The Young Old Lady', 'The Young Lady Just Out', and 'The Loquacious Young Lady'.[24]

'Curiosities of Medical Experience', too, was stretched out over eleven instalments, while 'Physiology of the London Idler' also used a serial format spread over several issues to introduce such characters as the 'Regent Street Lounger' and 'The Gent', the latter of whom would become a staple of Smith's comic prose in years to come. Smith was among the first writers in English to adapt the French *physiologies* format, in which small, seemingly trivial aspects of contemporary life were discussed and analysed in pseudo-scientific terms. The *physiologies* had been a staple of the *Charivari* writers (see note 18 on p. 200) in the 1830s and 1840s, but had been in existence since the 1820s – notable examples included Balzac's *Physiologie du mariage* of 1830.[25] Smith had certainly been exposed to this genre while living in Paris, and now adapted it to his writing for *Punch*: later in the decade he would use it as the basis for his 'Natural History' series of books.

Smith's articles for *Punch* between 1841 and his abrupt departure in early 1844 included 'The Gratuitous Exhibitions of London', 'Side-Scenes of Everyday Society', and 'An Act for the Abolition of Punishment by Tobacco-smoke, on board the River Steamers, and elsewhere'. He also contributed to the magazine's series of comic guides to various parts of Britain, writing the Brighton section of '*Punch*'s Guide to Watering Places' and the Tower Hill section of the 'Handbooks for Holidays Spent in and about London', both published in 1843. His work on these tongue-in-cheek guides exhibits tropes that would feature in his later novels and journalism, including a strong sense of the bathetic humour to be found in humdrum places, a tendency to poke fun at the antics of 'cockney' visitors, and a deep distaste for the great unwashed (as we will see, Smith was almost phobic about dirt, and considered the urban poor particularly filthy – something he tended to blame on their slovenly habits rather than on their lack of access to basic hygiene facilities). So in his guide to Brighton Pavilion, Smith notes that,

> Some of the carvings are curious, and record several visits made by the public when they were indiscriminately admitted to view. "J. Griggs" deeply cut with a clasp-knife into a sycamore table, gives greater effect to its buhl-work; whilst "Sarah and James" boldly slashed upon a state chair, considerably enhances its grandeur.[26]

This parody of the tone of a serious guidebook continues in his tourist guide to Tower Hill, from which he points out 'there is a fine view of the opposite coast of Bermondsey – Pickle Herring-stairs being distinctly visible with the naked eye'.[27] Lodgings and provisions in Tower Hill, Smith writes, are cheap, 'but washing is dear – if we may judge from the scarcity, upon the principle that all rare things are expensive'.[28]

Despite his prolific output for *Punch*, Smith found time in this same period to turn his Blanche Heriot story into a play, and to write another, *The Revolt of Bruges*, in collaboration with E. L. Blanchard.[29] *Blanche Heriot, or The Chertsey Curfew* was performed at the Royal Surrey Theatre in September 1842. Set during the Wars of the Roses, just after the Lancastrian defeat at Tewkesbury in 1471, it culminates with the hero, Neville Audley, being freed at the last minute before the curfew bell tolls to signal his execution. The play is replete with melodramatic dialogue. 'Miscreant! Release that lady instantly', Audley tells the villain, Hugh Laneret, who replies, 'Never! But with life! Beware how you oppose me. I am armed; and the energy of desperate passion nerves my arm.'[30] This did not prevent the *Illustrated London News* from giving it a positive review, noting that it was 'well written and full of striking incidents'. The reviewer described it as 'far above the run of dramas produced on this side of the Thames, both with reference to its intrinsic merits and the correct and tasteful manner in which it was put on stage'.[31]

Smith also translated *The Armourer of Paris*, a French romance set during the reign of Charles VI, for the *London Saturday Journal*, a two-penny journal published between 1839 and 1842. This fairly unremarkable piece nonetheless benefitted from Smith's intimate knowledge of Paris, and his ability to imaginatively reconstruct its history for a British readership. Although, like *Blanche Heriot*, it features some strikingly melodramatic lines ('I curse you, spurn you from my presence as I would a serpent', Charles tells his treacherous queen, Isabelle) it is nonetheless rather more successful than some of Smith's own later fiction in keeping the plot moving at a swift pace.[32] Smith also began to write lyrics for the popular singer John Orlando Parry, wrote a facetious piece for first volume of the *North of England Magazine* in 1842 called 'The Prevailing Epidemic', and from

September that year began the serialization of what would eventually become his first novel, *The Adventures of Mr. Ledbury and His Friend Jack Johnson*.[33]

Before *Ledbury* appeared in book form, however, Smith had already brought out his first book, *The Wassail Bowl*. Published by Richard Bentley in two volumes during the course of 1843, *The Wassail Bowl* is essentially a series of essays on aspects of London life, including Greenwich Fair, Bartholomew Fair, and the tradition of Christmas pantomimes. The latter article takes the reader on a nostalgic visit to a pantomime, insisting on going to the cheap seats in the pit, 'for we mean, in all good truth, to enjoy ourselves and scream with laughter'. The pit was the authentic place to be in the theatre, and 'we do not grumble, as usual, at the persevering apple-women, when they push by our legs between the rows, selling tenpenny books for a shilling; nor do we complain surlily of being too crowded; on the contrary'.[34] This attitude was in marked contrast to Smith's own approach when, years later, he put on his show at the Egyptian Hall – as we will see, he was particularly concerned to avoid discomfort and annoyance for his patrons, and to ensure that even the cheap seats were considered a respectable place to sit. Smith does seem to have become more concerned with conventional respectability and perhaps even a little choleric in later life, when he could be found writing indignant letters to *The Times* about the behaviour of street urchins and reacting querulously when latecomers interrupted the start of his Egyptian Hall performance. For now, though, he was happy to celebrate London life in all its colourful, rambunctious vulgarity. In his account of 'A Visit to Greenwich Fair', Smith describes setting off from one of his own favourite haunts, the Cheshire Cheese pub off Fleet Street, a location he says forms 'the link between the coffee-room and the menagerie, possessing the viands and the waiters of the one, and the saw-dust and feeding-time of the other'.[35] The subsequent train journey that takes Smith and his fellow passengers to Greenwich provides a dioramic view of London, as well as a tour through some characteristic tics of Smith's writing: his facetiousness; his fascination with the idea of a London that most observers do not see; and his recognition that poverty and squalor exist side by side with but largely hidden from the wealthier inhabitants of the city; not to mention his fascination with modern modes of transport and the very different experience of travel they offer. The passengers

> were much edified by the continuous brick-fields and gas-manufactures, whose localities they invaded, pronouncing the rapid dioramas of sectional habitations and domestic interiors which met their view, exceedingly interesting. The engine became a locomotive Asmodeus, hurrying them from roof to roof in quick succession, placing them on terms of close intimacy with the garret-windows, revealing endless birds-eye views of chimney-pots, back-yards, and water-butts, and causing the passengers of reflective minds to meditate upon the accumulation of

poverty and pig-sties that exist in the metropolis, unknown to the inhabitants in general, and Westenders in particular.[36]

Arriving at Greenwich, Smith describes the fair in a series of increasingly exaggerated and ludicrous snapshots, with attractions including 'an erection [...] nearly sixty feet long [which] contained they were informed, a live whale'. As so often in his writing, Smith is preoccupied by the gap between promise and reality, between the shameless claims of the hawkers and the rather deflating experience of the punters.

It was a theme he would return to many times both in his fiction and his journalism. In the two years 1842 to 1843, during which *Ledbury* was serialized, *The Wassail Bowl* was published, his two plays were staged, and his translation of *The Armourer of Paris* appeared, Smith also found time to contribute a version of *Beauty and the Beast* to a book of comic nursery rhymes and to produce another play at the Surrey theatre. *The Pearl of Chamouni* (not to be confused with Donizetti's opera, *Linda di Chamouni*, which was staged at Her Majesty's Theatre in March that year) was a translation by Smith of a French play, *La Grace de Dieu*, written by Adolphe Philippe Dennery and Gustave Lemoine and staged in Paris in 1841.[37] Meanwhile, he was still churning out material for *Punch*. However, tensions were rising in the *Punch* 'literary brotherhood', and the time was fast approaching when Smith would be grateful for the diverse experience and contacts that his other work provided.

5: GENTS, GENTLEMEN, SNOBS & COCKNEYS

The main object of the Gent is to pursue a position which he perceives to be superior to His own. Albert Smith, *Natural History of the Gent*

Albert Smith was 'a good kind creature', wrote the novelist, poet, and *Punch* contributor William Makepeace Thackeray in 1848, in a letter to his friend Edward Fitzgerald. But, Thackeray continued, 'Heaven has written Snob undisguisedly on his mean keen good-natured intelligent face.'[1]

Thackeray's views on Smith suggest the rather ambivalent nature of their relationship, but they also point to one of the underlying reasons for Smith's abrupt departure from the *Punch* 'brotherhood'. To put it bluntly, Albert Smith was considered just a little bit vulgar.

The term 'snob' did not really acquire its present meaning – 'a person who despises those whom he or she considers to be inferior in rank, attainment, or taste' – until the early twentieth century.[2] According to the *Oxford English Dictionary*, the word started out in the late eighteenth century as a colloquial term for a cobbler, or cobbler's apprentice, and around the same period was Cambridge University slang for a townsman – in other words, someone not from the university. From the 1830s it began to denote someone 'belonging to the ordinary or lower social class; one having no pretensions to rank or gentility', or a 'person who has little or no breeding or good taste; a vulgar or ostentatious person'. This meaning underwent a subtle shift from the 1840s, when 'snob' started to suggest 'a person who admires and seeks to imitate, or associate with, those of higher social status or greater wealth; one who wishes to be regarded as a person of social importance'.

It was this latter meaning of the term that Thackeray was using in his *Book of Snobs*, published in 1848 after being serialized in *Punch* in 1846-47, and which Smith himself was alluding to in his 1847 *Natural History of Stuck-Up People*. 'What do you mean by Stuck-up People?' Smith asked rhetorically in his Preface. The answer was 'those who believe that position is attained by climbing a staircase of money-bags', and who 'partake of the nature of mushrooms – inasmuch as they have not only sprung up with great rapidity to their present elevation, but have also risen from mould of questionable delicacy'.[3] It was also this kind of 'snob' that Smith referred to in his satires on 'gents'. Gents were, Smith told his readers, the type of people who spoke in an affected slang and wore loud, ostentatious clothes ('Albert' boots, large-sized, awkwardly cut yellow kid gloves, blue stocks, and 'rings in profusion, which we have seen them wear outside their gloves' were all unmistakable sartorial markers of the Gent). The Gent was marked above all by 'an assumption of style about him – a futile aping of superiority that inspires us with feelings of mingled contempt and amusement'.[4] Smith suggests that the gent is a creation of the present 'constant wearing struggle to appear something more than we in reality are, which now characterizes every body, both in their public and private phases'.

The term 'cockney', also in frequent use in the middle of the nineteenth century, has a similarly shifting etymology. Although it has long been used to denote someone born within the sound of Bow Bells (the *OED* records its first usage in this context as dating back to 1600) the word did not always have the connotations it acquired in the twentieth century. Images of costermongers dressed as Pearly Kings or chimney sweeps playing the spoons would not have been conjured up for a mid-Victorian reader coming across the word. During the period from the 1840s through to the 1860s, according to the historian Gareth Stedman Jones, the word 'cockney' changed its meaning from 'solid London burgher to sham-genteel swell'.[5] Its meaning at this time was thus similar to though not precisely synonymous with 'gent', and it was generally used to criticize not the urban proletariat but the 'plebeian smartness of the young journeyman, shop assistant, or lawyer's clerk' – those members of the lower middle classes who were increasingly enjoying the benefits of a whole range of social, political, and economic changes, among them the 1867 extension of the franchise, the 1870 Elementary Education Act, the growth of bank holidays and other forms of paid leave, and the new availability of relatively cheap travel both in Britain and abroad.[6] This same segment of society would later be important in Albert Smith's success during his lifetime, and in his legacy after his death – they were among the crowds who flocked to the Egyptian Hall to see his shows, and they formed a significant portion of those who travelled to the Alps to see the sights he had described. As we shall see, these travellers soon found themselves dubbed 'cockney' interlopers by more patrician visitors to mountain regions.

The problem for Smith was that, as Thackeray's letter suggests, he himself was considered by some contemporaries to be this type of individual. Descriptions of Albert Smith as a 'snob' and even more frequently as a 'cockney' began early in his career and have proven remarkably enduring. John Ruskin notoriously dismissed Smith's Mont Blanc climb as 'a cockney ascent of Mont Blanc', setting the tone for many subsequent descriptions of him and his adventures. 'I was speedily aware', William Howard Russell recalled in his memoirs, writing about a period in the early 1850s when he and Smith were fellow members of the Garrick Club, 'that Albert was not regarded by the *dei majores* of the morning room as quite the thing'. One elderly Garrick member, Russell remembered, 'alluded to him as "that bawster – no, shawman – doocid noisy fellow"'.[7] Later in the 1850s, looking for some financial stability, Russell approached the managing editor of his employer, *The Times*, to ask about giving public lectures. He was told pointedly that the newspaper's management would have no objection 'provided it was not in Albert Smith's style' – they might just as easily have said not too cockney.[8] As we will see, complaints about the 'cocknification' of the Alps in the wake of Smith's Egyptian Hall show began from almost the moment he took to the stage, and the characterization of Smith as a crass, brash cockney continued well into the late twentieth century. The French mountaineer and writer Gaston Rebuffat, writing in the early 1980s, described Smith's Mont Blanc escapade as '*la première vulgarisation de Mont-Blanc*', while Ranna Kabani, in her critique of Orientalist travel writing published in the same decade, described Smith on his Constantinople trip as 'content to present himself as a quick-witted if sharp-tongued Cockney, out for a good laugh on the Bosphorus'.[9] As recently as 2011, a former president of the Alpine Club, Stephen Venables, was describing Smith as 'a flashy entertainer with virtually no climbing experience [...] a bit of a charlatan, peddling a travesty of the real thing'.[10]

These jibes did not begin with Smith's Mont Blanc show, however. While Smith's contributions to the early volumes of *Punch* were clearly valued by his editors, his company at the *Punch* table seems to have been less appreciated. The editorial team at *Punch* quickly acquired a reputation for conviviality, dining every Wednesday evening with their publishers and enjoying other drink-fuelled evenings in haunts such as the Cheshire Cheese, off Fleet Street, the Cyder Cellars in Maiden Lane, and a tavern called Evans's at the western end of Covent Garden. A '*Punch* Club' met every Saturday evening at the Crown Tavern near to Drury Lane theatre, attracting not only contributors such as Smith, Douglas Jerrold, and the illustrator Kenny Meadows, but various other luminaries including Dickens and the artists Clarkson Stanfield and Edwin Landseer.[11]

'Among the *Punch* set – and particularly at the dinners – my father has told me that Albert Smith was far from popular', *Punch* co-founder Henry Mayhew's son recalled in the 1890s. Editor Mark Lemon was prone to playing practical jokes on Smith. On one occasion he pawned a black Spanish cloak that Smith had just bought, in order to pay for drinks the notoriously tight-fisted writer had refused to contribute to (according to one account of this incident, Smith was so infuriated that he reported the incident to the police).[12]

But it was Douglas Jerrold who was Smith's real nemesis at *Punch*. Jerrold, one of the most important contributors to *Punch* in its early days as well as a popular playwright, had joined the navy at the age of ten during the Napoleonic wars.

He wrote a number of plays, the most successful being *Black-Eyed Susan* (1829), a nautical melodrama about corruption and injustice in the navy. Politically liberal, he was a campaigner against capital and corporal punishment, and his views would later bring him into conflict with Thackeray and other Tory-leaning writers at *Punch*. He continued to write for the magazine until his death in 1857, however, and in the 1840s he was at the very heart of the *Punch* 'brotherhood'.[13] Physically small, his quick wits and sharp tongue were legendary, and he was in the habit of venting both on Smith.[14] Not everyone admired Jerrold; the journalist H. Sutherland Edwards (who was a friend of Smith's and therefore not entirely impartial) recalled that he 'uttered witticisms which were to wit what a truism is to truth; and he indulged in every opportunity in repartee which, sometimes facetious, generally sarcastic, was often in bad taste'.[15] But he was a key figure in the *Punch* circle and a force to be reckoned with both socially and professionally. Smith seems to have been uncharacteristically cowed by him, and contemporaries recorded a number of occasions when he was the butt of Jerrold's put-downs. The most notorious was Jerrold's question to Smith upon noticing that he had signed an article with his initials A. S. – 'Why do you only tell two-thirds of the truth?' On an occasion when Smith protested to Jerrold that 'after all, we both row in the same boat', Jerrold shot back, 'True, but with very different skulls'. Smith, no milksop in most situations, seems to have been genuinely intimidated by Jerrold. 'Pigmy as Jerrold physically was, Albert Smith quailed before him', Jerrold's grandson claimed.[16]

It is hard to gauge how much of the antipathy towards Smith was a result of his own sometimes bumptious behaviour, and how much was motivated by snobbery – in the modern sense of the word. The writer and publisher Henry Vizetelly, who detested Smith and made him the subject of a damning pen-portrait in his autobiography, claimed he was unpopular not just at *Punch* but in literary circles generally because of 'the imbecile canons of taste in literature and art which he so persistently enunciated', and in particular his insistence 'that Shakespeare was ludicrously over-rated, and that high art was all "rot"', but perhaps more pertinent is Vizetelly's claim that 'few of Smith's associates could stand his noisy self-assertion and boisterous behaviour'.[17] However, for every Vizetelly or Jerrold who found Smith intolerable there was a Sutherland Edwards who recalled him as a 'lively and agreeable man, full of good spirits, and full also of a mild, evening-party sort of fun'.[18] At least some of the derision aimed at Smith seems to have sprung from his relatively humble origins – even though Jerrold himself was the son of a jobbing actor and theatre manager. Upon discovering that Smith had an uncle who was an ironmonger, Jerrold composed the lines, 'My uncle Water Closets makes/ He is odorous of vapour,/And I who scribble books for Bogue,/Of course supply the paper.'[19] This kind of dig at Smith's social origins was typical of the jibes that he endured at the *Punch* table. His habit of easy familiarity with his colleagues also seemed to offend Jerrold's sensibilities. Hearing Smith address the illustrator John Leech as 'Jack', Jerrold pointedly asked, 'Leech, how long is it necessary for a man to know you before he may call you *Jack*?'[20] This suggests more presumptuousness on Jerrold's part than Smith's. Smith had known Leech since their days as medical students – Leech had been at St. Bartholomew's Hospital while Smith was at Middlesex – and they would continue to have a close working relationship, with Leech going on to illustrate most of Smith's novels and to work with him on *The Month*. Yet it does indicate how Smith had acquired the reputation, deserved or otherwise, of not knowing how to behave correctly in polite society, of being 'not quite a gentleman'.

Certainly, Smith seems to have been the object of a certain amount of derision throughout his life – even his friends would refer to him as 'Alabata Smith', referring to a white alloy of nickel, copper, and zinc that was used to make cheap cutlery look like silver.[21] 'It somehow became the fashion to look upon him as the type of all that was slangy and superficial', recalled Sutherland Edwards, 'and a writer who had anything nasty to say would generally say it of Albert Smith'.[22] But the intensity of the attacks by Jerrold had a particularly personal, visceral quality. It is not hard to imagine how Smith would have found himself transported back to his childhood experiences of bullying at Merchant Taylors', and the sense of vulnerability and impotence this would have engendered might explain the loss of his normal fighting spirit. Normally an assertive, even rather blustering man, Smith seems to have encountered some quality in Jerrold that rendered him docile. He tried to make light of their rivalry, buying a penny whip from a toy shop and 'boasting that he intended whipping little Master Jerrold at the first opportunity', but he fooled nobody and when it actually came to confronting Jerrold, Smith seems to have shrunk away.[23]

Smith's last piece for *Punch* – a short and inconsequential article called 'Important and Telegraphic' about toy soldiers being deployed to Ireland, whose humour has not survived the passage of time – was published in January 1844. He never wrote for the magazine again. The reason for his abrupt departure after three productive years is unclear: some accounts claim that he was sacked for plagiarism, in the form of direct translations of articles published in the French press; others that Mark Lemon became exasperated by Smith's habit of showing advance proofs of articles to his drinking companions in the Cheshire Cheese; others that Smith simply grew tired of the attacks by Jerrold, Lemon, and others. The son of one of Smith's contemporaries on *Punch*, the prolific comic journalist Gilbert à Beckett, dismissed the notion that passing off translations of French originals would have led to his sacking, pointing out that, 'it was not considered a very great crime this translating from the French in the early days of the nineteenth century [...] So if Albert Smith had "annexed" a few ideas from the Boulevards, I do not think it would have been considered such a serious crime'. Smith, he suggests, simply found Jerrold 'uncongenial company' and left of his own accord, which sounds plausible enough until one reads Smith's plaintive letters to *Punch*'s publishers William Bradbury and Frederick Evans, in which he expresses his bewilderment about what is happening.[24] Patrick Leary, in his minutely researched history of the *Punch* 'brotherhood', argues that Smith was probably a casualty of the transition to new ownership by Bradbury and Evans.[25] The magazine had begun as a cooperative, but when Bradbury and Evans bought it in 1842 they brought with them financial stability and the ability to service its printing requirements, as well as a new level of professionalism. *Punch*, in turn, allowed Bradbury and Evans, who up until that point had been jobbing printers, to transform themselves into a proper publishing concern – by the 1860s, the magazine was earning profits of over £10,000 a year, and the firm had grown to the point where it would publish many of Dickens's novels from *Oliver Twist* onwards as well as *Household Words,* the *Daily News* and a number of others publications.[26]

Whatever the reason, Smith seems to have been shocked by his exit from *Punch*, suggesting that he was either formally sacked or that the management simply stopped offering him work. His letters to the publishers display a genuine sense of hurt and dismay, although not so much as to prevent him from negotiating with them to publish his work in other formats. Writing to Bradbury and Evans in July 1844, ostensibly to discuss the possibility of publishing his medical student 'physiology' in book form, Smith's bewilderment at his treatment is palpable:

> I much regret that circumstances – of the nature of which I am entirely ignorant but which have originated in some great misunderstanding somewhere – have for some time kept me from seeing much of you at the office. As one of the oldest contributors to *Punch*, and one who at the same time undeviatingly did his best for its welfare, both in the early uphill work, and until after the almanac this year, I do not scruple to confess that I have felt this matter very deeply. Nor did I ever write for anything opposed to the interests of *Punch*, until I felt justified in doing so by the treatment I had received. Perhaps I regard this matter in a wrong light; but no opportunity was ever allowed for an explanation.[27]

These are clearly not the words of a man who had left his position at *Punch* of his own free will. Bradbury and Evans evidently took a circumspect line with Smith, claiming that they could not interfere with editorial decisions but at the same time encouraging him to send in further material to *Punch*, and keeping open the possibility of publishing his 'medical student' work separately. A few days after this letter, having received their reply, Smith was reassuring them that, 'I never, for a moment, wished to provoke any interference with the editorial arrangements of *Punch*. I only wished in some measure, to account for our have [*sic*] seen so little of each other lately. Be assured, in black & white, that it is not my fault', and accepting their suggestions for how to proceed with the 'physiology'.[28]

Bradbury & Evans may have encouraged Smith to submit further material for *Punch*, but they evidently chose not to order editor Mark Lemon to accept it or otherwise get involved in the editorial process on Smith's behalf. A couple of months later, in mid-September, Smith wrote to them again in tones of injured pride:

> The article which I thought would be most apropos […] has been returned to me from Mr. Lemon, in such a manner as will preclude me from again exposing myself to a similar insult. I can assure you I am very sorry for this, but having done all in my power, consistent with my position, to make up old breaches I hope you will acquit me of acting otherwise than from a wish for conciliation.[29]

Even at this stage, having clearly having had his friendly overtures and attempt to mend fences rejected in no uncertain terms by Lemon, Smith was pragmatic enough to add,

> I am quite ready to go over the "Medical Student" when you will be good enough to let me have the copy. And trusting that this little altercation may not in any way alter our excellent understanding with each other, in matters of business or otherwise, believe me to be my dear sir,
>
> Very sincerely yours,
>
> Albert Smith.

As it turned out, Smith's hopes that the controversy with *Punch*'s editors would not affect his business relationship with Bradbury & Evans turned out to be less forlorn than they sound in this slightly pathetic correspondence. When Smith and Leech launched *The Month* in 1851, Bradbury & Evans bankrolled it – despite Smith's earlier involvement in a rival publication called *The Man in the Moon* which spent much of its time mocking *Punch*, and his part in another squib called *A Word with Punch*.

Clearly, Smith's time at *Punch* was over. Never one to spend too long feeling sorry for himself, the twenty-eight-year-old writer quickly dusted himself down and began to look for new work, although he retained a grudge against *Punch* for many years, and was later delighted to accept work on *Punch*-baiting rivals. He briefly edited a short-lived publication called *Puck* and in the same year he was asked to write the prologue to a stage adaptation of Dickens's novel *Martin Chuzzlewit* being produced by Edward Stirling under the title *Mrs Harris* at the Lyceum.[30] Smith's verse prologue is a fairly conventional panegyric to the genius of the author – the original author, Dickens, not Stirling, a popular dramatist who specialized in unauthorised theatrical adaptations of Dickens's works.[31] It does, however, indicate how ably Smith could turn his hand to different genres – throughout his life he was adept at churning out verse on command:

> We owe this story of the present hour
> To that great master hand whose magic power
> Can call up laughter, bid the tear to start,
> And find an echoing chord in every heart;
> Whom we have learn'd to deem a household friend;
> Who midst his various writings never penn'd
> One line that might his guileless pages spot
> One word that dying he would wish to blot.[32]

Smith could – and did, when called for – produce this sort of thing by the yard. In the same year, 1844, he also produced a children's book, *The Adventures of Jack Holyday, With Something About his Sister*. Published as part of a series called 'Young England's Little Library' by W. S. Orr, *Jack Holyday* is a fairly conventional Victorian children's book in verse. The 'Little Library' series was praised by the *Mirror of Literature* for offering 'blameless amusement, and instruction associated with adventures of interest', and the book is every bit as unmemorable as this review would imply.[33] Again, however, it suggests Smith's versatility as a writer.

If Smith's departure from *Punch* in early 1844 marked a low point in his career, it was not to last for long. Two important events occurred in the same year that would influence his future – the publication of his first novel, *Ledbury*, in book form and his meeting with the celebrated American showman and huckster Phineas Taylor ('P. T.') Barnum. Barnum (1810-1891) was already famous in the United States and was starting to make his name in Europe, touring with his protégé the midget 'General' Tom Thumb (Charles Sherwood Stratton, 1838-1883). It is not clear precisely how he and Smith came into contact when Barnum and Tom Thumb arrived in England in 1844. Smith claims that they met by chance when staying at the same hotel in Birmingham, having already been introduced at the London house of a mutual acquaintance. However, Smith's reputation as a versatile comic writer and thrusting young man about town was growing by this stage, and Barnum was the sort of character who was always on the lookout for useful contacts. In retrospect, it seems impossible that the two of them could have failed to come across each other. In their sense of showmanship, their eye for the main chance, and their instinct for self-publicity they seemed so alike, although

Smith was rather less unscrupulous than Barnum and even gave the impression of being slightly shocked as well as impressed by the American's chutzpah.

Smith did not write up the details of his encounter with Barnum until three years later, when he published an article in *Bentley's Miscellany* titled 'A Go-Ahead Day with Barnum'. By then, however, he had already written a play for General Tom Thumb, and had used his Barnum experience in his 1845 novel, *The Fortunes of the Scattergood Family*, where he put some of the showman's opinions into the mouth of the character Mr. Rossett, and set some scenes in Coventry, Warwickshire, and Stratford, places he and Barnum had visited together.[34] Reading his account of travelling around the Midlands with the great showman, it is clear that at least some of Barnum's views rubbed off on him – or perhaps it would be more accurate to say that Barnum planted seeds on the already very fertile ground of Smith's character. Smith begins his account of the 'Go-Ahead day' with the remark quoted in Chapter 1 that, 'Before people see a person or place, they always form an idea to themselves of what he or it is like, and they are always decidedly wrong in their notions.'[35] He was referring to Birmingham, but of course as we have seen this could easily serve for Smith's writing about just about any location. Smith declares himself pleasantly surprised by Birmingham, having expected it to be dingy and depressing and instead finding 'a large clean town, with a pure country air blowing about its handsome streets', but it may be that in his remarks about being mistaken in preconceived notions of what something is like Smith was thinking of Barnum, as much as of Birmingham. The impression he gives after his day with Barnum is of being ever so slightly shell-shocked, even though he describes his jaunt as a relief from 'the pen that we had been chained to, like a galley-slave to his oar, in the continuously painful process, or rather intention, of always being "funny"'.[36]

Over the course of a day's sightseeing, Barnum explains to Smith his philosophy of keeping one step ahead of competitors and his pragmatic approach to fame and fortune. 'They call me a humbug now', he freely admits. 'Very good. I can afford it. They won't some day.' (Smith confesses that, 'We had so frequently heard Barnum called a humbug that we did not even venture the courtesy of saying, "Oh no! You must be mistaken".') Barnum continues, 'Humbug is nowadays the knack of knowing what people will pay money to see or support. Anybody who's up to this is safe to be called a humbug by everybody who isn't.'

In Stratford, where they pass a barber's shop called 'Shakespere, hair-dresser', Barnum tells Smith,

> You talk a good deal about your Shakespere [*sic*] being the pride of England, but I can see nobody knew or cared a cent about him while he was alive, or else you'd have known more of him now. If he'd been a living author, and I'd had

my exhibition, I'd have backed the general [Tom Thumb] to have shut him up in a week.

It's not clear if this conversation was the origin of Smith's supposed disdain for Shakespeare, and Smith recounts Barnum's words without much comment or elaboration.[37] Smith and Barnum move on to Warwick Castle, where 'Barnum wanted to buy everything that struck him, for his American Museum'. Barnum tries to buy a pair of elk horns, a Rubens painting, a pair of portraits of the Earls of Leicester and Essex, and another painting by the Italian Baroque painter Guido Reni. 'What'll you take now for the lot', he asks one of the castle's retainers who is showing them around, and upon being told indignantly that they are not for sale retorts, 'Just as you like [...] But I'll get up a better set than these within six months at my museum, and I'll swear mine are the real original, and bust up your show altogether in no time.'

At the end of their long day together, Smith professes himself tired. 'Well, I don't know what you call work in England', replies Barnum,

> but if you don't make thirty hours out of the twenty-four in Amerikey, I don't know where you'd be at the year's end. If a man can't beat himself in running, he'll never go ahead, and if he don't go ahead, he's done.

The Barnum of Smith's account comes across as loud, self-aggrandizing, and obnoxious, almost a cartoon version of the swaggering American huckster. Barnum gave his own version of his day with Smith, who he described as 'a particular friend of mine', in his 1855 autobiography, which tallies in most points with Smith's. In 'A Day With Albert Smith', he describes Smith as 'a jolly companion, as well as a witty and sensible author', and claims that 'during our journey I amused him with many of my adventures [...] which he afterwards served up in his *Scattergood Family*, making me the hero'.[38] In fact, it is hard to judge to what degree Smith was genuinely impressed by Barnum and to what degree he found him ludicrous and overbearing. The character of Rossett in *Scattergood* is a typical Smith concoction of the amusing and the ludicrous, with a considerable element of the charlatan and the braggart. He describes his methods as follows:

> If there was anything making a noise in the world, I got it. If I couldn't do that, I made one like it. Look at the mermaid, and the club that killed Captain Cook, with the very native who used it.

Rossett continues, 'as if wound up to enthusiasm by the recollection of former triumphs [...] in the same tone of voice that he would have used in addressing a crowd from one of his platforms':

The dolphin! the beautiful dolphin! There is no deception. The performing pig, and banded armadillo. The silver-haired Circassian, and pacific savage of the Indian seas. They were all mine![39]

Even leaving aside his use of Barnum as the basis for Rossett, Smith gave the impression of being rather exhausted by the whole experience and his sense of the ridiculous was finely enough attuned to see through at least some of Barnum's 'humbug'. Yet Smith's own subsequent career was to prove a fine example of the 'go-ahead' principle, and he certainly gave every indication that he did not mind being called a 'humbug' provided people were talking about him, reading his books, and coming to his shows. Albert Smith was not simply a British P. T. Barnum – his career was quite different to Barnum's in many respects – but he undoubtedly 'beat himself in running', as the American would put it, over the next few years. After his ignominious departure from *Punch* in 1844, Smith never looked back.

6: OUT OF GRUB STREET

'Travelling certainly broadens the mind', said Mr. Ledbury, 'but destroys many pleasant illusions'. Albert Smith, *The Adventures of Mr. Ledbury and His Friend Jack Johnson*

Having left *Punch* and struck out on his own, Smith was increasingly prolific during the rest of the 1840s. A brief overview of his output between 1844 and the end of the decade gives some measure of his extraordinary work ethic.

After the publication of *Ledbury* in 1844, he produced four more novels. His second, *Fortunes of the Scattergood Family,* appeared in monthly instalments in *Bentley's Miscellany* during 1845, followed by the *Marchioness of Brinvilliers* in 1846. In 1847 he published *Natural History of the Gent, Natural History of the Ballet-Girl, Natural History of Stuck-Up People,* various articles in *Bentley's* (including his account of the day spent with Barnum), and began to co-edit a publication called *The Man in the Moon* with Angus Reach. He also worked on a publication called *A Word with Punch*, on a short-lived periodical called *Curtain*, and still found time to nearly get himself killed in a ballooning accident that year. Then in 1848 *Christopher Tadpole* began publication in sixteen monthly stand-alone issues; during the same year, Smith published *A Pottle of Strawberries,* the *Natural History of the Idler upon Town, A Bowl of Punch* and *Comic Sketches from the Wassail Bowl,* and a pamphlet called 'Why our Theatres Are Not Supported'.

1848 also found Smith working on various other articles in *Bentley's*, and writing a comic piece called *The Social Parliament.* Smith's final novel, *The Pottleton Legacy,* was published in single volume by the publisher David Bogue in 1849; unlike his previous novels, which had illustrations by Smith's former *Punch* colleague Leech, *Pottleton* was illustrated by Phiz (Hablot K. Browne), who had just finished work on Dickens's *Dombey and Son* (1848).[1] During this same period, he dramatized Dickens's *The Cricket on the Hearth* and *The Battle of Life* for the stage (meeting his future wife, Mary Keeley, in the process) and either wrote or reworked various pantomimes and burlesques, among them *Cherry and Fairstar* (Princess's Theatre, 1844), *Aladdin* (Lyceum, 1844), *Valentine and Orson* (Lyceum, 1844), *Whittington and His Cat* (Lyceum, 1845), *Cinderella* (Lyceum, 1845), and *The Enchanted Horse* (Lyceum, 1845).[2]

Smith's comic writing during this period ranged from a mock law to regulate the giving and conduct of evening parties (*The Social Parliament*) through to

parodies of Samuel Johnson and James Boswell; in the latter, Boswell tries to provoke Johnson into a display of epigrammatic wit but is instead met with a series
of banal responses ('I wonder what time it is', muses Boswell. 'Sir, the time is after
two', replies Johnson).[3] All this plus numerous rhymes, riddles, poems, comic bal-
lads, and nonsense in between – Smith was seemingly inexhaustible.

Not only was Smith tireless, he was also determined not to remain anonymous. According to Patrick Leary and Andrew Nash, unsigned contributions to
newspapers and periodicals were almost ubiquitous until the 1860s, yet from the
1840s onwards Smith was insisting on signing (or at least putting his initials
to) his work.[4] This brought him criticism from some contemporaries, and gave
weight to those who considered him a pushy, ambitious 'snob', but it also helped
him become famous. Smith's refusal to publish anonymously, in defiance of the
conventions of the time, was an important source of his growing fame and success, and Smith himself certainly believed this.[5]

Inevitably, given his prolific output, the quality of Smith's writing is variable,
perhaps nowhere more so than in the novels, which are pithily described in his
Oxford Dictionary of National Biography entry as 'more notable for their wit than
their plots'. Smith's novels were very popular in their day, and can still be amusing in parts, but few modern readers would deny that they are excessively long,
overwritten, repetitive, and often risibly plotted. Henry James's description of
nineteenth-century novels as 'large, loose, baggy monsters' could easily have been
written with these books in mind. They do, however, present a particular class and
milieu – the striving lower middle classes, mostly in London or at least of London
origin – in vivid, unsentimental terms, and with a ring of authenticity.

Ledbury, a rambling, picaresque story whose action moves from London to
the Continent and back, taking in Paris, the Rhine, and the Alps, exhibits many
of the characteristics of Smith's subsequent fiction and indeed of his writing in
general – his use of characters and experiences from his own life; his tendency to
re-use material in different books and genres; and above all, perhaps, his breezy
irreverence for the sacred cows of the nineteenth-century tourist circuit, and his
insistence that 'guide-books are a collection of lies half-bound in cloth to deceive
travellers'.[6] This latter belief pervades the novel. 'I am considerably disappointed
in the Rhine', a fellow tourist tells Jack Johnson at one point. 'Everybody is, sir',
replies Johnson, 'that I ever met with; only they do not like to say so, for fear of
being shouted at. It's a mere popular delusion which the guide-books, hotels, and
steamers have an interest in keeping up.'[7]

The protagonists of this book are men and women of no great fortune, education, or breeding, but endowed with plenty of energy, ambition, and native wit,
and often living just on the right side of respectability. Titus Ledbury is a lawyer's

clerk with aspirations to greater things; his friend Johnson is a medical school drop-out who exists on 'some little property of my own. It has, hitherto, been sufficient to keep me out of debt.'[8] Johnson later resumes his medical training, becoming apprenticed to the disreputable private practitioner Mr. Rawkins, who, in addition to prescribing dubious medication to gullible customers, keeps a menagerie of rabbits, guinea-pigs, and ferrets, and performs feats of strength while posing as Hercules.[9]

Ledbury and Johnson fit neatly into the social milieu that Albert Smith focused on in most of his novels; what Jerry White calls 'that racy vulgar brash London of the new aspiring middle classes and those with whom they came into contact, above and below'.[10] Yet at the same time, Ledbury and Johnson are in a similarly ambiguous class position as their creator – disdainful of cockneys and snobs while perilously vulnerable to being described as such themselves. Ledbury is introduced as 'standing about five feet eleven in his improved Albert-boots ("gents new style")', marking him out as something of a 'gent' – the same species whose pretensions and absurdities Smith had poked fun at in his 'Physiology of the London Idler' article for *Punch*, and who he would skewer to comic effect three years later in his *Natural History of the Gent*. When Ledbury suggests visiting Gravesend and Johnson replies, 'Don't go there. Nasty place – swarms with hot clerks', the irony is not lost on the reader.[11]

The novel is full of 'cockney' humour, and at times it is not clear whether Smith the narrator is inviting the reader to laugh at the antics of 'cockneys' abroad or to laugh along with them. 'That's Cleopatra's needle', Johnson notes as they pass the Luxor Obelisk in the centre of the Place de la Concorde. 'They are going to bring over her thimble next year, and the Viceroy of Egypt has hopes of discovering the entire work-box.'[12] Upon being told that an Egyptian mummy he is viewing is three thousand years old, Johnson observes, 'Bless me! What an age they lived to in Egypt', and asks its curator, 'Pray, sir, is it Cheops?' '"No sir", replied the man, indignantly; "it's real bones and flesh"'.[13] (Smith loved this kind of humour, and a seam of it runs through all his work: 'You must have read *Childe Harold*', someone exclaims to the crooked lawyer Gudge in *Christopher Tadpole,* as they pass the Palazzo Mocenigo, Byron's erstwhile Venice home. 'No, I can't say I have', replies Gudge. 'I don't care much about children when they're not your own.')[14] Like his creator, Johnson is resolutely unimpressed by ancient ruins, spectacular sights, fairytale castles, and all the other standard appurtenances of European tourism. Travelling down the Rhine, Ledbury remarks that 'Those ruins of former times are very interesting', to which Johnson replies with characteristic bathos, 'Yes, but they are all alike […] The two tall chimneys at the base of Primrose Hill, and the round shot manufactory at Lambeth, cut into lengths, and perched on the tops of mountains, would furnish quite as many traditions. They are nearly all the same.'[15]

Yet Smith also displays the other, less hard-headed and reductive traits that are in evidence both in his subsequent novels and in his journalism; a fascination with the idea of life as a spectacular performance, which never quite disappears under the weight of his debunking scepticism, and a genuine interest in and affection for modern technology and modes of transport. On a voyage to Boulogne, Smith describes the ship about to leave dock in terms that suggest his ability to find wonder and beauty in seemingly unpromising places:

> A stream of vapour, visible in the light of the lamps on the bridge, was rising from the spare steam funnel, and breaking into occasional whiffs as the paddle-wheels sullenly turned a stroke or two backwards and forwards: like a musician indulging in a few notes and runs to himself, that he may ascertain all is right before commencing some great performance.

Smith's prose can be long-winded and downright dull in places, but he is also capable of lyrical turns of phrase and sharply observed, revealing descriptions of people and places. His vivid picture of a reluctant Ledbury getting down from a stage-coach 'with much caution, like a bear from the top of his pole at the Zoological Gardens, after he has been indulged with a bun by an intrepid little boy', or of 'a gentleman with a very hooky nose, having the air of a cockatoo in a suit of mourning' work with economy and precision.[16] His descriptions of food are another strong point – both in his fiction and his travel writing Smith was always interested in food, and could write about it in terms that were either mouthwatering or nauseating, depending on what he was describing. Here he is on the wares of a West End restaurant frequented by Ledbury:

> Strange cold meats of unintelligible origin and extraordinary shape, were exposed to view, with the remnants of yesterday's bill of fare on small plates. Round tough puddings, studded with plums at uncertain intervals, reposed with an air of indigestible solidity upon white and greasy earthenware dishes; and the soup-tureens were filled with a singular coagulation, resembling small pieces of fat and carrots set in dirty glue.

Ledbury was a commercial and to some degree a critical success. 'What *Pickwick* was to Dickens, *Ledbury* was to Albert Smith', recalled his friend Edmund Yates after Smith's death.[17] Comparing Smith to Dickens might seem far-fetched nowadays, but Yates was far from the only critic to make the comparison. John Hollingshead, a writer, theatrical impresario, and friend of Smith's, recalled him as 'a shrewd, clever writer, whose novels were admirable mixtures of Bulwer and Dickens – very readable', and even the *Athenaeum*, which was at times critical of Smith's work, reviewed *Christopher Tadpole* on its release as 'a story in invention not unlike *Oliver Twist* – cleverly conducted, with some passages of broad humour and whimsical scenes of foreign travel'.[18] The publisher George Routledge, advertising a set of cheap reprints of Smith's novels in the late 1850s, went even further, claiming,

> Charles Dickens and Albert Smith so assimilate in style, and their vigorous powers of conception are so great, that it would be a very difficult task for the nicest critic to award a preference as to their merits. Let it be said, therefore, that they are stars of great magnitude, shining with equal brilliancy.[19]

Unsurprisingly, not everyone agreed. The translator and dramatist John Oxenford, upon hearing Smith compared to Dickens, was reported to have said, 'If you were to pour a bottle of brandy into the Thames on one side of London Bridge, and draw up a bucket of water on the other side, you would find about as much flavor of brandy in the water of the bucket as there is of Dickens in Albert Smith.'[20]

Whatever the critical view, Smith was starting to build a reputation, and enlarging his social circle. Dickens wrote warmly to him in January 1844, thanking him for sending the three volumes that had just been published, although just a couple of years later he was complaining to Douglas Jerrold that he had been offended by Smith's allusion (in an advert for his forthcoming serialization of *Christopher Tadpole*) to the 'ponderous attempt' of some contemporary writers to improve society and persuade people who were 'contented' that they were actually oppressed. Instead, Smith had written, the purpose of writing books should be harmless amusement. Dickens understandably regarded this as a jibe at his own socially conscious novels, and complained to Jerrold that 'There was an impertinence in it that rather stirred my bile.'[21] Nonetheless, Dickens and Smith became good friends, and the year after *Ledbury*'s publication in book form saw them collaborating for the first time. That year Smith worked with the dramatist Tom Taylor on a production of *Cinderella*, starring Robert and Mary Anne Keeley, the celebrated actor-managers of the Lyceum. At the end of 1845, Smith adapted Dickens's Christmas novella *The Cricket and the Hearth*, working from Dickens's proofs so that the play could be staged at the Lyceum on the same day the book was published.[22] This production featured the Keeley's fifteen-year-old daughter Mary Lucy in her acting debut, as the blind Bertha Plummer.

The Spectator gave the play a positive review, despite its misgivings about the arrangement between Dickens, Smith, and the Keeleys, which it described as 'a practice equally injurious to the stage and to literature'. It conceded that Dickens had found in Smith 'the assistance of an expert operator […] whose version of *The Cricket on the Hearth* is a great improvement on the more paste-and-scissors process of mechanical botchers'. The journal praised the performance of Mary Keeley, who 'showed sensibility and cleverness, in addition to a handsome person'.[23] Smith himself seems to have been captivated by the girl from their first meeting. 'From the favourable impression created she will, we augur, become a star of no ordinary magnitude', he wrote about Mary's stage debut. 'Her features are pleasing and expressive; and when, at the conclusion of the piece, on being called before the curtain, we were permitted to see her eyes, which she had kept closed whilst playing the part of the blind Bertha, we found them as bright and intelligent as her mother's, and this is the highest compliment we can pay them.'[24] It is not clear at what stage they began a relationship, nor why they did not marry until 1859, by which stage Smith was already having an affair with another actress, Pattie Oliver, but they were evidently known to be a couple during the 1850s.[25] Mary never achieved the fame of her parents, and her life and career remain comparatively obscure. Shirley Brooks, who joined the staff of *Punch* in the early 1850s and later became its editor, was part of Smith's social circle and described Mary as 'a dainty, bright, saucy, yet kindly little thing',[26] and the actor and barrister Montagu Williams – who was married to her sister, Lousie Keeley – recalled that Robert Keeley was particularly fond of Smith.[27] But Smith himself left no account of their life together, and his relationship with Mary remains enigmatic.[28]

1845 also saw the serial publication of Smith's second novel, *The Fortunes of the Scattergood Family*. This was the novel in which Smith used – and perhaps to some degree exorcised – his experiences at Merchant Taylors' school, depicting it in terms unlikely to have brought an invitation to come back and speak at prize day. He describes the school as 'a long dingy brick building, with little claim to architectural beauty, occupying a large proportion of one side of the thoroughfare', while the house of the sepulchral Reverend Snap, where young Fred Scattergood is sent to board while attending the school – and where he is brutalized both by teachers and fellow pupils – has 'the stark, gloomy quietude of death'.[29] The scene where Fred runs away was directly based on Smith's own childhood experiences and here, at least, the comparison to Dickens is not strained; Smith writes of Fred's terrified escape, and his inevitable betrayal and forcible return, in prose that is all the more effective for its restraint, and which evokes the helplessness and fear of childhood trauma. He describes a school system where

> the spirits of the gentle are crushed and broken, or hardened in self-defence, by the overbearing tyranny of those who should be their associates; where the worst dispositions of the bully and the school despot are ministered unto and fostered by licensed opportunities; where every sacred feeling of home and affection is jeered at and despised.[30]

For once, Smith is not inclined to mock or debunk; his writing in this section of *Scattergood* is passionate, sincere, and coldly furious. From here on, however, the novel returns to more familiar comic territory, although it is notable for the introduction of what might be termed a Mr. Micawber character *avant la lettre*. Mr. Scattergood senior, the ineffectual head of the family who 'unvaryingly assert- ed that everything would come in good time, and that there was no occasion to worry', bears a striking resemblance to Dickens's invention in *David Copperfield* (1850).[31] As in his other novels, Smith is prone to Fieldingesque authorial inter- ventions on the role and prerogatives of the narrator, some of which are amusing but more often serve to slow down and disrupt the pace of the novel. He contin- ues his habit of recycling material (for example repeating in modified form a scene from *Ledbury* where someone annoys a turnpike keeper by asking him ridiculous questions), and demonstrates the same political conservatism that was to irritate Dickens in his *Tadpole* advert. Describing a stage melodrama, he notes that the most popular speeches by the actors were 'in support of a great right, viz. that "nature's aristocracy", have no right to pay any rent unless they like', which inevi- tably 'met with very great applause'. Smith notes that the authors of this kind of drama have 'only to abuse the superior classes of society, and insinuate the "we've- as-much-right-as-they-have" theory of possession into the bosoms of the pit and galleries' in order to achieve audience approval.[32]

Smith followed *Scattergood* with a historical romance loosely based on the true-life Marchioness of Brinvilliers (c. 1630-1676), who became the mistress of her husband's friend Godin de Sainte-Croix, and was eventually executed as a poisoner. The story had been revived by Alexandre Dumas in his *Celebrated Crimes*, which Smith probably read in the original French when it first appeared in 1839 or 1840. Herman Melville would later write a poem inspired by Charles Le Brun's portrait of the Marchioness.[33] Smith's *Marchioness of Brinvilliers* is a swashbuckling potboiler that clearly owes a great deal to the novels of Walter Scott. Like Smith's earlier translation of *The Armourer of Paris*, it benefits from his impressive historical knowledge of Paris, but, like much of his fiction, it suffers from his tendency to purple prose, as this brief extract suggests:

> Night came on: dark, cold, tempestuous. The fleeting beauty of the spring eve- ning had long departed; the moon became totally invisible through the thick clouds that had been soaring onwards in gloomy masses from the south; and the outlines of the houses were no longer to be traced against the sky. All was merged in one deep impenetrable obscurity. There were symptoms of a turbulent night. The wind whistled keenly over the river and the dreary flats adjoining; and big drops of rain fell audibly upon the paved court and drawbridge of the Bastille.

Smith makes full use of the Gothic potential of the catacombs of beneath the Parisian streets with their decaying skeletons, and creates numerous scenes of masques, balls, and other entertainments at the court of Louis Quatorze (Smith had a particular fondness for describing parties, balls, carnivals, fêtes, and soirées of every kind in his fiction, but his enthusiasm for such scenes tended to outstrip his ability to make them interesting and readable). He also introduces documents signed in blood, and villains who disappear into hidden passageways with 'loud and fiendish laughter'. Characters are prone to saying things like, 'Descend! – fiend! demon! murderess of my son! Descend! for you are mine – mine!'[34]

Ledbury, Scattergood, and *Brinvilliers* all began life in serial form in *Bentley's Miscellany,* but by the time Smith started to write his next book he was sufficiently famous that Richard Bentley was prepared to publish it as a stand-alone serial. The details of Smith's 1846 contract with Bentley, for a novel called *The Struggles and Adventures of Christopher Tadpole* to be published in twelve 'regular successive monthly portions containing thirty-two pages in the Octavo form of the same sized type and number of lines as the *Pickwick Papers* by Boz', not only indicate the continuing legacy of *Pickwick's* success in promoting serial fiction, but also demonstrate Smith's ability to command serious money for his writing. The contract specified that he would be paid thirty pounds for each installment, plus another five pounds for each monthly part which sold more than six thousand copies; another five pounds if it reached 6,500 copies; another five pounds when sales reached 7,000; then a final further five pounds if it reached 7,500, 'which last payment making a total of fifty pounds to be final'.[35] The serial was such a commercial success that the original agreement for twelve monthly parts was extended to sixteen, and Smith earned £800 – roughly £65,000 in today's terms – from the serialization alone, even before taking into account book sales.[36] '*Christopher Tadpole* was the first of my literary offspring that ran upon its own legs', Smith recalled in a preface to the 1854 edition, referring to the serialization of his previous novels in *Bentley's* as 'a sort of go-cart, by the aid of which they toddled on, relying on extraneous support'. *Tadpole,* by contrast, 'had to scramble on alone [...] and in spite of terrible supremacy, in the same play-ground, of a clever little boy named Dombey (who was a month younger but who had – and deservedly – a great many advantages), Christopher's parts, at a shilling each, at last enabled him to grow up a good stout book'.[37]

Despite Smith's reference to competition from *Dombey and Son, Christopher Tadpole* clearly owes a significant debt to *Oliver Twist,* with a hero who is born into poverty, abused and traduced by the adults around him, and cheated out of his inheritance, only to display natural gentility and courage and finally win his rightful place in the world. It even has its Bill Sikes character, in the person of the brutish salt-miner Rocky. As with his earlier books, Smith expends many pages on comical but usually excessively long depictions of balls, parties, fairs, and masques, and is particularly badly afflicted by logorrhea whenever a room presents itself to be described. A pivotal meeting between the crooked lawyer Gudge and the villainous aristocrat Sir Frederick Arden is delayed so that Smith can tell the reader that the back parlour where they confront each other

> had taken to itself somewhat the air of an expanded closet into which all sorts of things had been thrust to be out of the way, or in readiness. All the chairs had been transported to other regions, and so the floor was made into one large table and covered with half-demolished viands; and an inoffensive cheffonier [sic] was nearly weighed down by a flock of coffee cups, separated into detachments by candle-sticks which rose here and there in the glory of clean wax, recent leathering, and tinted ornaments, like the banners of the Lord Mayor's show amidst the procession.[38]

If *Tadpole* displays occasional flashes of the linguistic inventiveness that Smith at his best can deploy – a fairground mountebank's description of his hand-to-mouth existence as 'a sort of boey-constricty's life – one feed a month, and nothing betweens', for instance – it also suffers from Smith's tendency to recycle ideas and events.[39] He reuses his own experience with brigands to have one of his characters, Mrs Hamper, kidnapped and robbed, and once again has his protagonists ascend the Saint Bernard Pass, get into trouble, and have to be rescued by the monks and dogs, in an incident very similar to one already recounted in *Ledbury*.[40] Yet elsewhere in this novel Smith is writing at the height of his powers, especially in his description of salt mining in Cheshire and his evocation of the eponymous Christopher's first sight of Liverpool. Smith had visited the Marston mine in Cheshire while researching the book, and he conveys the eerie, netherworld quality of the mine and its environs powerfully:

> It was here less dark, and there were other things to guide him: lofty chimneys, whose mouths blazed forth like giant torches, high in air; cressets of coal fires that flared and trembled in the canal, and threw huge shadows of human forms upon the sheds and warehouses of the wharves; greedy furnaces that kept the engine at its unceasing work, devouring all thrown into their glowing throats, whose light streamed forth, through doors, and crannies, and untiled roofs, reflected on the jets of steam that burst forth so angrily from their mighty bondage to mingle with the air, and fall damp and cold upon the earth around.[41]

Smith's description of Liverpool captures the anarchic energy and the frontier quality of the port, with its 'Ships – ships – everywhere: crowding their lofty, quivering masts, and slender spars, and tense cordage in apparently inextricable complication.' Once again he is fascinated by modernity, technology, and the restless, expansive energy of a nineteenth-century trading port. The ships

> were the sources from which everything around rose – the lofty warehouses, and walls, and transit-sheds: the cranes, and oddly-fashioned carts, and solid

waggons; the crowds of toil-worn, thoughtful men of business: of careless sea-
men, and lynx-eyed officers that thronged the quays: the mighty docks, that
stretched so far along the shore, and could scarcely be said to finish anywhere.
For beyond their actual limits others were still forming. Huge piles arose to divide the rushing current of the Mersey far out from its banks, and blocks of stone
that appeared to defy all attempts to move them were lying about, on which the
clinking chisels of the masons were plied incessantly.[42]

Here, too, is Smith's ability to see beauty and magic in the seemingly quotidian, as in this description of travelling through London by river:

> If you have never passed a summer night upon the river as it flows through the
> metropolis [...] you cannot conceive how much of the beautiful, and even ro-
> mantic, still hangs about our cold, commonplace money-getting London. You
> must wait until the roar of swarming life has been stilled in the streets and on
> the bridges; and all traffic has ceased upon the water: until the house-fires have
> nearly all died away, and the moon is shining down from the clear heaven upon
> the sleeping city. And then Venice is scarcely more beautiful.[43]

Not that Smith was particularly enchanted by Venice – this was, after all, the
novel in which he compared it unfavourably to Wapping. But his description of
the Thames by night, like his pen-portrait of a steamer about to leave dock in
Ledbury, does illustrate how the corollary of Smith's irreverence towards the conventionally beautiful and spectacular – his dismissal of Venice, his comparison of
the Mer de Glace to a ploughed field – was his ability to see magic and romance
in unlikely places.

The success of *Tadpole* and of his 'Natural Histories' left Smith financially comfortable, although nowhere near as wealthy as he would become in the 1850s
as a result of his stage performances. To put the figure of £50 per monthly issue
into perspective, Smith was regularly making £30 a night from performing his
show *The Overland Mail* in the autumn of 1851, and for one performance at
Liverpool's Philharmonic Hall in the summer of 1851 he cleared £75.[44] Even
those sums would come to seem insignificant compared to the fortune he made
from his Mont Blanc show. However, for a man still in his early thirties, working
in the precarious literary profession, Smith had cause to be satisfied with both his
remuneration and his reputation. By the time *Tadpole* had finished its serial run,
Smith had also brought out his *Natural History* series, beginning with *The Gent*
and finishing with *Natural History of the Idler Upon the Town*. Henry Vizetelly
later denounced these as 'without a particle of wit', but was honest enough to
point out that he had turned down the opportunity to publish the series, which
was instead brought out by David Bogue, and was galled by the books' success.
'Quite a small fortune must have been made out of these wretched little books',

grumbled Vizetelly.[45]

It was. Bogue paid Smith only £10 for *The Gent*, but it proved to be such a success – reportedly selling two thousand copies on the day of publication – that Smith was able to command £100 for the subsequent *Natural Histories,* which continued to sell in great numbers to 'every run-and-read book-buyer', as one contemporary put it.[46] The humour of this series has not aged particularly well, but it is possible to imagine how Smith's precise delineation of particular social types struck a chord with his audience. *The Gent,* for example, describes a social phenomenon that Smith claimed was only about ten years old at that time, and he distinguishes between the eponymous gent and his predecessors, 'the "buck", the "gay blade", the "pretty fellow", and the "swell" or "man about town" or "knowing cove"'.[47] He is specific about the clothes and ornaments the gent wears ('blue stock; large breast-pins; snaffle coat-studs; curled hair […] large pattern trowsers; gay under-waistcoats'), the places he haunts, and the slang he uses (the fifth edition, published in 1847, has as its frontispiece an illustration of two 'gents' meeting, with one saying to the other, 'Come along my r-r-r-rummy cove, come along! how are you? how d'ye do? here we are my brickswywicksywicksy!!!')[48] As well as the delight of amused recognition, some of the success of *The Gent* and its successors may have been down to Smith's ability to make his readers feel he was up to the minute in his portrayal of the metropolitan scene. He suggests that the gent is a very contemporary creation of the present 'constant wearing struggle to appear something more than we in reality are, which now characterizes every body, both in their public and private phases'.[49]

This ability to make his readers feel he was tapping into the zeitgeist continued in the later *Natural Histories*. Smith was particularly good at rendering current argot, something that changes quickly and is difficult to capture. When he wrote in *Natural History of the Flirt* of how the 'flirt' arrives at a dinner party and 'is said by the girls "to think a great deal of herself" and by the young men leaning against the door to be "something nice"', he was clearly quoting back to his readers slang that they would recognize.[50] Smith's irreverence for the niceties of polite society probably appealed to his audience, too. In his *Natural History of Stuck-Up People*, for instance, he describes 'the season' and the custom of girls 'coming out' as 'that ceremony of inauguration into the mysteries of the Hymeneal Stock Exchange'.[51]

The success of Smith's novels and *Natural Histories* had pulled him up out of Grub Street to a position of wealth and a new social standing. By the end of the decade he would have succeeded in joining the Garrick Club, become editor of a monthly publication, and amassed sufficient funds to make a long journey to the Middle East – but not before another close escape from sudden death.

7: 'WE'RE ALL DEAD MEN'

We almost wanted a few perils to give a little excitement to the trip. Albert
Smith, 'Ascent of Mr. Green's Balloon from Cremorne Gardens', 1847

Smith's boyhood love of Vauxhall Pleasure Gardens never quite left him. By the
end of the 1840s, however, he gave the impression that it had been sorely tried.

Vauxhall continued to feature in Smith's writing. When the characters in
Christopher Tadpole want to go for an evening out, for example, they choose between Astley's and Vauxhall, eventually deciding on Vauxhall because it is possible
to stay there all evening.[1] By the time he published *The Pottleton Legacy* in 1849,
however, Smith's patience with Vauxhall was showing signs of wearing thin. One
of his characters, Wyndham Flitter, declines an invitation to spend the evening at
Vauxhall, saying,

> I know what 'great improvements' are at Vauxhall. The orchestra fresh painted;
> a view on the Rhine stuck up somewhere; and bad singing. The enterprise of the
> lessees consists in, season after season, seeing that what amused people thirty
> years ago doesn't do so now.[2]

Instead, Flitter and his companions go to see a balloon ascent from Cremorne
Pleasure Gardens, a rival venue to Vauxhall on the other side of the river in
Chelsea that had only been open since 1845 but which already reminded Smith
the narrator of 'a reduced nobleman compelled to turn clown for his livelihood'.[3]
Flitter eventually jumps into the balloon to avoid being arrested for debt, and in
true 'gent' style has to be dissuaded from lighting a cigar while in the basket. Yet
this cockney swagger soon gives way to a feeling of real wonder:

> His first feeling was that of wild exultation – his next, one of deep awe as the
> view below opened upon him. Hundreds of thousands of lamps were visible,
> marking all the localities of London, as though one had pricked out the lines of
> a map and put a light behind it.[4]

Smith once again demonstrates his instinct for a visual spectacle, but he was
not simply inventing Flitter's experience. Two years before *Pottleton* was published, Smith had made two balloon ascents, the first, like Wyndham Flitter, from
Cremorne. The second was from Vauxhall, and it very nearly marked the end of
Albert Smith's burgeoning career.

On his first, relatively uneventful flight from Cremorne in June 1847, Smith was taken up by the aeronaut Charles Green in his celebrated Great Balloon of Nassau, which had set a world record back in 1836 by flying from Vauxhall to the Duchy of Nassau in Germany, some 480 miles of continuous flight. Smith was accompanied by future *Punch* editor Shirley Brooks, Charles Ibbetson (who in 1849 would second Smith's candidacy for membership of the Garrick Club), and several other friends and acquaintances.[5] Smith later recalled his sensation that, instead of he and his companions rising, their balloon remained fixed and the spectators below them were falling away, 'until the cheers with which they greeted our departure grew fainter, and the cheerers themselves began to look like the inmates of many sixpenny Noah's Arks grouped upon a billiard table'.[6] The balloon sailed above the new Houses of Parliament, still being rebuilt after the 1834 fire, which from the air had 'the appearance of a delicate card-board model'.[7] The steamers on the Thames gave the impression of trailing long wings behind them, and the rowing boats reminded Smith of caraway seeds. They headed out over Chelsea, then were blown over Southwark, Rotherhithe, and the Isle of Dogs, towards Woolwich, then north to Barking Levels and Dagenham Marsh before finally coming to ground in Rainham in Essex, having crossed back and forward across the Thames a number of times as wind and air currents carried them. 'The strangest feeling of all, after our imperceptible journey', wrote Smith, 'was to find myself on the Essex marshes, with the shouts of Cremorne still in my ears'.[8] The group then walked to Rainham, about three miles from where they had landed, and got an omnibus and three horses back to London.

'From the delight we all experienced, we counsel everybody to go up in the balloon, and enjoy the journey – which they are sure to do – as much as we did', Smith advised the readers of the *Illustrated London News*. 'In spite of the apparent fragility of cane and net-work, nothing can, in reality, be more secure […] The stories of pressure on the ears, intense cold, and the danger of coming down are all fictions, invented by those who must make "adventures" out of everything that befalls them'.[9] He even joked that 'we almost wanted a few perils to give a little excitement to the trip; and have some notion, if possible, of going up the next time at midnight, with fireworks, in a thunder-storm; throwing away all the ballast, fastening down the valve, and seeing where the wind will send us'.[10]

Smith would soon have cause to regret this bravado. He arranged a second balloon ride, this time at night, with two balloonists named Gypson and Coxwell, who took trips up from Vauxhall Gardens. This was in a smaller vessel than the Nassau balloon, and incredibly it was indeed to involve trailing fireworks some thirty feet below the basket, then setting them off with fuses for the entertainment of the crowd below. As if this were not dangerous enough, the night chosen for the

ascent was 'uncommonly close and sultry [...] and lightning was repeatedly flashing about the skies, preluding [a] thunder storm'.[11] Smith had a bad feeling about
the preparations for the ascent, which seemed to his critical eye confused and
haphazard in comparison to the quiet professionalism that had marked Green's
ascent a couple of weeks earlier.

Faced with a night-time ascent in conditions of thunder and lightning while
trailing a cargo of fireworks, in a balloon prepared for its mission with doubtful
competence, a lesser man might have made his excuses and stayed on the ground
– perhaps retreating to a safe distance to watch with morbid curiosity as events
unfolded – but Albert Smith was never lacking in physical courage. He also had a
well-developed sense of his own dignity, and may have felt that to back down now
after his earlier boasts would be to court ridicule. In any case, he overcame his
misgivings and stepped aboard. The band played 'Off she goes', the crowd on the
ground at Cremorne cheered, and the balloon shot up in the air with what Smith
considered 'extreme velocity'. After one failed attempt to light the fireworks, they
were successfully ignited and shot out cascades of coloured flames from the ascending balloon.

'It is impossible to form the feeblest idea of what the appearance of London
is, seen by night, from the elevation we had now attained', wrote Smith, who at
that point was an estimated four thousand feet above the city.

> I can compare it to nothing else than floating over a dark blue and boundless sea,
> spangled with thousands of stars. These stars were the lamps. We could see them
> stretching over the river at the bridges, edging its banks, forming squares and
> long parallel lines of light in the streets, and solitary sparks, further and further
> apart until they were altogether lost in the suburbs. The effect was too bewilder-
> ing – too novel and extraordinary, to allow any of us even to speak; we could
> only gaze on them in rapt and deep attention.[12]

As they reached an altitude of 7,000 feet, the pilots noticed that the balloon
'was getting very tense, from the extreme rarefaction of the external air at the
elevation we had achieved'. The order was given to ease off the growing pressure
inside the balloon by allowing some gas to escape out of the top valve, but at this
point the valve blew and 'the lower part of the balloon collapsed rapidly, and appeared to fly up into the upper portion'. Coxwell exclaimed, 'We're all dead men',
and at the same moment 'the balloon began to fall with appalling velocity'. A
panicked cry went up to throw anything overboard that might lighten the balloon
and slow their descent; Smith threw two sandbags over the side, and the pilots and
other passengers proceeded to offload as much ballast as possible, yet the balloon
continued to fall:

> The wind still appeared to be rushing past us at a fearful rate; and to add to the

horror of these few moments, we came amidst the expiring discharge of the fireworks which floated on the air, so that little bits of exploded cases and touch-paper, still incandescent, attached themselves to the cordage of the balloon and were blown into sparks. The lightning [...] was playing about us uninterrupt-edly – it had done so during our ascent – and the whole machine soon began to oscillate frightfully.[13]

Smith described his feelings during this drama in terms which may exagger-ate his presence of mind, but it seems to me more likely that – as with his calm, precise account of his robbery at the hands of Italian brigands – he was trying to communicate the strange combination of intensity, fatalism, and the feeling of time moving very slowly which can characterize the experience of sudden mortal danger. 'I felt collected and tranquil to a degree almost preternatural,' he recalled,

but every impression, of the most trivial kind, appeared to be made with tenfold intensity. I have still the appearance of the lights on the earth before my eyes, almost as vividly as when I was looking at them – as though their forms had been so vividly impressed on the retina that they were retained there.[14]

The balloon hit the ground at terrifying speed, but miraculously neither Smith nor any other occupants were seriously hurt. Smith attributed their survival to the upper netting of the balloon having held in place and acting as a kind of para-chute to slow down their fall. When they hit the ground he was thrown out of the basket and became entangled in the netting. During the descent he had hoped they would land in the Thames but he later realized that if this had happened they would most likely have drowned while still entangled in the netting. 'Torn clothes, crushed hats, and a few grazes and bruises, were all the evils that resulted from a descent of a mile, without gas!'[15]

None the worse for his latest brush with death, Smith promptly gave a descrip-tion of the incident to an artist, to be turned into a dramatic illustration for an account in the *Illustrated London News* two days later. Never one to waste good material, and certainly never shy of re-using what had already been published, Smith later merged his accounts of the two ascents for an article in *The Town and Country Miscellany*, and also wrote a jocular version of his first balloon voyage in *The Man in The Moon* (see below). So far as is known, however, he never made another balloon ascent.

The same year, 1847, found Smith working on two new publications, both of them set up as rivals to *Punch* – or, in the case of *A Word with Punch*, as a kind of thinly-veiled threat to *Punch*'s writers by the theatrical impresario Alfred Bunn. Bunn was the manager of Covent Garden and Drury Lane, where he had enjoyed considerable success but was accused of vulgarizing the theatre by introducing, for example, lion tamers and tightrope acts. He got involved in a punch-up with the actor William Macready, was embroiled in a court case with the actress Jenny Lind, and ended up in deep financial trouble. The word most often used to describe Bunn's style is 'flamboyant', but *Punch* had other words, too, deriding him as 'the Poet Bunn' and 'Hot Cross Bunn' and mocking everything from his appearance to his librettos and poetry. Bunn decided to fight back, financing a publication in which he attacked the editors and writers of *Punch* in person, with help from Smith and George Augustus Sala, the latter only nineteen years old at that time but later to become a regular contributor to *All the Year Round,* the *Daily Telegraph,* and the *Illustrated London News.* Sala, a talented illustrator as well as writer, had had his submissions to *Punch* rejected by Mark Lemon in a rather peremptory manner; Smith, too, presumably relished the opportunity to eat his dish of revenge cold, three years after being banished from the *Punch* brotherhood. However, the level of invective in *A Word with Punch*, with its direct personal attacks on Douglas Jerrold, Gilbert à Becket, and Mark Lemon, seems more likely to have emanated from Bunn than Smith, who had always remained on good terms with à Beckett and later became reconciled with Jerrold. The first issue of *A Word with Punch*, its cover illustration showing Mr. Punch standing in the stocks, was listed as 'No.1 (to be continued if necessary)', and it was, as Bunn's *ODNB* entry puts it, 'virtuosically vituperative'.[16] The implied threat – that Bunn was willing to continue his assault for as long as needed – seemed to work. *Punch* left Bunn alone and no further issues were brought out.

The other anti-*Punch* publication Smith was associated with lasted longer. *The Man In the Moon* began in January 1847, jointly edited by Smith and Angus Reach. Reach would actually join *Punch* as a staff writer when *The Man in the Moon* folded two years later (his insistence that his surname was pronounced 'Re-ack' was mocked by Thackeray, who at a *Punch* dinner called across the table, 'Re-ack, pass me a pe-ack').[17] *The Man in the Moon* was, at least for a while, a more serious rival to *Punch* than Bunn's vehicle could ever have hoped to be. Contemporaries remembered it as 'the ablest and wittiest of *Punch's* rivals', and its staff writers included not only Smith and Reach but Shirley Brooks, the dramatists Tom Taylor and Dion Boucicault, and Charles Lamb Kenney, with occasional contributions from Sala and Robert Brough and illustrations by talented artists including 'Phiz' and Kenny Meadows (the latter of whom had worked for *Punch* since its earliest days).[18]

A typical *Man in the Moon* cartoon showed a man speechless with astonishment, with the caption 'Gentleman Finding a Joke in *Punch*', but the journal had more to offer readers than the reliably entertaining spectacle of hacks going for each other's throats.[19] In fact, the rivalry may have been less bitter than it seems in retrospect. Nigel Cross, writing about the bohemian lives of Grub Street hacks in the nineteenth century, notes that there was also a third publication called *Puppet Show*, started in 1848 by John Valentine Bridgeman with backing from Henry Vizetelly, and that some journalists wrote for all three magazines. 'In spite of their feuding and infighting', points out Gross, 'the most striking characteristic of the Bohemian community of comic journalists was their fondness for each other's company'.[20] This conviviality was certainly part of Smith's character, and it would become even more pronounced in the following decade with his membership of the Garrick and then the Fielding Clubs.

Subtitled *A Monthly Review and Bulletin, of, New Measures, New Men, New Books, New Plays, New Jokes, and New Nonsense*, its relatively small format meant that *The Man in the Moon* was suitable for journeys, and with this in mind its front page pointed out that it was 'Sold at every railway station in the Kingdom.' It had fold-out cartoons as well as full-page illustrations and various satirical and comical articles, and a common trope was to introduce a dreadful joke under a headline that read 'Bad, even for these times' ('Why is the fin of a pike like the hero of the Trojan war? Because it's a Jack's (Ajax)'), then underneath it print expressions of mock outrage: '"Get out", "for shame", and various other expressions of disgust, too numerous to mention'.[21] Throughout its existence, however, the magazine consistently poked fun at *Punch*, frequently accusing it of stealing its jokes: even in its final issue it found space to point out (under the headline 'Stop Thief') that 'Mr. Punch is up to his old tricks again. In No. 389 there is a cut representing a Marine Railway, stolen almost line for line from a similar view in Angus Reach's *Comic Bradshaw*. What can the police be about?'[22] It also indulged in less innocent fun, with an openly anti-Semitic cartoon depicting *Punch* as 'a peripatetic old Jew merchant', and some similarly heavy-handed anti-Semitism at the expense of Disraeli.[23] In this respect, it could be argued that it was simply reflecting the widely held prejudices of its time, although as we shall see Smith was to use a crude anti-Semitic caricature in his final novel, *Pottleton*, and grotesque caricatures of Jews crop up frequently enough in *The Man in the Moon* to suggest more than the usual degree of bigotry for the period. Other prejudices of the day were on display, too. The news that a woman, Elizabeth Blackwell, had received a medical diploma from the Geneva Medical College in the United States, was the occasion for much sniggering. 'A lady doctor! Good gracious! Only fancy the sort of thing becoming general. Why, it would never do. People – that is, male people – would always be ill, for the pleasure of being attended to by the dear creatures.'[24] Since the dear creature in question – Bristol-born Elizabeth Blackwell (1821-1910) – was the first woman in America to be awarded an M.D. qualification and went on to found the New York Infirmary for Women and Children in 1857, this all comes across as rather puerile, and Smith's humour sometimes struggles to transcend his medical student background. Elsewhere, however, the relish of *The Man in the Moon*'s writers for execrable jokes and puns – and the self-mocking style in which they were presented – can be infectious, even today. 'Why is a surgeon, since the aether discovery, like a swindler? Because he cuts off without *paying* (pain)', runs one riddle, followed by 'NB We are convinced that our readers won't stand many more of these.'[25]

Smith's public profile and professional reputation were further boosted by *The Man in the Moon*, although this was sometimes a mixed blessing. During the so-called 'Monte Cristo' theatre riots of 1848, he was attacked by a crowd who identified him as being on the 'Gallican' or pro-French side in a brief but bitter theatrical controversy. The proximate cause of the riot was a French theatre company's attempt to stage Alexandre Dumas's *The Count of Monte Cristo* at Covent Garden, in the face of widespread anti-French feeling after English citizens had been expelled from France in the February revolution.[26] Ironically, Smith himself narrowly escaped being arrested during the June Days Uprising later that year, when Parisian workers began a bloody insurrection that left thousands dead or injured, an incident he recounted in *Bentley's Miscellany*. However this came some months after his encounter with the London crowd, who according to one account pelted him with 'a huge jar of strawberry preserve, which wrought havoc with his waistcoat'.[27]

Smith's notoriety as a comic writer evidently led to some tiresome social situations, too. In *The Social Parliament*, his mock Act of Parliament 'to Amend the Laws relating to the giving of Dinner and Evening Parties', Smith stipulates that certain classes of person should be left off invitations at all costs – one of them being 'People who think that because one of the Guests has the misfortune to be a "Comic Writer", that they must always be making bad Jokes to him, or giggling at the most matter-of-fact Remarks he makes'.[28] For the most part, however, Smith found being famous rather congenial, and it certainly increased the volume and quality of offers of work he received. In 1849 he was asked to edit a volume called *Gavarni in London,* in which the French artist illustrated a series of essays by English writers. Gavarni – the pen name of popular caricaturist Sulpice Guillaume Chevalier (1804-66) – had made his name with lithographs of life in the Latin Quarter, and had illustrated several of Balzac's novels. He was in London partly to escape arrest for debt in France, but soon became fascinated and horrified in equal measure by the lives of the London poor (Smith shared his horror, but not his sympathetic interest).

Gavarni's illustrations were drawn on wood and then engraved by Henry Vizetelly, who later recalled in his memoirs that Smith had taken the opportunity to extend a hand of reconciliation to Douglas Jerrold, asking him to contribute to *Gavarni*. Jerrold, according to Vizetelly, 'declined in such offensive language that Smith's friends were sorely perplexed as to the way it could be resented'.[29] Thackeray, too, turned down a request to contribute to the publication, and editing it does not seem to have been a particularly enjoyable experience for Smith. He told George Hodder that he found Gavarni 'such a queer customer that I never know until the last minute what subjects he has fixed upon, and then everything has to be scrambled up by whoever I can put my hands upon. I shall be heartily glad to wash my hands of it'.[30] However, Smith went on in the same letter to tell Hodder that he was thinking of giving up writing and buying a farm instead, claiming, 'I would sooner make a pound by selling a porker than write a page of *Bentley*.'[31] The notion of Smith as a pig farmer is so improbable that it seems likely he was having a particularly trying day, rather than genuinely disillusioned with periodical journalism.

Whether or not he enjoyed the experience of working with Gavarni, it gave Smith the opportunity to display his abilities as a 'straight' journalist. *Gavarni in London* includes essays by Smith – as well as by other writers including Shirley Brooks and the playwright and journalist J. Stirling Coyne – on topics including 'Acrobats', 'Vauxhall', 'Greenwich Fair', 'The Parks', 'The Crossing-Sweeper', and 'Music in the Streets', which demonstrate his sharp eye for the theatre of the streets and his sometimes underrated powers as an observer. In 'The Crossing-Sweeper' he enumerates the multifarious people who live and work on the streets of London, from the coffee-stall keepers, who come out in the morning and set up their stalls near a cab-stand, to the fruit-merchants, vendors of cheap toys, and the crossing-sweepers themselves, of whom he points out that, 'The hour of their appearance [...] depends upon the quarter of the town in which they exercise their calling. Thus the crossings, from the Poultry to Cornhill, the Exchange, or the Bank, must be got ready long before those in Mayfair, Belgravia, or Tyburnia.'[32] Like Dickens, Smith walked around London, observing its denizens and their gradations, and using these observations in both his fiction and his journalism. Unlike Dickens, he was largely unsympathetic to the plight of the urban poor, as his piece on 'Acrobats' suggests. Writing of the 'swarms of children everywhere collected' in London's poor neighbourhoods, Smith remarks that, 'Their parents live huddled up in dirty single rooms, repelling all attempts to improve their condition – for "The People", we regret to say, are naturally fond of dirt.'[33] He may have regretted to say it, but Smith certainly made this point again and again in his writing. One of his less appealing characteristics as a writer was his stubborn belief – reiterated a number of times in his novels and journalism – that the poor actively preferred to live in dirt and squalor.

As Wendy Kolmar points out, the essays in *Gavarni in London* 'give a sense of a London in transition, hovering just on the brink of modernity with the old London still very much a part of people's experience'. Just two years before the Great Exhibition, Smith and the other writers

> invoke a Georgian London where people sought their amusements in Vauxhall Gardens, where a trip to the theatre at Sadler's Wells offered a clear view of London over green fields, and where orange sellers still greeted theatre-goers in Drury Lane. Yet they also anticipate an expanding and modern London served by railways and telegraph lines.[34]

Modernity – in particular the modernity brought about by the expansion of the railways – was also a key theme of Smith's last novel, *The Pottleton Legacy: A Story of Town and Country Life*. Whereas *Christopher Tadpole* had been set in a time when 'the railways were not yet in work out of London; it was what people conventionally call "the fine old coaching times"', the action of *Pottleton* takes place against the backdrop of a new railway line arriving in a sleepy provincial town; this railway not only allows Smith to make clear his unashamed preference for the new and the modern, it also allows him to create a gripping chase scene in the novel's denouement. Smith had already made clear in *Tadpole* and elsewhere that he had no nostalgia for the 'fine old coaching times' and that he regarded the expansion of the railways – a process taking place at great speed at this point – as an unambiguously good thing.[35] The arrival of the railway sets in motion a whole range of improvements in Pottleton, where the 'inhabitants found that if they did not move a little out of their old jog-trot style, they would be run down by the faster immigrants arriving daily among them'.[36] The Red Lion tavern finds itself competing with a proper hotel; locals start to order goods from London instead of buying them from the complacent and overpriced local dealers, and consumer goods are soon in greater supply and of better quality. By the end of the novel, 'Pottleton has improved daily. The houses are letting all about, and new ones are being built. Smart shops are here and there appearing; a large assembly-room is talked of, to join the Red Lion; and Farmer Grant is red-hot about a cattle-market close to the railway, on his five acres.'[37] The only people who object to the railway do so either from unthinking nostalgia or obstinate self-interest, such as the local shop-owner who, unable to compete with London dealers in wine and tea, 'became a confirmed radical – not from any honest political enthusiasm, but because, finding his hopes blighted of attaining that position he had frequently aspired to, and not seeing the slightest chance of ever doing so, he took to abusing it'.[38] This is a very typical Smith assumption – that political radicalism of any sort is caused by class jealousy and spite rather than based on real principle. He is similarly suspicious of foreign political exiles in London, whose 'struggle for liberty' in their home country, he believes, 'appears to be ruining its commerce, shooting its inhabitants, scaring away its visitors, hanging its authorities'.[39]

Pottleton displays Smith's improved skills at handling plot, and arguably greater mastery than in any of his previous novels of expository and illustrative dialogue. As his thoughts on political radicalism and foreign asylum seekers suggest, it also displays many of his characteristic prejudices, preoccupations, and bugbears, from his distrust of conventional wisdom (people become seasick as soon as they board a boat because that's what expected of them, he claims: 'many folks think there is an absolute duty and necessity for them to be sick, the instant they get on board a steam-boat'),[40] through to his resentment about having been taught classical rather than modern languages at school ('How many times, in society, have you wished that you had been taught Italian and German instead' of Latin and Greek).[41] Dealing with a different novelist, it might be naïve for the reader to assume that opinions expressed in a book – whether by characters or narrator – are necessarily those of the author. But Smith's views on most of his pet subjects were repeated so regularly throughout both his novels and his non-fiction that we can be confident that when he writes, for example, about the philanthropic Pongo Enlightenment Mission, and refers to Exeter Hall as 'the mighty reservoir for distributing gold to all parts of the uncivilized globe', he is transmitting his own views directly to the reader rather than presenting those of an invented character. Smith's scepticism about philanthropy of course anticipates that of Dickens in *Bleak House* (1853), with its references to Mrs. Jellyby and her mission to the natives of Borrioboola-Gha, 'on the left bank of the Niger'.[42] Smith writes about the Miss Twinches, the sisters who have dissuaded the distant 'savages' from 'eating every missionary upon his arrival'. Had these two spinsters 'followed many of their companions in charity to their homes, they would have found them to be persons who neglected their children, and were dead to kindly domestic feelings'.[43]

Smith's distrust extends not only to the kind of 'telescopic philanthropy' that Dickens would satirize in *Bleak House*, however, but also to attempts to improve the conditions of the poor in Britain. Here he is on the local workhouse, a passage that is worth quoting in full as it is must surely be one of the few occasions in the nineteenth-century novel when the institution – so controversial after the 'New Poor Law' of 1834 – has been defended so brazenly:

> The front of it, seen from the road, was rather gay than otherwise, with its banks of evergreens, and diagrams of grass-plots, and flower-borders of flints from the railway; but the gaiety stopped at the hall door. There was not a greater dif-ference between the spangled drapery and trophied columns of the outside of a dancing show at a fair, and the dingy patched canvas and rude benches of the interior. Yet it was clean and roomy, and indeed, comfortable, albeit there were always letters in the *Dibblethorpe Messenger* every week, detailing dreadful

enormities committed therein, which the Tower of London, the Bridge of Sighs, and the old original Bastille itself, all put together, could not have equalled in their chronicles. But the inmates all looked well. The old people were hale and hearty; the middle-aged ruddy and muscular; and the children as broad as they were long; and above all they were clean, which is not a reigning attribute of "The People". Not being a literary philanthropist, nor addicted to stirring up wild paupers with a long pen until they become troublesome, we may venture to say this.[44]

Dickens might have recognized some of his own misgivings about foreign missionary work presaged in Smith's writing, but it is hard to imagine the author of *Oliver Twist* having much patience with this view of the workhouse, and harder still to reconcile Smith's complacency with the widespread knowledge of horrific abuses taking place in workhouses. *Pottleton* was published just four years after the Andover workhouse scandal had been exposed by the very kind of outspoken, campaigning journalism that he dismisses in this passage, and just a year after the emergence of even worse abuses at the Huddersfield workhouse.[45] An 1846 Select Committee report into the Andover scandal had confirmed that inmates of the workhouse there had been so hungry they had resorted to chewing on the bones that they were supposed to be grinding down for fertilizer.[46] So much for Smith's portrait of 'hale and hearty' paupers enjoying a rigorous but beneficent regime.

There are other ugly attitudes on display in *Pottleton*, not least the character of Mr. Shem, an anti-Semitic caricature based on John Medex Maddox (1789-1861), the manager of the Princess's Theatre in Oxford Street. Shem's voice is described as 'that fatal accent which we, in a spirit so remote from the Christian, associate always with hired fancy-dressers, old clothes, and bad things generally'. From his pronunciation of 'w' as 'v' ("Vell, vot is it now?') to his constant attempts to save money and cheat others, and his mean, wheedling character, Shem is about as ugly a stereotype as can be found in the Victorian novel. He offers a hack writer called Scum a commission to write a song attacking someone who has been abusing him in print, then cheats Scum out of payment by having his own in-house copyist take down the lyrics from behind a screen when Scum reads them out.[47] In a strange case of life imitating art, the real-life Maddox was so incensed by his barely concealed portrait in *Pottleton* that he got his in-house writer (a character who was rumoured to be kept on the premises of the theatre, chained to a desk by his leg), to write some satirical verses about Smith, playing on his 'Alabata' nickname:

"Albata" Smith they've christened him, for wicked wags have said
That as Albata now is used for silver plate instead
So he has stolen the genuine wit that's found in Dickens's head
And for it substituted his own literary lead.[48]

Smith's portrayal of Shem/Maddox is scarcely unusual for the period in which it was written, but it is disquieting nonetheless. And yet for all the crude prejudice, reactionary politics, and smug complacency about the plight of the poor in this novel, it is hard not to enjoy Smith's sheer boisterous love of comic hyperbole. At times in *Pottleton* Smith almost seems to be winking at his readers in acknowledgement of his own verbosity, as in this bravura passage where he describes Wyndham Flitter's relief at getting out of a tight scrape:

> A man who comes up from a coal mine once more into an inexplosive atmosphere; a curious visitor, who finds himself on firm ground again, after making that frightful journey in the basket along the site of the suspension bridge at Clifton; a stranger landing from an American steam-boat, a balloon, or a diving-bell; a traveller arriving unattached at the end of his route between Naples and Terracina, or Madrid and Seville; a quiet man tranquilly finishing a month's sojourn in the Faubourg St. Antoine; a foreman at a powder-mill on Saturday night; an amateur hunter finding himself still in his saddle on the other side of an ox-rail; the summit of a human column of street acrobats when he finds the paving-stones under his feet again, instead of the crown of his companion's head, – all these persons can imagine Mr. Flitter's delight at this relief to his embarrassment.[49]

Smith wrote in his preface to *Pottleton* that 'eleven years of unceasing work' had 'induced me to think that I might venture to take an extended holiday – and accordingly I hope that the gratification of a long-felt wish to visit the Mediterranean, the East and the northern coast of Africa, is about to arrive'. Whether he knew it at the time or not, these words marked the end of his career as a novelist, and the beginning of a new phase of life.

As the brief survey of these last two chapters suggests, Smith's novels have a curate's egg quality. Read from the perspective of the twenty-first century, they can seem oddly out of time, their raffish protagonists and ramshackle plots incongruous beside the classic novels of the 1840s by the Brontës, Dickens, the early Thackeray of *Vanity Fair*, *Pendennis*, and *Barry Lyndon*, and Mrs. Gaskell's *Mary Barton*. They perhaps have more in common with the early Dickens of *Pickwick*, *Oliver Twist*, and *Nicholas Nickleby*, but in many respects they seem to share a sensibility with earlier, rougher chroniclers of London life such as Pierce Egan, whose *Life in London* series first appeared in 1821 and introduced the characters of Corinthian Tom and Jerry Hawthorn.[50] Successful and popular as Smith's novels were in their day, they were not destined to last long. Just over thirty years after Smith's death, Margaret Oliphant would write that 'Albert Smith, who achieved a kind of immortality for himself by his clever entertainments, in which department he perhaps never met his match, would scarcely have been remembered as the author of *Adventures of Mr. Ledbury*, the *Marchioness of Brinvilliers*, and other ephemeral stories.'[51] Even by the time of his death, the *Athenaeum*'s faint praise in its otherwise admiring obituary suggests that the books were not considered likely to achieve literary immortality: 'Some of his novels will not soon pass out of circulation', his obituarist predicted.[52]

In 1849, however, Smith himself was ready to move on to new pastures. The next stage of his life would prove to be the most successful.

8: 'DO YOU WANT THAT?'

'A Cockney – I don't deny it.' Albert Smith, *A Month At Constantinople*

Who exactly *was* Albert Smith – this ambitious, irrepressible young man who had made such a name for himself over the past decade?

The various accounts of Smith by his contemporaries suggest a personality full of contradictions: an instinctive conservative and a keen habitué of London's clubland, who nonetheless prided himself on his irreverence for convention and tradition; a man of considerable generosity and kindness who could also be distinctly stingy; a convivial extrovert who was often suspicious towards strangers, and who demonstrated in his writing a strong sense of the brutality and cruelty of life; someone who mocked any attempts to bring 'high' culture to the public as a pretentious waste of time, but who confessed to being moved to tears by George Eliot's story 'Amos Barton', and who also criticized the masses for their 'low' tastes; a religious sceptic who particularly distrusted shows of piety and moralism, yet who wrote to *The Times* deploring the 'blackguardism and depravity' of the behaviour he witnessed on the London streets at night; and a man who turned his back on a medical career as early as he could and often mocked the pretensions of doctors, but who retained an almost mystical reverence for the vocation of medicine and the duties of those who pursued it.

Most accounts and portraits of Smith date from the mid to late 1850s, after his Mont Blanc show had made him one of the most famous men in the country. These generally show a rather portly looking man with a heavy beard. Edmund Yates described Smith at this stage in his life as 'a man of barely middle height, thick-set, broad-shouldered, and stout. He had a fine head, with keen grey eyes pleasant in expression and full of sly humour, an aquiline nose, and a mouth hidden under his heavy moustache and large full brown beard'.[1] In a later memoir, Yates recalled Smith's 'large head, large body, short legs […] small hands and feet', and noted that he was 'always badly dressed',[2] while another account has him 'defiantly exotic in his dress'.[3]

Apart from the beard, which Smith grew for convenience during his travels in the Middle East, this also describes the Smith of the late 1840s reasonably accurately.[4] Portraits from that decade show a young man with pleasant but somewhat fleshy and otherwise unremarkable features, and a head of dark, wavy hair. He would most accurately be described as stout rather than fat but Smith certainly enjoyed good food and drink, though he claimed that alcohol never went to his head, and even insisted that the opium he tried in Constantinople had not affected him.[5] As we have seen, detailed descriptions of food were a staple of his writing. Some are downright horrifying: the dish of Irish stew on offer at the ferry terminal in Alexandria, for example, was 'a secret compound containing bones, onions, and flies, with shreds of unknown animal matter',[6] while the food on board ship during a Red Sea voyage in the late 1850s was 'a constantly-recurring, scrap-concealing mess. I have a horrid recollection of having one day detected the same peculiarly shaped bone on the occasion of its third appearance.'[7] But only someone with a genuine relish for food would have taken the trouble to describe in such detail the celebratory feast that ends *Christopher Tadpole*, when the characters enjoy

> 'beef, veal, ham, brawn, chicken, partridge, pheasant, tongue, pigeon pie, raised pie, apple pie, quince pie, puffs, turnovers, macaroons, biscuits, ratafias, figs, oranges, brandy cherries, chips, blancmange, trifles, jellies, custards, creams, grapes, bread', washed down with 'strong ale, stout, table beer, cyder, perry, port, sherry, champagne, elder wine, red negus, lemonade, punch, brandy, gin, rum, hollands, shrub, whisky, tea, coffee, cape, orange, and ginger'.[8]

What else do we know of the private Albert Smith? We know that he loved dogs, and hated a limp handshake ('There is nothing so sickening as the presentation of a limp hand which cannot return a grasp', he wrote, after describing the handshake of a character in *Tadpole* as feeling 'just like a cold boiled sole cut into slips').[9] We have already seen his almost phobic obsession with dirt, and how he associated it with the urban poor. We know that he distrusted organized religion, and in particular the ostentatious display of religious piety. 'Holding myself honestly to be neither better nor worse than the rest of the world, I *always* mistrust a display of religion', he wrote in his diary of his journey to China.[10] In *Pottleton* he refers to the 'clever schemers who so craftily turn our pure and holy religion into a matter of snug situations and lucrative popularity', and in *Scattergood* he introduces a family of social climbers, the Constables, who are 'well aware that no Sabbath could be properly kept in an obscure parochial church; and that the worship thus paraded before the great world was far more important than the silent religion of the heart, which eligible connexions could possibly know nothing about'.[11] Smith may have felt the need to nod in the direction of 'our pure and holy religion' in contrast to public displays of religiosity, but in fact there is little to suggest that he had any religious faith at all.

Whether in private or in public, Smith came across as a big, rambunctious personality. Henry James, who was taken to Smith's Mont Blanc show as a boy in the

1850s, remembered him years later as 'big, bearded, rattling, chattering, mimicking Albert Smith', and this was very much the persona Smith liked to project.[12] Despite his surprisingly high-pitched voice, he could sing well and was agreed even by his detractors to be a fluent and compelling public speaker (even Vizetelly, who scarcely had a good word for Smith, conceded that he was 'unquestionably an admirable *raconteur*, and, in spite of his cracked voice, had the rare art of rendering even the poorest stuff amusing').[13] He was described by one contemporary as 'full of life and jollity', and of his 'set' at the Garrick Club – which he joined in 1849 – as 'very pleasant if a little noisy'.[14] Another contemporary described him holding court at the Garrick, where he 'called every waiter by his Christian name, and seemed to enjoy himself amazingly'. In this same account, published under the pseudonym 'Belgravia' in the *New York Times* in the 1870s, Smith was recollected as always being the centre of attention, full of noisy bonhomie:

> You might have heard his hearty chuckling laugh all over the house and sounding high above the din of conversation. He contrived always to have a large party of his own intimates around him, and by joining together two of the ordinary dinner tables accommodation was provided for the whole of them.[15]

When Smith was in the midst of his Mont Blanc show, 'Belgravia' recalled, the start of each new season in the autumn 'was always inaugurated by a sort of supper, the like of which I have never seen before or since':

> A long table traversed the length of the hall, at which stood white-aproned attendants opening oysters, huge barrels of which were placed behind them. The 'tipple' was champagne, bitter beer, and soda water, all of which liquors were supplied in abundance; but no other food except oysters, with brown bread and butter, was to be had. At these repasts one would meet all sorts and conditions of men; everybody came, I think, who received an invitation. Peers, baronets, members of Parliament, and gentlemen from the provinces, mixed with actors, comic singers, showmen, artists, and many other London celebrities. This repast was annually provided by Mr. Rule of Maiden Lane [...] The wine came from Fortnum and Mason, and was the best that money could buy; and the flowers, of which there was always a lavish profusion, were the finest to be found in Covent Garden.[16]

This was the image that Smith loved to show to the world; brash, generous, ostentatious, gregarious. There are plenty of first-hand accounts of Smith showing great kindness and generosity, although he also had a reputation for sometimes being brusque with strangers – especially if he suspected they wanted to borrow money from him. Edmund Yates recalled Smith's thoughtfulness to his sixteen-year-old self at a dinner party given in London, while his erstwhile *Punch* colleague George Hodder described him as 'a most frank and agreeable companion among those whose idiosyncrasies he relished', and noted that 'he could be as kind and friendly as he was frank and cheerful'; the philanthropist, explorer, and 'urban missionary' John Macgregor recalled in his memoirs how Smith, at the height of his success in the 1850s, had allowed him to borrow material from his Mont Blanc show for a lecture to 'an assembly of shoeblacks and ragged children at the Field Lane Ragged School'.[17]

Even his pushiness – what Barnum would have called his 'go-ahead' quality – seems to have been greeted with amused tolerance by most of his social circle. Sutherland Edwards recalled Smith's habit of constantly taking notes for his columns and articles:

> If anyone told an amusing story or made a good joke in his presence, he would say, taking out his notebook, 'Do you want that?' In most cases the answer was in the negative. If, however, the narrator of the anecdote or the maker of the jest did want it, Albert Smith took it down all the same, and calmly remarked, 'You'll find it next week in the *Illustrated London News*.'[18]

Smith seems to have got away with taking such liberties through a combination of charm and chutzpah, but there were certainly those who, in Vizetelly's words, could not stand his 'noisy self-assertion'. Just as Smith had provoked Jerrold and other members of the *Punch* brotherhood in the early 1840s, he would come to irritate Thackeray and other figures in the Garrick during the 1850s (although his relationship with Thackeray was more complex and ambivalent than it has sometimes been painted). Smith retained throughout his life the habit of being careful with money, and according to one account even had a lithographed circular with the motto 'loan oft loses both itself and friend', which he would send in reply to anyone who asked to borrow money.[19] Understandably this did not always go down well, particularly when everyone knew how lucrative Smith's various publications and shows had been. After his death, Edmund Yates defended him loyally against the charge of being mean, arguing that Smith – who had lived frugally on two pounds a week when he first moved to London, and had a life-long horror of falling into debt – was misrepresented in part because of 'the blunt manner in which he invariably refused any attempt on his purse which he thought savoured of humbug'. Smith, Yates argued, was 'punctiliously honourable in all money matters', and 'was essentially a kind-hearted man, fulfilling his duty to his relatives with far more than ordinary care and affection, exercising a wide and generous hospitality to his acquaintances, and constantly showing his regards for his friends in many delicate attentions'.[20]

Smith certainly had more friends than enemies, but he was far from universally popular. The response in the *Punch* editorial office to the news of his death in 1860 was recorded in *Punch* writer Henry Silver's diary, and suggests just how intensely some people disliked him.[21] 'No doubt he half killed himself by guttling and guzzling', wrote Silver, who noted that his colleagues were 'savage' at the rumour (untrue, as it turned out) that Smith had left more to his mistress than his wife in his will.[22]

Less frequently it was others who found themselves on the receiving end of Smith's own hostility. The army officer, writer, and man-about-town William Pitt Lennox recalled how Smith was initially hostile when they first met, believing that Lennox had been responsible for blackballing his Garrick membership: 'When first introduced to him by a friend, with whom I was strolling along Piccadilly, the hero of Mont Blanc looked as cold and frigid as one of the mountains he was wont to discourse upon, and without deigning to reply to a common-place remark I made, "moved on"'.[23] When Smith came up for re-election a few weeks later, and Lennox let it be known that he had not blackballed him before and had no intention of doing so this time, Lennox recalled that Smith relented and 'we became warm friends'.[24] With the exception of Douglas Jerrold – who, as we have seen, seems to have intimidated Smith with his sharp tongue and force of personality – Smith was rarely cowed by anyone and was happy to retaliate in kind to personal attacks. He told Henry Mayhew that, 'when a man attacked him in the papers he always found the best course to be "to drag him out by name, and say all you know against him"'.[25] For the most part, however, his approach was robust rather than outright aggressive. Dickens, whose friendship with Smith ebbed and flowed over the years, considered him 'a very good, kind fellow, under certain oddities of manner', but clearly found him trying at times.[26] In a speech given in 1854, when Smith was guest of honour at a banquet celebrating the anniversary of the charitable Commercial Traveller's Schools, Dickens jokingly but pointedly alluded to Smith's bossiness. 'Mr. Albert Smith, who is present among us here tonight, is undoubtedly a "traveller"', said Dickens. 'I do not know whether he takes many orders, but I can testify, on behalf of the children of his friends, that he gives them in the most liberal manner.'[27]

Smith had abandoned medicine as soon as he could make a living as a full-time writer, and on the face of it he never seemed to regret the switch of career. There are plenty of quacks and snake-oil pedlars in Smith's novels, like Mr. Blandy in *Pottleton* who inoculates an entire school against hay fever with 'three dozen draught bottles (which Mr. Blandy's assistant had purchased of an old tramp, and washed clean that morning, with shot and potash)'.[28] But there are also a striking number of conscientious, serious-minded physicians – Mr. Roopy, who attends the impoverished hack writer Scute's terminally injured daughter in *Pottleton*, or Dr Ashton in *Tadpole*, who speaks 'in that soothing tone of apparent unconcern which all his profession can assume with such admirable effect, when coolness and presence of mind are found in none other of the bystanders'.[29] In a relatively rare note of solemnity in his treatment of medical students in *Ledbury*, Smith steps away from the high jinks and low-life comedy to muse on the responsibilities ahead of those destined for a medical career:

> They alone upon whom the responsibility has fallen of attempting to arrest the last gleam of flitting existence in its own darkening tenement – to kindle by their own breath the dull remaining embers of life, which too eager or precipitate a course might extinguish for ever – who have felt they were regarded by the surrounding crowd as dispensers of life and death, upon whose will it depended, whether the senseless object of their earnest care became once more a thing of vitality and reason like themselves, or a clod of decaying earth – they alone can understand the deep and all-absorbing feelings of the surgeon, whilst superintending the process of restoring suspended animation [...] those trying moments can be but faintly imagined beyond the circle of that profession, whose pilgrimage on earth is doomed to pass but amidst the most distressing scenes of anguish and mortality.[30]

For all his irreverence about the escapades of medical student life, Smith had clearly been inculcated – whether by his father or his own hospital training – with the sense that medicine was a vocation as well as a career. He also demonstrates in his novels a striking awareness of the harsh reality of London street life. Smith enjoys the comedy and theatre of the streets, but he is under no illusions about what tough places they can be for those who stand out from the crowd or who cannot defend themselves. 'Mind the moon, daddy-longlegs', someone cries out to the tall, lanky figure of Sprouts in *Tadpole*, while a 'small five-year-old in an apron and shirt-sleeves' eggs on the crowd with the cry, 'Hit him hard, he's got no friends'. Sprouts is only saved from further abuse when the mob's attention is drawn to a drunken bricklayer who they can pick on more easily.[31] This is a world in which anyone who looks different or is unable to fight back is fair game, even to young children. It's a more brutish world than that envisaged by Dickens, for example, and sometimes seems to have more in common with Regency or eighteenth-century London. Smith certainly doesn't share Dickens's sentiments about the innocence of childhood, perhaps because his own had been shattered so brutally at school (Dickens's own childhood had, of course, been overshadowed by the demoralizing experience of the blacking factory, but he was largely spared the sheer physical brutality that Smith endured at Merchant Taylors'.)

This unsentimental worldview can sometimes come across as harsh and unfeeling. Smith's political views are clear from his novels, and they came through in his journalism and even in his stage shows. His old editor John Timbs, writing about Smith's shows during the 1850s, recalled his unashamed populism. 'He succeeded in pleasing the public,' wrote Timbs, 'because he represented ordinary Englishmen so well, and fell in with so many of their opinions […] He swam strongly, but it was with the tide. He used to inform his hearers that he was no scholar, and even took credit for not knowing the learned languages'.[32] His politics, Timbs recalled, were rabble-rousing ('the only "clause" wanted is the claws of the British Lion, which will rend the Bengal Tiger', he reported Smith declaring, presumably during the Indian Rebellion of 1857), and he enjoyed name-dropping, particularly when letting people know of the connections to royalty he cultivated in the 1850s:

> Put all these things together – popular politics in their most grotesquely popular form, frankness as to his own pretensions, and a discreet conjunction of the Egyptian Hall and Buckingham Palace – and no one can deny that Mr. Smith knows how to find his way to the hearts of an English audience.[33]

Smith's political and social views, however, were not simply calculated to please his audience. At times he displays a visceral distaste for the poor. Here he is, for example, reporting the reaction of Mrs. Gudge in *Tadpole* on the death of her husband. She had responded

> with that perfect want of control over the feelings so common in uneducated women, had never left the bed to which she had been carried in her fainting fit, but had passed the time in tearless howling, and appeals of that conventional sort which anyone experienced in the behaviour of the lower classes in times of sudden trouble can so readily call to mind.[34]

A portrait of the 'lower classes' enjoying themselves at Hampton Court in the novel drips not only with contempt for their vulgar tastes, but also with disdain for any suggestion that ordinary people might benefit from access to culture:

> It is delightful, we know, to talk upon paper of the infusion of a love of high art into the minds of the lower orders: and the impression that such is done by throwing open first-class galleries of pictures is, in truth, a pleasant one to cherish. But would you wish the spell broken – go to Hampton Court: place yourself by the side of the commonest types of the usual holiday visitors you can find; listen to their remarks as they wander by the paintings; and glean from their comments some notion of what they think of them. You will find that art, or artist, has nothing to do with their attention – that the subject alone attracts; and that by the interest of the situation the picture describes, or the familiarity of its import, is the admiration of the masses regulated.[35]

Nor was Smith's pessimistic view of the lower orders and their capacity for culture confined to his novels. In an 1851 article in *The Month*, a magazine he jointly edited with John Leech during that year, he turns his attention to Greenwich Fair on Whit Monday. 'We have never entertained very great notions of "the people"', begins 'An English Holiday', and Smith's sour tone throughout the article is at odds with his celebrations elsewhere of the joyful exuberance of street life and popular entertainments. Smith is careful to point out that by 'the people' he is not referring to the respectable artisan classes, but to,

> the riff-raff of the million – the "I'm as good as you" class of snobs, among whom the cant of cheap bad literature has found its chief supporters, who "sympathise" with runaway patriot scamps from foreign countries look upon respectability as a crime, and bawl about "the rights of the poor man" with gin-shop enthusiasm.[36]

As a result, he writes, 'when we see that "a great holiday of the working classes" is coming on, we prepare to witness a most humiliating national spectacle of beery, dreary, weary incapacity for amusement'. Nowhere, Smith claims, 'did we ever witness such a scene of unmeaning attempt at fun, snobbish riot, and unmitigated vulgarity, as this festival presented [...] It is long since we ourselves have seen anything so contemptibly degrading'.[37] Smith's complaints were not only about the behaviour of the visitors but also about the quality of the shows themselves.

> The shows were on a level with the people. Outside one of these was displayed an enormous animal with an elephant's head and ox-hoofs, attacking two negroes. Tempted by this we went in and saw the original – a malformed abortion of, we expect, a cow, hung in a bottle about six or eight inches square.[38]

Nonetheless, he gave the distinct impression here and elsewhere that 'the people' neither expected nor deserved entertainment of any higher quality than this. Writing to the Scottish publisher John Blackwood, who published Smith's first account of his Mont Blanc ascent, he declared his intention to be at the reopening of the Crystal Palace in 1854 (the original structure had been built for the Great Exhibition of 1851 in Hyde Park, but was reconstructed on Sydenham Hill and officially opened there by Queen Victoria in 1854). 'You must not misunderstand my feelings about it', Smith wrote:

> I think it will be the greatest show ever started, but it will not play and the cant of calling it 'the people's palace' is rather sickening. It won't amuse them so much as Cremorne. What the deuce will the old woman who comes up from Banbury, with a basket, know (or care) about the Renaissance.[39]

This attitude – that the poor can neither know nor care about culture – imbues much of Smith's writing about the 'lower orders', and while it is consistent with his reactionary politics it is also yet another example of his paradoxical nature. Populist and even something of a vulgarian himself, he nonetheless condemned the popular, vulgar pastimes of the poor; and while damning them as degrading and squalid he consistently mocked any attempts to improve the condition of the poor or to offer them anything better than 'cheap bad literature'.

Even Smith's own populism – his supposed irreverence towards Shakespeare, his complaints about the uselessness of a classical education – was by no means consistent. Visiting ancient sites in Athens he wrote that 'the exceeding beauty of the ruins can scarcely be overpraised', but noted that the traveller's appreciation would be dependent on his or her own 'early classical training'.[40] As mentioned in the Introduction, George Eliot asked for a copy of *Scenes of Clerical Life* to be sent to Smith when it was published by Blackwood in book form in 1858. Smith might seem a strange choice for the cultivated and high-minded Eliot, until one discovers that he had already written to Blackwood the previous year when her stories were published anonymously in *Blackwood's Magazine*. Smith had been particularly impressed by the first story, 'Amos Barton', the publisher reported to Eliot, and 'had never read anything that affected him more than Milly's death'.[41] This rather complicates the picture of Smith as an unabashed vulgarian, sneering at anything sophisticated or complex.

Perhaps nowhere is Smith's paradoxical nature better illustrated than in his travel writing. In between his journalism, fiction, comic writing, and stage work, Smith had been travelling in Europe whenever he got the time throughout the 1840s. In 1842, for example, he had visited the Rhine and the Rigi, a Swiss mountain that had become a popular tourist attraction by this stage, using his experiences in various articles and in his novels, and later parlaying it into material for his Mont Blanc show. In 1848 he had found himself in Paris during the June Days Uprising, and later wrote a compelling account of the anxious time he spent there, under constant fear of arrest. 'The city was in a state of siege', he recalled.

> Every place of amusement was closed; people were shot dead at noonday in the public streets, from courts and windows; and the eye was as wearied with the constant view of soldiers, National Guards, Mobiles, Marines, and insurgent prisoners, as the ear was with the ceaseless riot of [...] infernal performances upon the drums which the French are so particularly attached to.[42]

Smith described his various encounters with the labyrinthine and capricious bureaucracy set up in the wake of the failed revolt, and the tense days during which he attempted to get his exit visa and leave the country. It is not clear how much real danger he was in as a foreign visitor, but he does point out that at least one other Englishman had been detained after being denounced to the authorities for having 'been seen on the wrong side of a barricade'. Undaunted by this experience, by 1849 he was preparing to undertake a more adventurous trip, with the eventual goal of reaching Constantinople.

Smith's travel writing displays the contradictions of the man in sharp relief. He combines the qualities of sophisticated traveller who speaks French and dines with the British ambassador to Constantinople, with an oafish John Bull who thinks all foreigners are smelly and compares sunset over the Bosphorus unfavourably with that to be seen from Chertsey Bridge. 'I should be very sorry to class foreigners, generally, as a dirty set of people when left to themselves', he wrote in his account of his Middle Eastern travels, 'but I fear there is much reason to suppose that (in how many cases out of ten I will refrain from saying) a disrelish for a good honest plunging wash is one of their chief attributes'.[43] As we shall see in the next chapter, he appears to have been unmoved by witnessing slaves being bought and sold openly, and his insouciance about slavery is deeply disturbing for modern readers (and would also have horrified many of his contemporaries). Yet behind his air of mocking irreverence and casual indifference to the suffering of slaves and other unfortunates, Smith the traveller was an acute observer, and Smith the journalist could turn a phrase that conjured up a vivid sense of place. Here he is in the souk at Smyrna:

> Here, were huge morsels of 'the best Turkey sponge', redolent of ocean depths, and heavy with the sea-sand that still filled their pores; there, were baskets of yellow rhubarb, cakes of aromatic opium, and bags of fresh clammy dates, ready to burst with their very sweetness [...] Anon were beautiful arms from Damascus – arabesque and glittering blades, with jeweled handles and velvet-covered sheaths [...] Then came rich carpets, and quilted coats of silk, scarlet caps, and costly pipes of every shape and fabric.[44]

In passages like this in Smith's travel writing, the hard-bitten cynic who refuses to be impressed by what everyone else has seen gives way to a wide-eyed youth, transported back to his childhood reading of the Arabian Nights (Smith refers to the Arabian Nights stories on a number of occasions, and they had clearly left an impression on him when first read at an early age). In 1849, having completed his career as a novelist, Smith was ready to make his first visit to the Middle East. It would prove to be the springboard to a new, even more successful career as a showman.

9: 'BEHIND THE SCENES OF A GREAT "EFFECT"'

No nation in the world makes so much fuss as our own about the comforts of home, and there is none so notoriously anxious to run away from them. Albert Smith, *Pictures of Life at Home and Abroad*

Smith set off on his travels once more in early June 1849, arriving in Constantinople at the beginning of September. He travelled through Germany and Switzerland to Italy, before sailing from Naples to Malta, where he connected with one of the *Paquebots Poste de la Méditerranée*, the mail boats that sailed regularly from Marseilles to Malta, Smyrna, and Athens. From Smyrna (at that time part of the Ottoman Empire, nowadays the Turkish city of Izmir) he sailed through the Dardanelles to arrive at Constantinople.

The book he published after his return, *A Month At Constantinople* (1850) is in many respects an archetypal Smith production. Rather than presenting new, unexplored places or people to his readers, he was taking a fresh look at territory already quite familiar to the reading public. Thackeray's *Notes of a Journey from Cornhill to Grand Cairo* had been published in 1846 under a pseudonym. Before that Alexander William Kinglake's *Eothen, or Traces of Travel Brought Home from the East* (1844) and Eliot Warburton's *The Crescent and the Cross* (1845) had already set the stage for irreverent, entertaining tales of Eastern travel, replete with sweeping Orientalist assumptions about the cultures they claimed to be interpreting.[1] Significantly, Kinglake's book, recounting his travels during the 1830s, had initially been rejected by the publisher John Murray 'on account of its irreverent style'.[2] In some respects, Kinglake took an approach that might be more readily associated with Smith, although there are also passages of lyricism and even a kind of mysticism to be found in *Eothen*. He certainly shared Smith's disrespect for conventional wisdom and expected pieties; travelling between Belgrade and Constantinople, he writes, 'There are few countries less infested by "lions" than the provinces on this part of your route. You are not called upon to "drop a tear" over the tomb of "the once brilliant" anybody, or to pay your "tribute of respect" to anything dead or alive'. 'Lions', in this context, refers to sights that simply must be seen by the traveller – Smith and Thackeray also used the word in this sense in their travel books.[3] Thackeray, too, took a fairly irreverent view of what he saw on his travels – claiming, for example, that he had been 'made so miserable in youth by a classical education, that all connected with it is disagreeable in my eyes', and therefore finding Athens 'a disappointment'.[4]

Smith was not attempting or claiming to break new ground, but he also seemed keen to distance himself somewhat from these recent examples of Eastern travel writing. He wrote in the Preface that he believed 'the funny school has been rather overdone of late', and warned those of his readers who were hoping for a 'Comic Constantinople' that they would be disappointed. Instead, he wrote, he wished to 'present a book of First Impressions – describing all things, as plainly as may be, just as they struck me upon my journey; colouring nothing for the sake of a page of poetical description or conventional enthusiasm'.[5] Ever alert to shifting tastes and to the moment when a particular fashion had become spent, Smith seems to have sensed that the time for comic travelogues about the region had passed. The reviewer of *Blackwood's Magazine* congratulated him on having written 'an amusing book on so hackneyed a text as a visit to Constantinople', but for the most part the book is amusing in the sense of being entertaining and an easy read rather than being particularly funny.[6]

A Month At Constantinople displays many of the characteristics of Smith's writing from the 1840s – his fascination with visual spectacle, and with the contrast between expectation and reality – and also prefigures some of the features of his Mont Blanc book, such as his care in setting out for his readers the practical details of how they could make the same journey. Both here and in *The Story of Mont Blanc* (1853), Smith adds appendices with useful information on options for boats to make the voyage out, relative costs, and even the bill of fare for dinner in particular places. He gives a detailed breakdown of all the expenses he incurred between London and Constantinople, down to individual day's meals and board costs, and then another breakdown of his living costs during his time in Constantinople. He recommends specific local guides, and even sets out the latest quarantine regulations at Mediterranean ports. In this respect, Smith is presenting his readers with a hybrid of travel memoir and guide-book. He is also emphatically moving away from a Romantic tradition of writing about travel, in favour of a more prosaic, pragmatic approach that is as concerned with the best place to buy clothes in Malta as it is with tales of the Golden Horn or the Seraglio.

In his Preface to the second edition of the book (which came out later in the same year) Smith is unrepentant about this approach, noting that 'a few of the more lofty-minded critics have made two objections to my book – the first, that it abounds in "cockney comparisons;" the second, that I have ridden roughshod over many old poetical and oriental associations, in great independence of previous estimation'. He cheerfully pleads guilty to both charges:

I always professed that I was, as I was – a traveller for amusement only; a Cockney – I don't deny it; very slenderly gifted with enthusiasms of any kind – but making no pretension to more than I have.[7]

Yet Smith also retains his eye for a striking scene – the '*coupe d'oeil* of the harbour' at Malta, the 'bazaars of the sunny, bustling, beauty-teeming Smyrna' – not to mention his fastidious distaste for the squalid lives of the poor. Noting the presence of 'dirty urchins' on Malta, Smith describes them as 'cousins Maltese of the boys who seek for halfpence in the mud of Greenwich and Blackwall'.[8] And anchored at the Dardanelles, he displays the lingering influence of his own classical education, alongside his concern for practical details and his tendency towards boastfulness. Smith and his fellow passengers note that they are anchored at the point where Byron swam across the Hellespont in 1810, and the discussion turns to the story of Hero and Leander. 'No one knew where to look for Sestos and Abydos; nor is the course the young lover took at all decided', recalled Smith. In the legend, and in Christopher Marlowe's 1598 poem, Leander swam from his home at Abydos across to where Hero lived in a tower at Sestos (the story had also been revived in an 1819 poem by Leigh Hunt). Byron had made the crossing in the opposite direction, from Sestos to Abydos. 'He came over diagonally with the current, which made the distance about four English miles from starting to landing', estimated Smith, in his distinctly unromantic fashion, 'and the distance was accomplished in an hour and ten minutes. Had we waited longer, I should have tried it myself [...] for there did not appear any remarkable difficulty about it – certainly nothing to make its accomplishment a matter of record'.[9]

This kind of cool scepticism, and Smith's determination to impose a prosaic British reality on exotic locations that had traditionally been the subject of romantic hyperbole, continues throughout the book: the *Athenaeum* remarked in its obituary of Smith that this book had 'washed a great deal of colour out of the Oriental turban'.[10] His description of his first sight of Constantinople is particularly telling. At half-past-seven in the morning, he caught his first glimpse of the Ottoman capital, 'with its white buildings and minarets glittering in the sun, at the extremity of the Sea of Marmora'. Smith's first instinct was to debunk – he had read and heard so much of the city's beauty that upon first sighting St. Sophia he initially exclaimed to himself, 'And this is all!' Yet as the boat continued into the Golden Horn, Smith found his scepticism replaced by a familiar sense of wonder:

As we rounded the Seraglio Point, and slowly glided into the Golden Horn, where the whole gorgeous panorama opened upon me in its unequalled loveliness, the feeling of wonder and admiration became absolutely oppressive. I had never been so strangely moved before but once – when I looked down upon London, by night, from a balloon.

Smith then continues for several pages to describe the picturesque scenes he witnessed upon his arrival, concluding that 'for once, and once only, the realization of some glittering scene from childhood's story-book visions appeared to be accomplished'.[11]

Almost immediately after this rather surprising concession, however, Smith's boat lands and he and his fellow travellers are taken up the steep lane to the district of Pera, at that time the most westernized part of the city, where most of the European residents and the diplomatic community lived. 'In an instant, I felt that I had been taken behind the scenes of a great "effect"', he writes:

> The Constantinople of Vauxhall Gardens, a few years ago, did not differ more, when viewed, in front from the gallery, and behind from the dirty little alleys bordering the river. The miserable, narrow, ill-paved thoroughfare did not present one redeeming feature – even of picturesque dreariness.[12]

Here again we see Smith's life-long interest in visual spectacle, and his equally consistent awareness that a dull reality might lie behind the glittering façade. He was predictably disappointed by many of the most vaunted sites of Constantinople: the Sultan's palace, the Seraglio, St. Sophia, all of which he claimed 'had been so ridiculously written up, and over-praised, that expectation could not possibly be gratified'. Seeing the Sultan attend a mosque, Smith felt let down by the encounter, turning once again to the *One Thousand and One Nights* for his reference point: 'A dream of the Arabian Nights had been somewhat harshly dispelled. I had seen a Sultan – a great monarch, holding as high a rank as the father of Aladdin's Princess Badroulbador – and but for his fez, he might have passed for a simple foreign gentleman from Leicester Square.' This is fairly typical of Smith in his John Bull mode, as are his sentiments when he meets an acquaintance from Surrey who is working in Constantinople. They find themselves watching 'a magnificent sunset behind Stamboul, which called forth my liveliest admiration', when Smith's friend observes, 'I would sooner see a sunset from "The Cricketers" at Chertsey Bridge'. Smith recalls,

> Immediately our feelings were the same. There is no nation of the world so great in distant enterprise and love of wandering as the English – none which ever turns with such deeply-rooted and constant affection, unchanged by any time or distance, to its home.[13]

This is harmless enough nostalgia, understandable in a man who had been travelling constantly for several months by this stage, and Smith was scarcely the first travel writer to make this observation; nor was it the last time he made it, since, true to form, he reused it in a slightly altered version in *Pictures of Life at Home and Abroad* two years later (that quotation is the epigraph to this chapter).

But a more boorish side of Smith was on display when he witnessed a group of so-called 'Whirling Dervishes', members of the mystical Sufi order who performed a kind of whirling dance as a devotional act. With no understanding or sympathy for the religious and cultural context of what he was seeing, Smith found the spectacle alienating, even infuriating:

> There was something inexpressibly sly and offensive in the appearance of these men, and the desire one felt to hit them hard in the face became uncomfortably dominant [...] I suppose, altogether, a greater set of rascals do not exist; and I came away not quite sure as to whether I had been most amused or irritated at their performance.[14]

Smith was equally baffled by another set of Sufi mystics, the so-called 'Howling Dervishes', who performed the *dhikr,* or ritual devotion, by chanting:

> I could not exactly understand what induced these men to make such fools of themselves. Certainly it was not for money, for none was given by the spectators, nor indeed was any solicited. Neither can I suspect it to have been for religious motives, for, to all appearances, a greater set of scamps had seldom been collected together. I must leave the explanation to those familiar with the mysteries of Eastern worship.[15]

This kind of crassness was by no means unique to Smith. British travellers to the Ottoman Empire had a long history of expressing disdain for what they regarded as 'a spectacle of apparent fanaticism, barbarity, and deceit'. Since the late eighteenth century, the Dervishes had regularly been accused by British visitors of fraud, hypocrisy, or fanaticism.[16] But for Smith – a writer who would often complain about the ignorance and lack of curiosity of his own countrymen abroad – to demonstrate such a failure of imagination is surprising. Whatever else Smith was, he was generally an excellent journalist and a curious observer of all that he came across on his travels, but something about the Dervishes seems to have upset and disturbed him to the point where his curiosity was displaced by alienation.

Much more disturbing for the contemporary reader of Smith's book is his response to encountering slaves. Slavery remained widespread in the Ottoman Empire until the late nineteenth century, although it became increasingly clandestine as foreign criticism grew throughout the century; when the *New York Times* published an article in 1886 exposing the practice, its correspondent in Constantinople noted that the Turkish authorities 'deny its existence when approached by Europeans'.[17] Smith's first encounter with slavery came at Smyrna, where he visited the Slave Market with a group of fellow travellers, seemingly in the same spirit that they went to the souk and the camel bazaar. This was his response to seeing human beings for sale:

Two black men, a black woman with a baby, and a little boy, were its only occupants, and they had squatted together in the fierce sun, until their brains must
almost have dried up and rattled, like nuts, in their skulls. The men grinned at
us, and held out their hands for money; the woman took no notice, but continued unconcernedly nursing her baby; and the boy nestled in the dust, and played
with it. There was nothing to excite compassion; in fact, the Slave Market was
pronounced a failure. One of our companions tried to get up a little virtuous
indignation, and began to talk about the degraded condition of human beings,
with other Exeter-Hall conventionalities; but he could not excite the sympathies
of the party, and the American having made a daring observation to the effect
that if he saw one of these slaves and an elephant side by side, he should think
the latter the more intelligent of the two, we all hurried out to stop the argument
which was evidently impending.[18]

By 'Exeter-Hall conventionalities', Smith was alluding to the activities of the
British and Foreign Anti-Slavery Society, founded in 1839 as a successor to the
Anti-Slavery Society that had originally campaigned for abolition of the British
slave trade. The slave trade had been outlawed in Britain in 1807, and full emancipation in the colonies took place between 1834 and 1838, in the wake of the
Slavery Abolition Act of 1833.[19] The Anti-Slavery Society's meetings had traditionally been held in Exeter Hall on the Strand, and the Hall became synonymous
with the campaign against slavery, and more generally with progressive causes
and nonconformist Christianity. It also had for many people a certain whiff of
sanctimony and condescension; Smith had already mocked its ethos of earnest
philanthropy with his portrayal of the Pongo Enlightenment Mission in *Pottleton*,
and Dickens's Borrioboola-Gha mission in *Bleak House* was in part an allusion
to the ill-fated 1841 missionary expedition to Niger, which had had its origins
in an Exeter Hall meeting. Dickens had written after the Niger mission ended
in disaster that, 'It might be laid down as a very good general rule of social and
political guidance, that whatever Exeter Hall champions, is the thing by no means
to be done.'[20]

But Smith was going considerably further than mocking the self-righteousness
of Exeter Hall. Instead, he seemed to be suggesting that only a prig or a fanatic could
summon up compassion for slaves. Nor was he any more distressed by the sight
of a group of galley-slaves chained up in pairs at the Arsenal in Constantinople.
'These fellows were more fearful to look at than any criminals I had ever seen',
he wrote. 'They were of all nations – Turks, Greeks, Negroes, Arabs, Maltese,
and Levantines generally, and filthy beyond expression. They were employed in
drawing heavy timber to land, and treated precisely as so many brutes.'[21] As usual,
it did not seem to occur to Smith that the slaves were filthy through circumstances beyond their control. In his account, their filthiness almost becomes part
of the justification for their enslavement, just as the filthiness of the urban poor in

Britain renders pointless any philanthropic attempts to alleviate their condition.

On a subsequent visit to the Slave Market at Constantinople – like his Smyrna experience, carried out in a matter-of-fact fashion as if it were just another tourist excursion – Smith could not help being reminded of his American companion's comments about elephants back at Smyrna:

> I do honestly believe that if any person of average propriety and right-minded-ness were shown these creatures and told that their lot was to become the prop-erty of others, and work in return for their food and lodging, he would come to the conclusion that it was all they were fit for – indeed, he might think that they had gained in exchanging their wretched savage life for one of comparative civilization. I would not pretend, upon the strength of a hurried visit to the city, to offer the slightest opinion upon the native domestic and social economy; but I can say that whenever I have seen the black slaves abroad, they have been neatly dressed and apparently well kept.[22]

Judging the attitudes of the past by the standards of the present is always dif-ficult. As with his casual anti-Semitism, Smith's indifference to, even approval of, slavery was far from unusual at the time. Kinglake had dealt with slavery in a similarly offhand manner in *Eothen*, treating the slave market in Cairo as a tour-ist attraction in the same spirit that Smith had visited comparable institutions in Smyrna and Constantinople. Warburton was rather more thoughtful and sym-pathetic in his treatment of the matter, but nonetheless concluded that 'a wide distinction should be drawn between the slavery of the East and of the West', and that the institution of slavery was less cruel in the former.[23] And three years after Smith's book was published, Thackeray was travelling in another country where slavery was widespread. Thackeray wrote from Charleston, South Carolina, com-plaining about how unfairly the South was portrayed in the literature of anti-slav-ery campaigners: 'It's all exaggeration about this country – barbarism eccentrici-ties nigger-cruelties & all [...] The negroes are happy whatever is said about them at least all we see & the country Planters beg and implore any Englishman to go to their estates & see for themselves [*sic*].'[24] In the same year, Thomas Carlyle repub-lished his 1849 essay, 'Occasional Discourse on the Negro Question', under the calculatedly offensive new title, 'Occasional Discourse on the Nigger Question'. Carlyle's pamphlet has been the subject of much debate, and his defenders would argue that his wider purpose was to address the inequality and injustice back home in Britain which he believed anti-slavery campaigners ignored in their fo-cus on overseas emancipation. But this was at its core only the same point Smith was making in *A Month At Constantinople* when he claimed to know of a man who publicly expressed sympathy for the poor and oppressed, 'but who would abuse his wife and brutally treat his children' in private.[25] The argument that slavery is justifiable because some of its opponents ignore the plight of the poor in Britain or behave badly in their private lives was as specious in the 1850s as it would be today. It is also important to be clear that Smith was writing at a time when slavery had already been outlawed in his own country, and the anti-slavery movement had enjoyed widespread support for decades. And while Thackeray may have sympathized with the slave-owners of the southern states, there were plenty of other writers – including Dickens, with his depiction of the former slave Cicero in *Martin Chuzzlewit* (1843-44), or in the United States Harriet Beecher Stowe in *Uncle Tom's Cabin* (1852) – who took a very different attitude. Walter Keeley, who would later become Smith's father-in-law, caused controversy during his American tour in 1837 by expressing his outrage at slave ownership in the South.[26] It is one thing to accept that attitudes in the past were different to those of today; quite another to justify attitudes that were benighted and callous by the standards of their own time. Smith's ability to look at people for sale in a market place and conclude that 'it was all they were fit for' is probably the single most unpalatable aspect of his complex, often contradictory character, and it cannot simply be explained away by its historical context.

From Constantinople, Smith sailed to Alexandria in Egypt on a vessel of the Austrian Lloyd's Company (the largest shipping company in the Austro-Hungarian empire, based in Trieste and not connected to Lloyd's of London). During the voyage he became acquainted with an English engineer employed by the line, who proceeded to tell him a comically convoluted and inconsequential anecdote. This chance meeting would form the basis of one of the most popular and enduring characters in Smith's later stage shows, Edwards the Engineer ('He told me the stupidest story I heard in my life', Smith would tell his audience. 'Now, ladies and gentlemen, with your kind permission, I will attempt to tell it to you'). Upon arrival at Alexandria, Smith and the other passengers were forced to undergo a miserable period of quarantine, then he took another boat up the Nile to Cairo. This vessel

> swarmed with rats as big as kittens; spiders that led one to place credence to the full in the bird-catching powers of some of their race, and darted in and out of gaps in the wood, whenever the shutters were let up or down; cockroaches, fleas, and their more important associates, with millions of mosquitoes, to whose stings clothes offered no protection.[27]

Smith liked Cairo, but did not include his experiences there in his book, instead saving most of his Egyptian material for 'The Overland Mail', the stage show he launched in May 1850. Upon his return to London in the autumn of 1849, he quickly wrote up his experiences in the book (published by Bogue the following year, and later republished in the United States under the title *Customs and Habits of the Turks*), then set about creating the show that would open up the next stage in his career.

Smith also succeeded in becoming a member of the Garrick Club, despite a previous experience of being blackballed and the concerns of some members about the beard that he now sported.[28] 'The comfort of a beard, when travelling, to the abolition of shaving tackle may be readily conceived', he pointed out, but the Garrick's membership committee was evidently not convinced. Edmund Yates recalled that although 'clean faces were uncommon', in the late 1840s, men's facial hair was usually confined to 'a pair of "mutton-chop" whiskers'. Anything more hirsute, such as 'a pair of mustachios', was 'never seen, save on a cavalry officer, a dancing-master, or a "snob"'. The cultivation of a full beard like Smith's was 'wholly confined to foreigners', and it was discreetly made known to Smith that 'his beard was most objectionable'. Smith 'distinctly refused to be terrorized into shaving, but declared he would have no objection to modify the hirsute adornment after his election', recalled Yates.[29] Once Smith was safely elected he simply kept the beard, and within a short time events had caught up with his facial hair – the 'beard movement' in Britain got underway from the early 1850s, as beards 'spread from the social margin inhabited by artists and Chartists into the respectable mainstream', becoming associated with solid masculinity rather than with bohemianism.[30] Smith joined the Garrick on 15 December 1849, and would remain an active member of the club for the rest of his life.

Smith was now a successful novelist and travel writer, and had been accepted into a club that combined exclusivity with an air of cultured bohemianism, allowing him to rub shoulders with distinguished theatrical and literary figures. But he had his eye on new challenges. Smith was about to combine his youthful experience of travelling around with his 'Alps in a box' with the fruits of his travels in the East, and his instinct for grand visual spectacle. In May, 1850, the Overland Mail was born.

10: 'THE OVERLAND MAIL'

A pleasant evening may be spent in the company of Mr. Albert Smith, who, if not very instructive, is very entertaining. Illustrated London News, review of 'The Overland Mail'.

'The Overland Mail: A Literary, Pictorial, and Musical Entertainment' opened at Willis's rooms, in King Street, St. James's, on 28 May 1850.[1]

The show's title was a reference to the new route that had been opened up between Britain and India, shaving some three months off the voyage out. A former naval officer, Thomas Waghorn, had set up a series of rest-houses along the Egyptian desert between 1835 and 1837, allowing travellers to make the formerly gruelling journey between Alexandria, on the Mediterranean coast, and Suez, if not exactly in comfort then with relative ease. Waghorn ran a postal and passenger service which covered the route, and from the early 1840s faced competition from the Peninsular & Oriental Company (P&O). Relatively easy access to Suez, and from there through the Red Sea to the Gulf of Aden, avoided the need for a long sea voyage down the west African coast and around the Cape, allowing the journey to India to be completed in just under a month. Strictly speaking, the only 'overland' section of the journey was that between Alexandria and Suez, and it was this that Smith's show focused on. The route was still fresh in the public mind, partly because of accounts by travellers including Thackeray (who travelled with P&O), and partly because Waghorn had died that January.[2]

Smith recruited the scene painter William Beverley, already renowned for his work at the Princess's Theatre and the Lyceum, to paint a series of dioramic scenes with realistic three-dimensional effects. Unlike the Mont Blanc show that was to follow it, 'The Overland Mail' featured a diorama rather than a moving panorama, and Beverley's scenes of Eastern travel were displayed on a screen while Smith performed his 'monopolylogue'.[3] Edmund Yates defined the monopolylogue as a performance 'in which the actor, sometimes with and sometimes without change of costume, takes the whole burden of the performance on his own shoulders, and constitutes himself the sole representative of the *dramatis personae* when the introduction of such characters is necessary'.[4] This fairly accurately summed up Smith's performance.

In contrast to *A Month At Constantinople*, 'The Overland Mail' focused on the journey between Suez and Alexandria (and to a lesser extent on the journey out from Europe) and unlike most previous panoramic performances the moving pictures were a backdrop to the performer rather than the main event. Smith turned out to have a talent as a raconteur and mimic to rival his skills as a writer, and an ability – which was remarked on by a number of those who witnessed this and his Mont Blanc shows – to make prepared material delivered on stage seem spontaneous and intimate: 'Smith gave the impression of being a raconteur in a private drawing room, spontaneously reminiscing by free association.'[5] As well as a lecture about his Egyptian travels, Smith interspersed the performance with comic songs and what one review called 'histrionic representations of his fellow travellers'.[6] *The Times* ran a positive review of the first night, with equally enthusiastic reviews later in the *Illustrated London News* and other publications, and the first season at Willis's Rooms continued until 10 July, when Smith took the show on tour, giving over one hundred performances and still finding time to spend a couple of weeks at Chamonix that summer.

The performance was divided into two acts, with an interval of just ten minutes between them. The first act comprised eight sections, each illustrating a stage or tableau in the 'Overland Mail' journey between Suez and the Mediterranean: 'Suez to Alexandria'; 'The Desert By Sunset'; 'The Middle Station of the Desert'; 'A Street in Cairo'; 'The Kandjia, or Nile Boat'; 'The Sphinx and the Pyramids'; 'The Locks at Atfeh'; 'The Frank Square at Alexandria'.[7] The second act was more concerned with the European stages of the journey home, with five sections representing 'Malta Harbour', 'Marseilles', 'The Great Cutting on the Avignon Railway', 'The Diligence Changing Horses', and 'Boulogne'. Beverley's paintings of these scenes – some of them from sketches by Smith, others based on photographs brought back from his travels – were an important element of the show's success, with their evocation of archetypes of Oriental mystery and splendor. They were, *The Times'* critic wrote, 'distinguished for knowledge of effect and a finished execution rarely attempted in works of this kind'.[8] Beverley's illustration for the 'Desert by Sunset' section, for instance, was described by another contemporary reviewer as follows:

> The painting of this wild and untenanted waste, with the glowing tints shed by the earlier sunset upon the distant horizon, and reflected by the few fleecy clouds visible amid the expanse of blue, is of the highest order; and life-like as it is possible to conceive are the figures in the foreground, wearied with travel, still stealing onward upon their lonely journey.[9]

However, at least as crucial a factor in the show's success was the performance of Smith, who introduced various characters who would recur in his later Mont Blanc shows. Edwards the Engineer, at this stage simply described as 'An English Engineer and his complicated dilemmas', and 'Undecided Mr. Parker, the tourist, who never knew his own mind' both made their appearance for the first time in 'The Overland Mail'. Smith's comic songs were, according to the critic of *The Times*, 'exceedingly well written, displaying a nice feeling for smooth metre, and great power in compressing a number of salient points into a small compass'.[10] Smith demonstrated how to smoke a shisha pipe, described the scene at the pyramids at Giza where travellers were constantly pestered to buy souvenirs or take camel rides, and as always mixed his colourful descriptions of exotic scenes with a reminder that much of what was said and written about these places by others was exaggerated. So Smith acknowledged to his audience that 'the most vivid associations of the traveller are those which he connects with the personages and scenes of the Arabian Nights' Entertainments', and claimed that in 'the exceeding beauty and attractive bustle of Cairo' these associations were constantly stimulated by 'a series of living illustrations to that delightful story-book'. Yet in the same show, he mocked a recent book that described the ascent of the Great Pyramid (still permitted to tourists at this stage) as 'not without difficulty and danger', and claimed that 'I went, unaided, from the base to the summit in twenty minutes; and returned, also, alone'.[11] According to Smith, it was to be regretted that 'all authors, with the exception of Mr. Thackeray, lose every sense of the practical and commonplace the instant they begin to write about the East'.[12]

Smith's timing in staging 'The Overland Mail' was, as so often in his career, propitious. Richard D. Altick, in his monumental study of London entertainments and exhibitions, calls the early years of the 1850s 'The Age of the Panorama'. Although panoramas and dioramas had been around for decades at this point, they were enjoying something of a renaissance. As Smith's satirical 1850 article on 'The Panoramania' suggests, there was still a considerable public appetite for these visual spectacles (see Chapter 3). At the Egyptian Hall, where Smith would later enjoy such success with his Mont Blanc show, a dioramic portrayal of 'Colonel Fremont's Overland Route to Oregon and California' was playing until July 1851, and was then replaced by a diorama of the Holy Land, accompanied by 'Grand and Appropriate Music'.[13] Another show, 'The Overland Route to India', had opened over Easter 1850 at the Gallery of Illustration on Regent Street, and was already enjoying considerable success; it would go on to run for 1,600 performances.[14]

Smith's show was to some extent competing with these and similar attractions, but of course it had the added benefit of his unique narration. The 'monopolylogue' format employed by Smith had been around since the time of the comic actor Charles Mathews in the 1820s, and was still popular with performers including W. S. Woodin and John Orlando Parry. However, many of these performers relied on costume changes for their shifts between different characters: Woodin, for example, 'would dive into an extra-sized carpet bag as Martha Mivens, a domestic servant, and jump out of it as Major Bluster, a swaggering half-pay solder'.[15] Smith, according to Yates, had 'a horror of what he called the "ducking down business", the old-fashioned process of diving under the lecture table, and by rapid assumption of wig and costume, reappearing immediately as someone else'.[16] With his considerable sense of his own dignity, Smith behaved with more gravitas, for all his adoption of amusing voices and comic persona, and performances of 'The Overland Mail' – which Smith always gave in full evening dress – were considered a respectable entertainment option for mid-Victorian audiences: 'the audience was numerous and fashionable', according to the *Illustrated London News*.[17] This respectability would prove to be another factor in Smith's success throughout the 1850s, encouraging those who were wary of the sometimes rowdy atmosphere of the popular theatre to attend his lectures, and to feel that they were not only being entertained but also educated. The sharp distinction between the legitimate and illegitimate drama was becoming blurred by this stage in the nineteenth century, and the atmosphere in most London theatres was gradually becoming more genteel, but there were still members of the middle classes who would not have attended, for example, a popular melodrama but would happily have gone along to Smith's more refined and supposedly educational entertainment. As Judith Flanders points out, nonconformist religion had become an increasingly important influence on middle-class sensibilities in the course of the nineteenth century, and the theatre – like the novel – was still considered by many to be 'too much concerned with the passions, and too little with morality'.[18] A respectable atmosphere and a patina of improving, educative content could go some way towards allaying those suspicions. This would also be the case with Smith's Mont Blanc shows, where 'the amusement afforded was of a kind that offered no impediment to the presence of the most strait-laced of moralists', as his friend William Ballantine recalled.[19] In reality, of course, the volume of educative material in Smith's shows was fairly limited; he had made his views on combining education with entertainment clear in his article on 'Science and the Show-Folks' (see Chapter 3). Even the *Illustrated London News*, generally friendly to Smith, wrote in its review, 'Verily, a pleasant evening may be spent in the company of Mr. Albert Smith, who, if not very instructive, is very entertaining in his "Entertainment".'[20]

Smith also developed a range of publicity materials to accompany the show. Handbills and souvenir programmes were already a feature of other entertainments, but to these Smith added explanatory booklets with extra information about the places he described in the show, an innovation he would develop even further in his Mont Blanc show. He created his own stamp for letters, with an image of a man – possibly intended to be Smith himself – riding a camel at speed across the desert (in a private joke in an 1851 letter to his friend and collaborator John Leech, Smith appended this image to his signature, doctoring the picture so that it showed him trailing a cart with large bags of money, each with £100 signs on them – presumably a gleeful reference to how profitable the show was proving by that stage).[21] Relatively little of this accompanying material has survived, compared to the wealth of publicity material for his later Mont Blanc shows, but those that do exist suggest that Smith had already grasped the importance of advertising, publicity, and merchandising.

'The Overland Mail' resumed in 1851, opening at the Music Hall on Store Street, a short walk from Smith's Percy Street home. The Music Hall at number 16 Store Street had been opened by piano maker Robert Wornum for concerts in the 1830s, and had capacity for up to a thousand people. However, Smith was by now competing with the upcoming attraction of the Great Exhibition, which opened in Hyde Park in May of that year. He was also about to launch a new publication called *The Month* with Leech, with backing from Bradbury and Evans. As a result, the time seemed right to take 'The Overland Mail' off the London stage, although it was not dormant for long and Smith was certainly not inactive. Six issues of the *The Month* appeared before the new publication folded in December that year, produced during a period when Smith not only climbed Mont Blanc but also spent most of the time between September and December 1851 touring the provinces with 'The Overland Mail'. Letters written by Smith to Leech during that autumn – from Liverpool, Huddersfield, the Isle of Wight, Wakefield – are full of short, throwaway ideas for illustrations or comic articles, testimony to his extraordinary energy and ability to juggle multiple projects.

That summer, Smith succeeded in his longstanding ambition of climbing Mont Blanc, to be discussed in the next chapter. Upon his return, he set off on an extensive regional tour with 'The Overland Mail'. His schedule took him from Tunbridge Wells on 1 September, though many of the large towns of southern England, on to the Isle of Wight, back to Winchester, Chippenham and on to Wells at the end of September. October took him to Plymouth, Torquay, Teignmouth, Clifton, Exeter, and other towns and cities of the south-west. By late October, Smith was travelling north to Worcester, Wolverhampton, then on to Manchester. November found him heading to Ashton-under-Lyme, Stockport, Liverpool, Birkhenhead, then on to the main Yorkshire towns and cities, then to Newcastle and other centres in the north-east in December. This packed schedule finally ended with a return to the south-west, where – as Smith wrote to John Blackwood in the middle of December – 'The Overland Mail dies tonight, at Exmouth, after 288 engagements.'[22]

Meanwhile, Smith had been collaborating with Leech on *The Month: a View of Passing Subjects and Manners, Home and Foreign, Social and General*. Bankrolled by Bradbury and Evans, the new publication was initially well received, although it never gained the readership that Smith and Leech had hoped for it, and was wound up in December that same year. Smith wrote to Bradbury and Evans after the first issue was released in July, noting that there had been 'a great puff of *The Month* in the leader of the *Standard*', and enclosing a clipping from the *Liverpool Post* which said that, 'The contents, redolent of true wit and humour, are distinguished by a refinement of tone, and freedom from personalities, somewhat rare in comic publications.'[23] The first issue mocked the excitement surrounding the Great Exhibition, with a section called 'Nursery Rhymes of the Great Exhibition' ('Koh-i-noor, Koh-i-noor, go away home/You're duller than ever beneath your gilt dome').[24] It also demonstrated that Smith had lost none of his contempt for those who sympathized with the urban poor. The very first article, which was expanded into a regular feature in subsequent issues, was called 'London Labour and the London Rich' and was framed as a comic riposte to Henry Mayhew's *London Labour and the London Poor*, serialized in the *Morning Chronicle* in the 1840s and then published in three volumes in 1851. Mayhew's detailed and formally innovative chronicle of London's working classes famously gave a voice to the poor, interviewing hundreds of people in various situations – from street entertainers to rat catchers, prostitutes to sewer scavengers – and transcribing their own words in an attempt to establish the sheer scale and variety of poverty in the metropolis. He backed up his case studies with census data and other statistics, creating a compendious portrait of poverty in the capital that was revolutionary both in its methodology and in its implications; Mayhew's book forced many people to acknowledge for the first time the sheer scale of urban poverty.

Smith, predictably, was unmoved, and his response was an admittedly very well-executed parody of Mayhew's study, in which the urban rich become the object of the same kind of anthropological curiosity Mayhew had brought to bear upon the poor. 'The interest excited by the details of the manner in which the London Poor don't get their living, about the streets, has induced us to send a Commissioner forth to study the habits of an equally interesting and hardworking class of people – the London Rich.' Instead of street traders or beggars, Smith's subjects were, for instance, the 'Hyde Park Belle', a wealthy young lady in the market for a husband, who begins her self-introduction, 'I shall be nineteen in August, and have been out two years and a half.'[25]

Smith's work on *The Month* also brought him into conflict with the actor and theatre manager Charles Kean, son of the famous thespian Edmund Kean. Charles Kean was himself considered a great tragedian, and during his tenure at the Princess's Theatre from 1850 he put on a number of highly regarded Shakespeare productions. Smith, no respecter of persons, mocked him in the final edition of *The Month*, in December 1851, evidently leading Kean to snub him at the Garrick. He had, Smith wrote, 'mistook his trade when he turned actor, trusting to the *prestige* of his immortal father's name, without one qualification, intellectually or physically, for the purpose'.[26] Kean's refusal to shake Smith's hand at the Garrick evidently took place some time after publication, since in a letter dated 20 February 1853 Smith took Kean to task, saying he had offered him his hand because 'you were the only professional person in London with whom I was on bad terms'. Kean replied the following day that he had expected an apology from Smith, and accused him of indulging in 'personal scurrility, with individual spite in every line of it'. Smith then brought the correspondence to a close, writing loftily, 'I have no apology to offer, and really not caring a straw about the matter either way, now, I beg with this letter to close the correspondence.'[27] This would seem to have been a rather embarrassing spat given that Kean's joint lessees at the Princess's Theatre were the Keeleys, who would become Smith's mother and father-in-law a few years later. However, part of Smith's purpose in the original article appears to have been to emphasize the role of the Keeleys in the success of the theatre: 'Does he [Kean] conceive that there has been one single sixpence paid at the doors of the Princess's Theatre', demanded Smith, 'of which the Keeleys have not attracted four-fifths?'

Smith and Leech worked hard on *The Month*. During his autumn and winter tour with 'The Overland Mail', Smith was firing off ideas to Leech, such as this 'notion for a cut' in a letter from Huddersfield in November: 'Girl and swell in country house. Swell: I must be off, Julie. I'm going to draw a badger. Julie: Can't you draw it here, Willy. There's my colour box.' This became a cartoon by Leech in the final volume of *The Month*, with an almost identical caption.[28] But for all their efforts, *The Month* did not sell in sufficient copies to make a profit, and by later that month Smith was writing to Leech from Wakefield: 'My dear Jack. We must give up *The Month* – or rather, I must. I cannot work any longer, nor take money from the proprietor, under such disheartening circumstances.'[29] He wrote around the same time to Bradbury and Evans,

> It must be given up. I regret this very much, but I will no more throw all my pains into a work that does not command a large audience (and I never scamp anything), than I will receive your money, so liberally given, for what is evidently not bringing you even an average return. A literary man may, sometimes, have a gentleman's delicacy: and were we to continue I should look upon myself as a mere "bloodsucker", only anxious to get as much out of you as I could, irrespective of your contingent gain.[30]

It is impossible to know to what extent Smith's determination to close *The Month* was, as he claimed, down to moral fastidiousness about taking his publishers' money without returning them a profit, and to what extent he simply wanted to get on with his next idea, which would turn out to be his Mont Blanc show. But he sounds sincere when he writes to Leech that 'the only thing that grieves me in the matter is giving up co-operation with you: but we will do some books together with Bogue', and when he tells Bradbury and Evans that, 'now we have only to hope to be more fortunate in something else, some day. I am most vexed at the failure because I <u>know</u> how good the books have been'. Smith told his publishers that he thought *The Month*'s pricing had been misjudged ('I wish the book had been sixpence. I know that *The Man in the Moon* sold, and how well, with the smallest care, it would have paid'), and to Leech he intimated that he thought his next project might be to set up a weekly publication.

What seems clear, however, is that by November of 1850, over a year before *The Month* folded and while 'The Overland Mail' still had a long run ahead of it, Smith was not only planning his ascent of Mont Blanc the following summer but had already decided he would turn the experience into a show. In a letter dated 1 November, to a recipient whose name is illegible, Smith wrote: 'My Mont Blanc will be a go – <u>safe</u>. William Beverley comes with me to Chamonix [...] I shall bring it out more elaborately than 'The Overland Mail' and yet at less expense.'[31]

It is impossible to tell to what extent Smith had plotted out the precise nature of the show he would put on in the wake of his Mont Blanc ascent, but he evidently had decided to take Beverley along with a view to making images of the climb. His belief that the projected show would be 'a go' turned out more than fully justified. First, however, he had to get himself up Mont Blanc.

11: 'PLUCK WILL SERVE ME'

There is not much mistake about Chamouny. However disappointed travellers may feel at the first sight of the majority of the continental show places, with which they have only been acquainted through the medium of Annuals and dioramas, yet few pens or pencils can do justice to the exceeding grandeur of this valley. Albert Smith, *Christopher Tadpole*

Smith had not been idle during his visit to Chamonix in the summer of 1850. As a regular visitor over the previous seven or eight years, to the extent that 'the guides came to look upon me as an *habitué* of the village', he had become increasingly fixated on the prospect of ascending Mont Blanc. While he was visiting that year, he looked on with envy as Erasmus Galton (older brother of the scientist Francis Galton) returned from a successful ascent. Before he departed from his 1850 visit, Jean Tairraz – son of the innkeeper who he had met on his first visit back in 1838 – 'made me half-promise that I would come back again the following August, and try the ascent with him'.[1]

As his November 1850 letter indicates, Smith was soon planning his next visit, with a view not only to climbing the peak but also to taking along William Beverley, whose dioramic views had been an important factor in the success of 'The Overland Mail'. He and Beverley set off on 1 August 1850. The night before their departure an excited Smith dined with George Hodder at the Cheshire Cheese. 'His animal spirits were tuned to a high key, and he spoke in rapturous terms of his intended visit', recalled Hodder, 'but I had not the least idea that he proposed to do more than spend a few weeks at his favourite resort'.

'Off tomorrow morning!', Smith exclaimed, 'and I shall make the ascent of Mont Blanc in a day or two'.

'Bold thing to do', suggested Hodder, 'for a man who has not been in training, and you are rather heavy for a mountain climber'.

'Never mind', replied Smith. 'Pluck will serve me instead of training; and I haven't the slightest fear.'[2]

Smith and Beverley left London on the same mail-train from London Bridge as a party that included the Lord Mayor and various members of the Corporation of London travelling to a function in Paris. Smith was carrying his possessions in the old knapsack he had used back in his days as a student traveller, and upon arrival he was gleeful to discover that the dignitaries' luggage had been lost while he was able to carry on his journey with the knapsack that had been stowed under his seat. True to form, Smith lost no opportunity to let his readers know how he had stolen a march on less wily travellers when he wrote up his experiences for *Blackwood's Edinburgh Magazine* a few months later.

The feat Smith hoped to undertake was still relatively unusual in the early 1850s. Depending on which historical sources you choose to believe, Smith's ascent would be the thirty-sixth, thirty-seventh, thirty-ninth, or the fifty-sixth successful attempt on Mont Blanc.[3] A Genevan savant, Horace Bénédict de Saussure, had tried and failed to climb it in the 1780s, and offered a cash prize to anyone who succeeded; a Chamonix doctor, Michel-Gabriel Paccard, and a local hunter and crystal-gatherer, Jacques Balmat, finally reached the summit in 1786. Saussure himself climbed the mountain the following year, accompanied by Balmat, and later that summer Colonel Mark Beaufoy became the first Briton to climb it. The Napoleonic Wars of 1799-1815 put paid to further attempts by Britons for a while, although various other people managed to reach the summit during this period, including Maria Paradis, the first woman to climb the mountain, in 1808.[4] By the second and third decades of the nineteenth century, Britons were returning to the Alps in greater numbers, inspired in part by Romantic literature, particularly Wordsworth's accounts of his 1780 walking tour.

As more visitors attempted to climb Mont Blanc, a number of accidents inevitably took place, although rather surprisingly the only fatalities were those incurred by the Hamel expedition in 1820.[5] Even by the 1850s, however, the mountain was considered sufficiently perilous that, according to the mountaineer Edward Whymper, 'men commonly made wills before starting for it, and wrote heavy accounts of the dangers of the enterprise when they came down'.[6] As late as 1850, *The Times* would report that a successful ascent by 'Mr. Gretton, late of the 5th Fusileers [sic], and Mr. Richards, of the County of Wexford' had been preceded by the climbers making out their wills, leaving behind their watches and other valuables, and that 'nothing else was thought of in the town' until they were seen from the valley safely on the summit, whereupon a cannon was fired to hail their success.[7] The great majority of visitors to Chamonix contented themselves with excursions to the Mer de Glace and perhaps to the 'Jardin', the island of rock that juts dramatically up out of the Glacier de Talèfre. The influence of Romantic literature on Alpine tourists remained considerable at this point in the nineteenth century, and Mary Shelley's description of the 'terrible precipices of solid ice' and the tremendous and ever-moving glacier' could still lead many visitors to believe that the relatively accessible peak of Montenvers – the popular viewing point for the Mer de Glace – was quite wild enough for their tastes.[8]

The Mer de Glace. The glacier would have been much more extensive in Smith's day, but even after his first visit to Chamonix he dismissed it as resembling a ploughed field. Author photo.

Potential Mont Blanc summiteers consulting their *Murray's Handbook* would have found little encouragement. Murray, clinging to the imagery and sensibility of Shelley and other Romantic-era writers, suggested excursions to the Mer de Glace and Jardin, the object of which was 'to enter more into the heart of Mont Blanc, to penetrate into its profound valleys, and witness scenes of wilder horror and more savage solitude; and there is no excursion from Chamouny that excites these sublime emotions more powerfully'.[9] For anyone foolhardy enough to consider actually climbing 'The Monarch of the Mountains', however, Murray had these stern words:

> The Ascent of Mont Blanc is attempted by few; of these, the records are to be found at Chamouny. When Saussure ascended to make experiments at that height, the motive was a worthy one; but those who are impelled by curiosity alone, are not justified in risking the lives of the guides. The pay tempts these poor fellows to encounter the danger, but their safety, devoted as they are to their employers, is risked for a poor consideration. It is no excuse that the employer thinks his own life worthless; here he ought to think of the safety of others; yet scarcely a season passes without the attempt.[10]

Even by 1852, the year after Smith's attempt, the *Handbook* was claiming, 'It is a somewhat remarkable fact that a large proportion of those who have made this ascent have been persons of unsound mind', although it did also concede that the climb had become more popular since Smith's ascent the previous year.[11]

Those who ignored these warnings and attempted the climb faced a variety of what mountaineers now call 'objective' dangers – in other words, dangers that are inherent in the mountain environment and cannot be wholly eliminated by planning, skill, or experience. Perhaps foremost among these was the risk of ava-lanches. but there were a number of other such dangers, including rock falls (a risk that becomes higher later in the day, as the sun melts the snow and ice holding rocks in place); electrical storms, which were particularly dangerous for climbers carrying metal-tipped alpenstocks or other metal gear; and cornices (overhanging ridges of snow, usually on the leeward edge of a mountain, which can appear solid but collapse under the weight of a human body). And all this is before one takes into account the problems caused by the mountain's 4,810-metre altitude.

Despite his bravado when speaking to Hodder, Smith admitted that he 'had not undertaken the least training for my work', and Jean Tairraz evidently cast a doubtful eye over him when he arrived at Chamonix. Then as now, a safe attempt on Mont Blanc was dependent on reasonable weather, and Tairraz was concerned that the favourable conditions would break before Smith was prepared. Edmund Yates described Smith at this stage in his life as 'short, stout, and middle-aged'.[12] Thirty-five years old was indeed middle-aged in a period when male life expectan-cy was in the low forties, and Smith was scarcely in ideal condition to be attempt-ing an ascent of the highest peak in western Europe, even in good conditions.[13]

Smith set about getting in shape for the ascent, but his training regime seems to have been fairly desultory, consisting of a couple of strolls up the relatively easy path from the valley to Montenvers, and on one occasion crossing the Mer de Glace, an excursion he had made on previous trips accompanied by local guide Julien Devouassoud.

It was not simply Smith's lack of fitness that was the problem. The effects of altitude were imperfectly understood at this stage, but it had long been noticed that ascending above a certain height could lead to a variety of symptoms, from headache and nausea, through to dizziness, shortness of breath, vomiting, and disturbed sleep. The first recorded reference to the malady of altitude sickness is believed to be from a Chinese chronicler two thousand years ago, describing the 'Great and Little Headache' mountains on the Silk Road, and since then a series of travellers had speculated on its causes.[14] The Jesuit missionary and explorer Joseph de Acosta had described the symptoms of what is now known as acute mountain sickness (AMS) in 1590, and the invention of the mercury barom-eter in 1644 led to the discovery that barometric pressure declined with altitude. Saussure reported that on his ascent of Mont Blanc in 1786 he had to stop for breath every fifteen or sixteen steps.[15] Saussure recorded the details of pulse rate, body temperature, and respiratory rate during his climb, but neither he nor any other early climbers were in a position to conduct more sophisticated experiments.[16] As more people started to climb mountains (and to make hot-air balloon ascents) during the nineteenth century, speculation grew about the precise cause of these symptoms. The Hamel expedition had been intended to study levels of oxygen both in the air and in human blood at the summit of Mont Blanc, but the avalanche that killed three of its members put paid to that ambition.[17] It was not until 1878 that the French physiologist Paul Bert finally identified low partial pressure of oxygen as the definite cause of altitude sickness, a discovery he wrote about in his book *La Pression Barométrique* the same year.

The best way to cope with altitude sickness was the subject of a great deal of debate and speculation throughout the nineteenth century, and as mountaineering became an organized, codified activity with its own organizations and publications, the potential of the human body to acclimatize to high altitudes would often be discussed in the pages of mountaineering club journals.[18] Even today, the physiological effects of altitude are not fully understood. What is certain is that altitude sickness tends to happen with a rapid ascent to 2,500 metres or above, as the partial pressure of oxygen falls with the drop in barometric pressure; the barometric pressure at the summit of Mont Blanc, for example, is around half that at sea level.[19] It is difficult to predict how well any given individual will cope with altitude, and physical fitness is not in itself an indicator, but the way mountaineers usually acclimatize nowadays is by ascending gradually, and if possible spending the night at moderate altitudes, then retreating to a lower level before climbing higher after an interval. So a typical ascent of Mont Blanc might involve the climber spending a night or two at a mountain hut at around 3,000 or 3,500 metres, climbing to higher elevations higher during the day but descending to this altitude to sleep at night. This would be followed by a descent to the valley, then an attempt on Mont Blanc itself over a two- or even three-day period, depending on the route chosen. Even with this level of preparation, the lack of oxygen near the summit makes exertion difficult, but this approach to acclimatisation will generally improve the chances of reaching the summit without extreme symptoms.[20]

None of this was known to the climbers of the 1850s, however, and even if it had been there was no network of mountain huts which would have allowed them to spend the night at altitude in relative comfort and safety in order to acclimatize. It was not even understood that consuming alcohol, for example, hinders one's ability to cope with altitude – a gap in knowledge that would have an effect on Smith's condition by the time he reached the summit. And while better physical fitness would not have helped Smith with the altitude, the fact that he was out of condition made the sheer physical effort of climbing up the mountain much harder for him.

Smith, then, was starting out at a considerable disadvantage. Not a man to be daunted, he set about looking into hiring guides for an assault on the mountain. The rules of the municipality since the formation of the Compagnie des Guides de Chamonix in 1821 (in the wake of the Hamel disaster) meant that guides had to be taken from the roster on a 'taxi cab' basis, with visitors obliged to accept the guide or guides whose turn it was that day. Later in the century this system would be the cause of complaints by many British mountaineers, who felt that they were sometimes obliged to use less competent and experienced guides than they would have liked. Eventually the obligation to climb with guides was abolished, but up until the 1870s it was standard practice for visiting mountaineers – even those who, unlike Smith, already had considerable climbing experience – to be accompanied by local guides. Until at least the 1880s, the practice of climbing without guides was condemned by some (even among members of Britain's main climbing institution, the Alpine Club) as reckless.[21] For Smith in 1851, the possibility of climbing the mountain without guides did not even arise – the only question was how many to take.

At this point a chance encounter took place that improved Smith's prospects of achieving his ambition. A reading party of Oxford undergraduates, the Hon. William Edward Sackville-West, Charles G. Floyd, and Francis Philips, also happened to be staying at the Hôtel de Londres. A few days earlier, they had been swimming in Lake Geneva when they spotted Mont Blanc in the distance. 'The exclamation, "How awfully grand!" burst almost at the same moment from our lips', recalled Francis Philips in his memoir of their trip. The friends decided there and then to travel to Chamonix and try to climb the mountain, but they had to wait for a week until the weather cleared. They used the time to set about training for the climb, meanwhile 'steadily resisting the allurements of hot French rolls', confining themselves to one or two cigars a day, and ordering 'bifstek a l'Anglais' for dinner. During their enforced wait, Smith evidently heard of their plans, and – no doubt thinking of the benefits of sharing the cost of guides and porters – suggested that they join forces. The undergraduates were initially reluctant:

> The garçon had informed us that a "Mr. Smith of London" wished to accompany us. As we had no acquaintance with such a person, we declined the honour; and it was not till some days after that we found out it was Mr. Albert Smith, the well-known comic author, when we at once took the liberty of introducing ourselves.[22]

It was agreed that they would climb together. The party bought green spectacles and veils to prevent snow blindness, acquired thickly studded boots, and took along rugs and warm blankets in preparation for a planned bivouac at over

3,000 metres on the rocky outcrops known as the Grands Mulets.

Philips suggested in his account that Smith 'fully intended to expose the whole affair as an imposition, fancying the guides were leagued together in representing it as much more hazardous than would prove, on trial, to be the case'.[23] However, Smith makes no mention of this motive in his own accounts of the climb, and it seems unlikely given his cordial relations with the Tairraz family, his subsequent praise of the conduct of his guides, and his continued association with the town of Chamonix in years to come. The fact that his party had chosen to hire four guides for every one client – twice the minimum number required by the rules – also makes this seem improbable. As early as the 1890s, a reviewer of Philips' book in the *Alpine Journal* was suggesting that Smith was probably joking with his companions when he told them this and that he simply 'could not resist the temptation to mystify them to some extent' (the reviewer added, 'They were innocent enough for it.')[24] In any case, an impressive roster of sixteen guides and eighteen porters was hired, and an even more impressive list of provisions assembled.[25] Smith reproduced the bill of fare in his account of the climb:

60 bottles of vin ordinaire	4 packets of prunes
6 bottles of Bordeaux	4 packets of raisins
10 bottles of St. George	2 packets of salt
15 bottles of St. Jean	4 wax candles
3 bottles of Cognac	6 lemons
1 bottle of syrup of raspberries	4 legs of mutton
6 bottles of lemonade	4 shoulders of mutton
2 bottles of champagne	6 pieces of veal
20 loaves	1 piece of beef
10 small cheeses	11 large fowls
6 packets of chocolate	35 small fowls
6 packets of sugar	

This cost a total of 456 francs.[26] Smith has often been mocked for this seemingly extraordinary list of provisions, but it is worth pointing out that when his predecessor John Auldjo wrote the account of climbing Mont Blanc in 1827 that had inspired the young Albert Smith, he enumerated a very similar list. For a party of just nine people, Auldjo took along a banquet that included twenty bottles of vin ordinaire, a bottle of champagne, sixteen chickens, and a couple of bottles of brandy, plus a great deal more. Smith's provisions, by comparison, were required to feed nearly forty people, at least in the initial stages of the climb.[27] Henrietta d'Angeville, who in 1838 had become the second woman to climb Mont Blanc, had also taken along a similar list of supplies, 'to which she added a blancmange in a flask for her private use', according to one account.[28]

Generous provisions purchased, guides and porters hired, all that the party could do now was wait for the weather to clear. It had started to rain not long after Smith's arrival, and there seemed no break in sight. Smith had to retire to bed after getting soaked on his Montenvers excursion, but upon recovering he visited the home of an elderly member of the Balmat family to consult a celebrated local weather guide. This 'turned out to be one of the little Dutch houses, with the meteorological lady and gentlemen occupiers' – in other words, an elaborately designed barometer, from which the female figure would emerge if the pressure was high, and the male figure if pressure was low. To make matters slightly more complicated, the device was called Le Menteur (the liar) because it was known to predict the exact opposite of what would then happen. 'The lady in her summer dress was most provokingly abroad, and the worst fears were entertained', recalled Smith. For once, however, Le Menteur turned out to be honest. Just as Smith and his companions had decided that they could wait no longer, and agreed to leave Chamonix the next day, 'all the fog rolled away clean out of the valley as if by magic'. A window of settled weather had opened, and there was no time to lose. A few hours of frantic preparations got underway, and the aspirant mountaineers 'walked about Chamouni that night with heads erect, and an imposing step. People pointed at us, and came from the hotels to see what we were like. For that evening, at least, we were evidently great persons.'

The day had come at last. After years of dreaming about it, Albert Smith was going to climb Mont Blanc.

Smith's route up Mont Blanc. Author photo.

12: THE MONARCH OF THE MOUNTAINS

Mont Blanc is the monarch of mountains,/They crowned him long ago/On a throne of rocks, in a robe of clouds,/With a diadem of snow. Lord Byron, *Manfred.*

Smith may have enjoyed being the centre of attention in Chamonix for a few hours, but he had still not fully recovered from the effects of his soaking and he was too anxious to sleep that night.

In the morning he evidently had a moment of sober reflection on the dangers he was about to face. He made a small parcel of his money and a few other valuables, handed it to Beverley, who was not going to accompany the climbers, and asked him to take care of them if he should not return. 'I am afraid my attempt to be careless about the matter was a failure', he confessed.

What Smith believed, probably correctly, to be 'the largest caravan that had ever gone off together' from Chamonix left the town at around half-past-seven on the morning of the twelfth of August. In addition to the four climbers, sixteen guides, and eighteen porters, there was also 'a rabble rout of friends, and relations, and sweethearts, and boys, some of whom came a considerable distance with us'. All the British visitors to Chamonix also turned out to see the party set off. The principal guides were Jean Carrier and the two Tairraz cousins, both called Jean. Francis Philips described Carrier as 'a very fine man of twenty-six years of age, so compactly built that it was not till you stood close to him that you discovered his height, which was upwards of six feet'. The elder Jean Tairraz 'had a facetious expression of countenance, and evidently thought himself a wag'. He lost no opportunity to use his one word of Italian, 'andiamo' (let's go). His younger cousin was described simply as 'a short man, strongly built, and able to undergo great fatigue'.[1]

The first stage of the climb was through the steep pine woods that lay between the lower stretches of the Glacier des Bossons and the Glacier des Pélerins. Smith began the trek on a mule, hoping to conserve his strength, although the path soon became so steep that riding was almost as challenging as being on foot, and after about two and a half hours he was forced to dismount. They were now at the highest human habitation on the mountain, known as the Chalet de la Para, and from here onwards the vegetation started to thin out and the track became narrower. Another half-hour of steep walking took the party to the rock known as the Pierre à l'Echelle, where a ten-foot ladder was left *in situ* to allow climbers to ford the crevasses they would encounter once they reached the Bossons glacier.

After a brief rest stop, Tairraz announced 'andiamo' and the group continued on towards the glacier, but before they had even reached it Philips slipped on a patch of snow and slid down a steep incline. He was able to arrest his descent by digging in his heels and using his walking pole, but the guides decided it would now be prudent to rope up. The use of ropes in mountaineering had not become standardized at this early stage, and some guides did not bother with them at all. Others tied their clients to the ropes – using a simple loop around the waist, as harnesses had not yet been developed – but carried the other end of the rope casually in their hand. Some guides even ordered their clients to untie in particularly steep places, to avoid the whole party being pulled off if one person fell.[2] Smith and his young friends were therefore fortunate in having guides who took a rather less desultory approach to ropecraft. The party was tied on to a series of ropes, with three guides at the front including Carrier, then Philips, with another three guides behind him. West and Floyd were separated by another three guides, then three guides tied on to the rope in front of Smith, and the remainder of the party behind him. Each man was separated by about eight feet of rope. In this way, each inexperienced climber could potentially be held by a group of more surefooted and experienced guides if he fell.

The first part of the trek up the Bossons glacier – the largest icefall in Europe, which in the 1850s extended down to the valley from its origins high up on the north side of the Mont Blanc massif – was relatively easy, although the fierce heat of the sun and its blinding glare off the ice was uncomfortable, even with the veils and glasses the climbers wore. As they ascended, the route became more broken, and detours were required to avoid crevasses and séracs (large blocks of glacial ice, some as big as buildings, which have the potential to fall down at any moment and thus present a serious danger to anyone crossing a glacier). Although this was not known at the time, the steepness of the Bossons glacier means it moves almost twice as fast as the Mer de Glace, and this rapid progress in turn leads to a high incidence of crevasses and séracs. In what was for him a relatively unusual detour into the vocabulary of the Romantic sublime, Smith described how this glacier was

> rent and torn and tossed about by convulsions scarcely to be comprehended; and the alternate action of the nightly frost and the afternoon sun on this scene of splendid desolation and horror, produces the most extraordinary effects.

Smith's account of his climb has sometimes been described as entirely irreverent and boisterous. 'Albert Smith invented a new treatment', wrote Edward Whymper, contrasting Smith with those who had written about the mountain before him. 'In his hands the whole thing was a joke – a piece of sport. He made merry over his troubles, jested at the funny persons he met, and laughed at everything.'[3] It is certainly true that Smith took a new approach, disregarding the conventions of both Romantic depictions of mountains *and* the scientific discourses which had developed in the first half of the nineteenth century as people began to investigate the structure of glaciers and other physical phenomena. But it is worth quoting at some length Smith's description of the Glacier des Bossons, a passage where he was clearly still writing under the influence of Romantic assumptions about mountain scenery.

> Huge bergs rise up of a lovely pale sea-green colour, perforated by arches decorated every day with fresh icicles many feet in length; and through these arches one sees other fantastic masses, some thrown like bridges across yawning gulfs, and others planted like old castles on jutting rocks commanding valleys and gorges, all of ice. There is here no plain surface to walk upon; your only standing-room is the barrier that divides two crevices; and as this is broad or narrow, terminating in another frightful gulf, or continuous with another treacherous ice-wall, so can you be slow or rapid.

Even making allowances for a degree of hyperbole, this is not the language of someone who is dead to any aesthetic sense. For the most part, however, Smith's account – like his later stage performance – was more concerned with action than scenes of natural beauty, and it soon returns to the business of climbing the mountain. Smith was impressed by the sure-footedness of the guides, who 'took the most extraordinary jumps, alighting upon banks of ice that shelved at once clean down to the edge of frightful crevices, to which their feet appeared to cling like those of flies'. Crampons were not yet in common use at this time, and the guides, like their clients, were shod in hobnailed shoes or boots.[4] Progress was nonetheless slow, and the party sometimes stopped and regrouped for a quarter of an hour or so while the guides decided which was the safest route to take, in order to avoid crevasses and séracs. Many crevasses were narrow enough to stride across, while others had natural snow bridges that could be crossed one person at a time, but before long the ladder from the Pierre à l'Echelle was required to straddle a wider crevasse. Francis Philips admitted that the prospect of following the guides across it was daunting:

> I am not ashamed to own that I felt a slight degree of tremor on approaching the margin of the deep abyss, but, knocking off the snow that adhered to my shoes on the first cross-bar of the ladder, I fixed my eye on the further side, and making three rapid strides stepped in safety on the firm ice.[5]

Smith, too, acknowledged how intimidating this manoeuvre was. 'There is no great difficulty, to be sure, in doing this when a ladder lies upon the ground', he noted; 'but with a chasm of unknown depth below it, it is satisfactory to get to the other side as quickly as possible'.

Thus far, the party had followed a slightly different route from that of the early pioneers, Balmat and Paccard, who had climbed up through the steep forest slopes on the other side of the Bossons glacier known as the Montagne de la Côte. But once they reached the point known as La Jonction, between the Bossons and Taconnaz glaciers, they were back in the footsteps of the early pioneers, heading across the expanse of fractured ice up to the great rocks of the Grands Mulets, which 'rise like island peaks from the snow and ice', as Smith put it. This was their destination for that day. They were forced at one point to surmount a large bergschrund – a deep crevasse with a wall rising above it, formed by the movement of glacier ice away from compacted ice above it – and during this process Smith cut his wrist open on a sharp piece of granite frozen into the ice. 'The wound bled furiously for a few minutes; but the excitement of the scramble had been so great that I actually did not know I was hurt until I saw the blood on the snow', he reported. Tying his handkerchief around the cut staunched the blood flow, but the wound was deep enough to leave a permanent scar.

About half-way to the Grand Mulets the porters left the four men and their guides – whether by previous arrangement is not entirely clear. Smith claimed that they had been in rebellious mood for some time and now refused to go farther, and that 'promises and bribes were now in vain', but in Philips's account the porters simply deposited their loads as agreed and then descended for Chamonix, leaving the clients and guides to their bivouac and the remainder of the ascent. In any case, the group reached their bivouac site at about four in the afternoon. A couple of years after Smith's ascent, the Chamonix town council would build a refuge at the Grands Mulets, and Smith would be one of the guests at the opening ceremony. For now, however, the party had to rest in the open on two flat ledges of rock. Stopping for lunch earlier, they had discovered that knives and forks had been left behind – each guide thought that one of the others was bringing them – so they had to make do with pocket-knives to cut up their food. Now they made a far more serious discovery – the leather drinking cups that their guides had carried up in their pockets smelled so strongly of tobacco that it threatened to spoil the taste of the champagne that was chilling in the snow. Disaster loomed until Smith had the bright idea of emptying a bottle of champagne into the copper saucepan that had been carried up to melt snow, then passing it round as a giant communal tankard.

The bivouac site was extremely hot, with the rocks retaining the warmth of the afternoon sun, and the party stripped off their wet clothes and placed them on the surrounding rocks to dry. A cannon salute from Chamonix told them that they could be seen from the valley, and they acknowledged the watchers below by tying a handkerchief onto the end of a long walking pole and sticking it into the snow. They set about working their way through some of the massive stock of food and drink they had brought, and were unexpectedly joined by a young Irishman and his mountain guide. Smith's younger companions seem to have resented the fact that this individual had benefitted from following the steps of their party, and were inclined 'to give him a reception in keeping with the glacier' but the convivial Smith felt that 'it would be hyper-punctilious to show temper here, on the Grands Mulets rocks, up and away in the regions of eternal snow' and instead invited him to join the party. Unfortunately a row then ensued about the sharing of provisions, and the Irishman took himself off to an adjacent rock with his guide.[6]

This squabble evidently did not put a dampener on the group 'holding high festival', as Smith put it, at the Grands Mulets bivouac site. 'The consciousness of success thus far, the pure transparent air, the excitement attached to the very position in which we found ourselves, and the strange novelty of the surrounding scenery produced a flowing exhilaration of spirits that I had never before experienced', recalled Smith, although drinking champagne at over 3,000 metres above sea level may also have contributed to the high spirits. The guides sang the Marseillaise, Smith regaled the group with a composition of his own called 'Nina la Marinière' ('In her light bark advancing,/She whom we all adore!/Darts on as the diamond spray/Falls flashing from her oar./Nina, Nina, dearest Nina,/I am waiting on the shore'), which would later appear in *The Month*, and 'a fine diversion was afforded by racing the empty bottles down the glacier'.[7] This last activity was accompanied by much excitement, as the group took bets on whether the bottles would have enough momentum to overshoot crevasses and carry on sliding down the ice until lost in the distance.[8] Settling his accounts back at the hotel after his descent, Smith would discover he had been charged 50 francs for the loss of 103 bottles (he was unusually philosophical about this, deciding that 'it was better to throw them away than to fatigue the men with the thankless task of carrying them down again').

Even when the sun set and the air got colder Smith – clad in two shirts, two pairs of wool socks, a thick pair of 'Scotch plaid trousers', and a wool balaclava, and wrapped in a railway rug, with his knapsack for a cushion – was still comfortable. As the sun went down, he gazed out over 'a scene of such wild and wondrous beauty – of such inconceivable and unearthly splendour' that 'with every sense, and feeling, and thought absorbed by its brilliancy, I saw far more than the realization of the most gorgeous visions that opium or *hasheesh* could evoke, accomplished'. Smith's companions were now illuminated by a small fire they had lit on the rocks, and by this and the brilliant starlight he watched them fall asleep one by one. It was clearly a magical experience, and Smith again drops his debunking, 'cockney' tone to describe it in language that seems closer to the conventions of the sublime than to mid-Victorian commonsense:

> Often and often, from Chamouni, I had looked up at evening towards the darkening position of the Grands Mulets, and thought, almost with shuddering, how awful it must be for me to pass the night in such a remote, eternal, and frozen wilderness. And now I was lying here – in the very heart of its icebound and appalling solitude. In such close communion with nature in her grandest aspect, with no trace of the actual living world beyond the mere speck that our little party formed, the mind was carried far away from its ordinary trains of thought – a solemn emotion of mingled awe and delight, and yet self-perception of abject nothingness, alone rose above every other feeling.

Hard to credit that this was written by the same man who earlier that evening had been crashing empty bottles down the glacier and regaling his companions with songs.

The climbers set off again just after midnight, leaving most of their provisions at the Grands Mulets to collect on the way back down. They took with them just a few bottles of wine, some small loaves, and two or three cold fowls. Lanterns were rigged up with candles to illuminate the route, and one of the Tairraz cousins attached to himself a kind of Chinese lantern for Smith to follow from behind him. The group was roped together again, and they climbed in zig-zag formation for about three hours until the moon suddenly rose, illuminating the vast bulk of the mountain in front of them. The quality of snow varied widely, in some places hard and firm, in other places so soft that the climbers sunk to their knees at every step.

Another hour found them on the Grand Plateau, an area that offered more level ground to walk on but was frequently menaced by avalanches; it was here that the Hamel tragedy had taken place back in 1820. The three guides who died – Auguste Tairraz, Pierre Balmat, and Pierre Carrier – had all been relatives of the men guiding Smith and his companions, and the elder Jean Tairraz was Auguste's brother. Tairraz told Smith 'through his teeth, almost in a whisper' that 'It is here, Monsieur, my brother was lost, with Balmat and Carrier. Their poor bodies are still there.'[9] Smith described the three-quarters of an hour spent trudging across the Plateau in terms reminiscent of his earlier accounts of being robbed by highwaymen and surviving a balloon accident:

> Once or twice in my life I have been placed in circumstances of the greatest peril, and I now experienced the same dead calm in which my feelings always were sunk on these occasions. I knew that every step we took was gained from the chance of a horrible death; and yet the only thing that actually distressed me was, that the two front lanterns would not keep the same distance from one another – a matter of the most utter unimportance to everybody.

After safely negotiating the Grand Plateau, the group once again deviated from the original route of Balmat and Paccard (now known as the 'Ancien Route'). About eight o'clock in the morning, they reached the rocks known as the Rochers Rouge and moved on to the less dangerous 'Corridor Route' pioneered by two English climbers, William Hawes and Charles Fellowes, in 1827.[10]

It was now close to daybreak, but with the slopes they were climbing on still in darkness, and a fierce north-easterly wind whipping up small crystals into the mountaineers' faces, it remained bitterly cold. Smith had not slept properly for two nights, and despite the generous provisions they had brought up to the bivouac site the altitude had suppressed his appetite, so that he had eaten little more than part of an egg, a small piece of chicken, and a hunk of bread since the previous morning. Smith could not resist some more hyperbole in his description of the climb from the Rochers Rouge, which he claimed 'was as hazardous a one as a man might make along a barn-top with frozen snow on it'. Carrier took the lead, cutting steps with his axe for the others to step into.

The next stage of the climb was up the steep slope of the Mur de la Côte, less than four hundred metres from the summit of Mont Blanc. But by now Smith was suffering from acute mountain sickness, and he found himself 'in such a strange state of mingled unconsciousness and acute observation – of combined sleeping and waking – that the old-fashioned word "bewitched" is the only one that I can apply to the complete confusion and upsetting of sense in which I found myself plunged'. He hallucinated that people he knew from London were beside him and calling his name; that he was involved in a complex negotiation involving two bedspreads; and that one of his literary friends was warning him that the King of Prussia had forbidden them to pass over his territory on the way to the summit. He staggered and reeled, fell down in the snow at the foot of the Mur de la Côte, and told Tairraz that he could go no further.

Smith was by no means the only victim of altitude sickness that morning. Since reaching the Rochers Rouge, both he and Charles Floyd had been suffering from nausea, and Floyd had complained of a headache – both common symptoms of altitude sickness, and probably not helped by the decision to fortify themselves with red wine before crossing the Grand Plateau. Everyone in the party suffered to some degree; all reported loss of appetite, and two aspirant guides who had joined the party to gain experience had to return to the Grands Mulets; Floyd and West's faces were described as being 'nearly the colour of ink', and when Philips pulled off his gloves he was alarmed to discover that his hands had turned a shade of deep purple.[11] 'Albert Smith was utterly exhausted', Philips reported, 'and it was only by the most undaunted courage that he ever reached the summit'.[12] The ostracized Irishman, who had set off before them, was discovered lying on the snow at the

Rochers Rouge, vomiting and bleeding badly from his nostrils. He turned back, and was still recovering at the Grands Mulets when the party descended later.

It is notable how much the other climbers suffered that day, as Smith has sometimes been mocked and derided for the difficulty he experienced in getting up the mountain and for briefly passing out when he reached the summit. The younger men – who Smith described as being 'in first rate fibrous muscular condition' – also suffered badly from the altitude, and Philips, too, briefly fell asleep on the top (upon awakening he promptly downed a refreshing cup of champagne). The whole affair has also been presented as a kind of drunken spree, with some accounts implying that Smith staggered up the mountain half-cut and collapsed on the top in an alcoholic stupor. Admittedly, the full complement of ninety-three bottles of wine and three of brandy seems to have been guzzled, although Smith recorded that some of the wine was consumed on the descent. Even allowing for the porters having tippled, say thirty bottles of wine on the way up, that would still suggest that the twenty guides and clients each drank an average of three bottles of wine over the course of their Mont Blanc climb. Nonetheless, it seems unlikely that Smith or any of his companions any of the group were seriously intoxicated; had this been the case, they almost certainly would not have reached the summit, nor would Smith have left such a vivid, detailed account of his impressions. Even small amounts of alcohol could potentially have exacerbated the effects of altitude, but it was far from unusual for climbers and other people engaged in hard physical activity at this time to fortify themselves with wine and spirits.

Tairraz and Balmat, no doubt accustomed to what Smith called 'these little varieties of temper' on the part of clients at high altitude, simply pulled Smith to his feet and told him to get a grip on himself, warning him that the whole party would be endangered if he did not. Smith marshalled his strength, reminded himself that 'success in scaling this awful precipice was entirely dependent upon "pluck"', and climbed on. The Mur de la Côte seems to have been for Smith the most challenging part of the whole ascent. 'Should the foot slip, or the baton give way', he claimed, 'there is no chance for life – you would glide like lightning from one frozen crag to another, and finally be dashed to pieces, hundreds and hundreds of feet below in the horrible depths of the glacier'.

Charles Edward Mathews would later debunk Smith's description of this section of the climb, claiming that the Mur de la Côte 'is perfectly safe, and the traveller, if he fell upon it, would be landed on soft snow at the bottom', and estimating the angle of the slope – which Smith described as 'all but perpendicular' – as closer to forty-five degrees.[13] This seems to me a little unfair on Smith. For one thing, few climbers even today would describe taking a fall anywhere on the upper slopes of Mont Blanc as 'perfectly safe', especially for a party without crampons or proper ice axes.[14] For another, Smith was scarcely the first or last writer to have overestimated the steepness of a mountain. It had been widely remarked on by the late nineteenth century, when Mathews was writing, that novice mountaineers found it difficult to accurately judge the angle of slopes. Writing in the 1880s, for instance, the mountain photographer William Frederick Donkin noted that the 'tendency to exaggeration [in the beginner] is only natural; did we not estimate the steepness of our first snow-slope as being much greater than the reality, and feel decidedly hurt when a scientific companion with a clinometer declared it was only forty degrees, though we thought it nearly perpendicular?'[15] A section of the ascent that might appear unremarkable to Mathews – a pioneering Alpinist whose climbing career spanned over forty years and who climbed Mont Blanc at least a dozen times – would naturally have been perceived very differently by Smith. This is not to deny that Smith was prone to hyperbole – his descriptions of the dangers of the climb are clearly designed to thrill and impress his readers – but it is not fair to judge him by the standards of experienced mountaineers some forty years later. Nor were Smith's claims about the dangers of the climb groundless. The Grand Plateau is indeed an area of high avalanche risk, and the Grands Mulets route to the summit is nowadays considered unsafe in summer, even with the far superior techniques and safety equipment available to modern mountaineers (it can be used in winter by ski mountaineers, when the risk of séracs and crevasses is diminished).

Smith was supported by his guides for most of the remaining trudge up to the summit of Mont Blanc. There were those who claimed that he was actually carried up in one of the big provision baskets, and even his friend and admirer Edmund Yates wrote that his performance on the mountain 'was less like that of the leaping chamois than that of a sack of oats which is lifted from the wagon to the granary by means of a crane'.[16] Smith himself did not deny that he 'was perfectly done up' and that Tairraz 'had no sinecure to pull me up after him, for I was stumbling about as though completely intoxicated'. In his confusion, Smith became angry, scolding his companions when they tried to point out Monte Rosa in the distance, and at the same time he struggled to keep his eyes open or even to plant his feet in a straight line.

Finally, nine hours after leaving the bivouac site, he was on the summit. Smith had done it. His lifelong ambition was finally accomplished. How did he celebrate his moment of triumph?

> The ardent wish of years was gratified; but I was so completely exhausted that, without looking round me, I fell down upon the snow, and was asleep in an instant.

13: A COCKNEY ASCENT OF MONT BLANC

There has been a cockney ascent of Mont Blanc, of which I believe you are soon to hear in London. John Ruskin, letter from Chamonix, August 1851.

Smith only slept for a few minutes, and when Tairraz woke him he felt well enough to get up and take in the view. Like many Mont Blanc climbers before and after him, he found it both overwhelming and at the same time oddly disappointing:

> There was too much to see, and yet not enough: I mean, the view was so vast that, whilst every point and valley was a matter of interest, and eagerly scanned, yet the elevation was so great that all detail was lost [...] In the first place, it must be understood, as I have just intimated, that the height greatly takes away from the interest of the view, which its expanse scarcely makes amends for.

The elevation of the mountain above the surrounding landscape has the paradoxical effect of flattening out the view, making it seem somehow less dramatic than might be expected. Many climbers before and after Smith remarked on this phenomenon. When Saussure had finally made it to the summit in 1787, he initially felt disappointment and even irritation. 'Since I had for the last two hours under my eyes seen almost all one sees from the summit, the arrival was no *coup de théâtre*', he admitted. 'It did not even give me all the pleasure one might have imagined', and he confessed that when he 'trod the highest point of the snow that crowned the summit I trampled it with a feeling of anger rather than pleasure'.[1] Over eighty years later, Edward Whymper remarked on the 'disappointing nature of panoramic views' and singled out Mont Blanc as a particularly egregious example:

> That seen from Mont Blanc is notoriously unsatisfactory. When you are upon that summit you look down upon the whole of Europe. There is nothing to look up to; all is below [...] The man who is there is somewhat in the position of one who has attained all that he desires – he has nothing to aspire to; his position must needs be unsatisfactory.[2]

Leslie Stephen wrote a couple of years later that 'the ordinary view from Mont Blanc is not especially picturesque', and in the early twentieth century William Edward Durham noted that 'mountains do not look their best when regarded from above, and from Mont Blanc one looks, of course, over everything'.[3] This was Smith's experience, too – surely one of the few matters he and the patrician, cultivated, and ascetic Stephen would have agreed upon. 'Of the entire *coup d'oeil* no descriptive power can convey the slightest notion', wrote Smith. 'Where everything is so almost incomprehensible in its magnitude, no sufficiently graphic comparison can be instituted.'

The party forced themselves to eat a little food and drank a series of toasts in champagne and wine, while the guides lit their pipes. By now everyone's faces had a dark tinge that reminded the former medical man of the effects of cholera, and Smith was suffering from frostbite in his right hand, having removed his glove on the ascent to get a better grip on his walking pole. He does not seem to have realized at the time how potentially serious this was, but fortunately his guides did and spent five minutes rubbing it vigorously until circulation was painfully restored. He was left with permanent numbness in his little finger, but spared any worse effects (untreated frostbite could easily lead to the amputation of fingers, or even worse to gas gangrene).

Smith was almost aggressively keen to point out that the expedition made no claim to a scientific purpose. 'We made no "scientific observations" – the acute and honest De Saussure had done everything that was wanted by the world of that kind', wrote Smith, and it was true that Saussure had spent four and a half hours on the summit during his Mont Blanc ascent, taking readings with thermometers, barometers, and other instruments, checking the boiling temperature of water and the pulse rates of his companions, and even setting up a mini-laboratory inside a tent.[4] But Smith went on to claim that 'those who have since worried themselves during the ascent about "elevations" and temperatures, [have] added nothing to what he told us sixty years ago'. Smith was distancing himself from scientific narratives of mountain climbing, of which there had been a number in the preceding decades.[5] In this, he was at the forefront of a trend that would gather pace over the next few years. Although some mountaineers – notably the physicist John Tyndall – would continue to propound scientific motives for Alpine climbing, the period from the 1850s saw a distinct shift in the motives for mountaineering. Both the transcendent experience of the sublime claimed by Romantic poets, and the disinterested spirit of scientific investigation into the physical nature of mountains and glaciers took a back seat after the formation of the Alpine Club in 1857, supplanted by a sporting, recreational approach which viewed the Alps as – to quote from the title of Leslie Stephen's 1871 memoir – a playground for hearty outdoor exercise.[6]

Yet as we saw in the previous chapter, Smith was by no means wholly impervious to the claims of the sublime, as his closing words about the summit of Mont Blanc make clear. Having dismissed the significance of any scientific purposes for climbing the mountain, he continues:

But we had beheld all the wonders and horrors of the glacier world in their wild-
est features; we had gazed on scenery of such fantastic yet magnificent nature as
we might not hope to see again; we had laboured with all the nerve and energy
we could command to achieve a work of downright unceasing danger and difficulty, which not more than one-half of those who try are able to accomplish,
and the triumph of which is, even now, shared but by a comparative handful of
travellers – and we had succeeded!

As this passage suggests, Smith was standing on the cusp of two different approaches to mountains and two very different reasons for climbing them. On
the one hand, he retains some of the conventional imagery and language familiar to readers of Romantic accounts of Alpine travel in the late eighteenth and
early nineteenth centuries – the 'wonders and horrors' of glaciers, the scenes of
'fantastic yet magnificent' nature. At the same time he emphasizes the arduous
physical struggle to complete the climb, and the exclusive, almost competitive nature of this accomplishment. These new facets of mountain travel would become
more important in the decades to come, as those who chose to climb increasingly
dwelt on the physical challenge of the activity, and the pleasures and benefits to
be gained from that challenge. Smith at this stage in his career still had a foot
in both camps, and of course he was always *sui generis* to some extent, neither
truly a Romantic traveller nor a typical Victorian mountaineer; after all, his previous travel journalism owed precious little to Romantic convention, and he never
climbed another mountain in his life after Mont Blanc. As Peter Hansen points
out, Smith 'was so popular in part because both on stage and in print he blurred
the boundaries between the genteel and the vulgar, the sacred and the profane'.
Smith's presentation of his Mont Blanc experience, Hansen argues, 'contributed to
the declining cultural authority of the picturesque and the sublime in the Alps'.[7]
This is undoubtedly true, but there was still a trace element of the Romantic in
Smith's writing about scenes 'of splendid desolation and horror'. Although he was
arguably one of the key figures in ushering out the aesthetic of the sublime, its
long, lingering twilight can be detected his own writing.

Having finally achieved his ambition of standing on top of Mont Blanc, Smith
now had to get down safely. His account of the descent initially presents it in
less dramatic terms than the climb, describing the process of glissading down the
snow slopes as 'capital fun':

Sliding, stumbling, and staggering about, setting all the zigzags at defiance, and
making direct short cuts from one to the other – sitting down at the top of the
snow slopes, and launching ourselves off, feet first, until, not very clever at self
guidance, we turned right round and were stopped by our own heads.

But once they reached the glacier the descent would turn out to be a more serious affair than this suggests. They had intended to spend some time resting when they got back to the Grands Mulets, but Tairraz decided that the sun was melting the glacier so fast that there was no time to lose – the danger would increase as the day went on. Having drained the final bottle of wine, the party set off on what Smith claimed (probably with some justification) would turn out to be 'the greatest danger of the undertaking' – the descent of the Bossons glacier. The glacier was now melting into 'perfect sludge', and the group sunk almost to their waists. Smith noted that the guides, no doubt concerned about the dangers of crevasses, looked uneasy, and the party was soon roped together again. Nowadays it would be standard practice to use the rope for any glacier crossing, but the group had been descending unroped and spread out across the glacier until now. At one point Floyd was leaping across a crevasse when the guide jerked the rope, pulling him back into it – he 'hung suspended by the rope over this fearful abyss' until being pulled out.[8] Then one of the Tairraz cousins had a narrow escape as he jumped across a crevasse and found that the snow on the other side was not solid. As it gave way beneath him, he managed to wedge his alpenstock transversely across the crevasse, arresting his fall. Smith was pulled off his feet by the shock, and realized that if Tairraz had plummeted into the crevasse he and the other climbers on the same rope would have followed him. 'I was more startled by this little accident than by any other occurrence during the journey', he wrote.

Finally they reached the foot of the glacier, returned the ladder to its home at the Pierre à l'Echelle, and after a brief stop for water they began the final descent down the track to Chamonix. As they approached the town, the elder Jean Tairraz insisted on the group walking in procession and, repeating the injunction 'andiamo', he set off at their head, 'flourishing his alpenstock like a drum-serjeant flourishing his baton when at the head of his band'.[9] A few people had already come out from Chamonix and the surrounding hamlets to greet them, and the party 'went merrily through the fields that border the Arve, in the bright afternoon sunlight, receiving little bouquets from the girls on the way, and meeting fresh visitors from Chamonix every minute'. As they entered the town they were greeted by a 'tableau vivant' of two young men playing the violin and a young woman playing the harp; the crowds thickened, parting to let them through; an English visitor jumped out of the crowd shouting, 'Three cheers for the travellers!', and continued 'Hip! Hip!', before realizing that nobody was going to join in and retreating in embarrassment. Edouard Tairraz, who was now the landlord of the Hôtel de Londres, welcomed them with a speech and banquet, more champagne was drunk, and someone began letting off a cannon in the garden below the hotel, while further cannon fire was heard from the roof of the new Hôtel Royal.

Smith, suddenly exhausted, retreated to a warm bath, and after a hot dinner he was ready for some much-needed sleep. Looking out from his balcony, watching the final glow of sunset on the mountain, Smith 'could hardly persuade myself that the whole affair had not been a wonderful dream'.

Despite a troubled, feverish night's sleep, during which he dreamed he was tumbling down precipices, Smith felt well enough the next day to walk up to the Montenvers path again, and despite a raging thirst and painful sunburn he was able to attend a celebratory dinner for the guides in the hotel garden that evening: 'and what with toasts, and speeches, and songs, excellent fare, and a warm-hearted company, the moon was once more on the summit of Mont Blanc before we parted'. If Smith ever had intended to 'expose the whole affair as an imposition' and accuse the guides of exaggerating the dangers, he had certainly changed his mind by now. In the 'fuhrerbuch' (the official book where clients recorded their recommendations or otherwise of each guide) of Pierre Francois Favret he wrote that the guide 'recommended himself to my notice, during our ascent of Mont Blanc, by his courageous conduct'.[10]

One reason the celebrations were so exuberant was that Sir Robert Peel (who had become third baronet the year before, upon the death of his more famous father) was in town, and had arranged for some of the cannon fire and musical interludes to welcome back his cousin, Charles Floyd. Peel's presence would encourage criticism of the whole affair in the weeks to come. The *Daily News*, which had been founded by Dickens in 1846 as a liberal alternative to the right-wing *Morning Chronicle*, was unimpressed by the escapade and seems to have been especially provoked by Peel's role in the post-climb revels. 'The aimless scramble of four pedestrians to the top of Mont Blanc', it thundered,

> accompanied by Sir Robert Peel's orgies at the bottom, will not go far to redeem the somewhat equivocal reputation of the herd of English tourists in Switzerland for a mindless and rather vulgar redundance of mere animal spirits.[11]

This would not be the last criticism of Smith's Mont Blanc adventure by any means. Smith's first act after the post-climb celebrations was to write to *The Times* pointing out that his group had formed 'the largest party ever assembled on the summit'.[12] The ever-fastidious John Ruskin, who was also staying at Chamonix at the time, was horrified both by the boisterous nature of the ascent and the subsequent celebrations and publicity. 'There has been a cockney ascent of Mont Blanc, of which you are soon to hear in London', he wrote to his father.[13] Ruskin's comments about 'cockney' visitors to the Alps would be echoed over the decades to come by a range of mountaineering writers. The *Daily News*' concerns about the aimless nature of mountaineering would prove to have less longevity, although such criticisms would recur in the wake of the Matterhorn tragedy of 1865.

Surprisingly, Francis Philips himself seemed to have misgivings about this aspect of his ascent. He closed his account of the climb with this warning:

> I strongly recommend any one who may feel ambitious of ascending Mont Blanc, to consider well before he attempts an expedition which cannot be productive of any good to himself or others, and which is attended with fearful risk, not only to himself, but to those persons who, allured by the desire of gain, endanger their lives in his service.[14]

Smith himself was as unruffled by the criticism as always. A few days after the ascent he was on his way back to London, and by the first of September he was back on tour with 'The Overland Mail', opening at Tunbridge Wells and then performing in Canterbury, Dover, Folkestone, and Hythe each successive night. Even before heading off on tour, however, the indefatigable Smith was negotiating with John Blackwood about an article on his Mont Blanc experience. This would become the first full account of the climb, published in *Blackwood's Edinburgh Magazine* in January 1852, but Smith was keen to ensure that he did not lose the opportunity to expand the material into a book.

His subsequent correspondence with Blackwood gives an insight into Smith's business acumen and the attention to detail he gave to his work. Any notion of Smith as a prolific but chaotic hack, dashing off articles in slapdash fashion, is dispelled by the care with which he addresses Blackwood's queries about his copy, asks to see and correct galley proofs, and plays him off against the London publisher David Bogue. Writing from Percy Street at the end of August, Smith agrees to Blackwood's request for 'an article on my late ascent of Mont Blanc, for the magazine', but points out that he had met with Bogue a couple of days earlier to discuss turning the material into a book. 'Could I come to any arrangement with you respecting the copyright of the paper, so that at a future time, I might work it into my volume, which I thought of calling "A Week at Chamonix"?', suggests Smith.[15] Blackwood evidently gave provisional agreement, and Smith began writing the article in between performances of 'The Overland Mail'. In mid-October he wrote to Blackwood from Teignmouth in Devon, apologizing for not having been in touch sooner but explaining that he had 'been stuck fast on the Grands Mulets for ten days. I have got to that point, and am so occupied with my Entertainment, that I cannot get a quiet spare half hour by any possibility'. For any other publisher, Smith added, rather obsequiously, 'I should scamp my writing: but for my debut in your pages I should choose to be very careful'. About a month later, Smith sent Blackwood the first section of his article, up to the point of the Grands Mulets bivouac, with detailed suggestions as to how it should be divided into sections. He also pushed the publisher for a quick decision on whether or not the material was acceptable, warning that, 'If not to your liking, I shall at once bring the account out, as a book, with illustrations, similar to my *Constantinople*, against Christmas, and Bogue will publish it.' In typically plain-speaking fashion, he added, 'I need not tell you that, pecuniarily, the latter is to me the most advantageous; but I am anxious to have a new audience in your respectable pages. I put all this plainly that you may see I am not praying your decision with mere impatience.'

This correspondence with Blackwood is interesting in that it shows Smith operating strategically as a writer, passing up the chance of another quick profit from a book published by Bogue in favour of the opportunity to reach a new, 'respectable' audience. Blackwood was evidently not put off by Smith's unsubtle negotiating style, and by mid-December Smith was correcting page proofs and giving detailed replies to the publisher's comments and queries. Blackwood had queried Smith's use of the word 'gemmy', presumably to describe the starlight; Smith agreed to cut it, but pointed out a precedent from Tennyson's 'Lady of Shallot', in which the lines 'The gemmy bridle glitter'd free/Like to some branch of stars we see/Hung in the golden Galaxy' appear. Smith also agreed to amend the word 'todge' – which he described as 'a London, and indeed southern word' – to 'sludge' when describing the condition of the Bossons glacier on the descent. He also answered Blackwood's query as to why he had not called his article, 'Narrative of an ascent &c', pointing out that virtually every previous account of climbing Mont Blanc had that title.[16]

The account was duly published – Smith happily informing Blackwood that 'the cheque has arrived safely, and I am obliged to you for it, as well as for your kind opinions of the narrative' – and Smith and Blackwood clearly stayed on good professional terms. Three years later, the Edinburgh publisher asked Smith to write 'from observation' about popular fairs, but Smith, while claiming to have 'turned over the subject a great deal, in my hours of leisure head', had to refuse as he was so busy with his Egyptian Hall show.[17] Hardly surprising; by 1854, when the correspondence took place, Smith's show was the talk of London, and Smith was busier, wealthier, and more famous than ever before.

Smith would duly publish a book-length version of his Mont Blanc story with Bogue in 1853, but as his tour of 'The Overland Mail' came to an end in December 1851, and he and Leech wound up the final issue of *The Month*, his main focus was on the new show planned for the following year. Beverley, who had accompanied him to Chamonix, was working on the panoramic scenes that would be an integral part of the spectacle. The next step was to find a suitable venue, and Smith decided on the Egyptian Hall on Piccadilly.

The Egyptian Hall had been one of London's main exhibition spaces since being opened in 1812 by William Bullock, a collector who had brought his natural history museum from Liverpool to London a couple of years earlier. Bullock had started out as a jeweller and goldsmith, but soon began to concentrate his energies on his collection of curiosities, some of which had been brought back by Captain Cook from his South Sea voyages. The Hall was designed in faux-Egyptian style by the architect Peter Frederick Robinson, who had begun his career working on the expansion of the Brighton Pavilion in the early nineteenth century. The interior was a replica of the Temple of Karnak near Luxor, while the façade was supposed to be based on the Temple of Tentyris, as depicted in Vivant Denon's 1802 book on Napoleon's Egyptian campaign, and huge statues of the ancient Egyptian deities Isis and Osiris stood on a plinth above the entrance.[18] The building was the product of a brief vogue for all things Egyptian in Britain in the early nineteenth century, of which very few architectural examples survive: the Egyptian House in Penzance, Cornwall and the Odd Fellows Hall in Devonport, Plymouth are probably the only remaining buildings in this style.[19]

Bullock's collection, known as the London Museum, was housed in the Hall until 1819, and over this time various exhibits were added to it. Napoleon's coach was displayed in 1816, after being brought to England by the Prussian major who captured it at Waterloo, and was reputedly viewed by some 800,000 people during its residency at the Hall.[20] The rooms on either side of the entrance to the hall housed a chemist and a bookshop, and after passing them visitors went along a passageway into the main exhibition hall, and from there into a 'basaltic cavern similar to the Giant's Causeway [and then] into an Indian hut situated in a tropical forest', this second chamber of the Hall being known as the Panherion and mostly devoted to tropical flora and fauna.[21] The main section, however, was 'a great three-domed hall where changing exhibits were mounted'.[22] When Bullock sold up in 1819, he continued to lease the Egyptian Hall out for other exhibitions, and it played host to an extraordinary range of attractions, from Théodore Géricault's painting *The Raft of the Medusa* (1818-19) to the artefacts brought back from the Valley of the Kings by Giovanni Belzoni in the early 1820s; from historical paintings by Sir George Hayter through to the 'Poecilorama', a series of dioramic images painted by Clarkson Stanfield and viewed through lenses.[23]

A brief survey of some of the exhibits from the departure of Bullock's collection in 1819 through to Smith's arrival in March 1852 gives an idea of the sheer range and the often bizarre nature of the hall's exhibits.[24] 1822 saw the display of a group of Laplanders, complete with reindeer, an exhibit that enjoyed takings of £100 a day for the six weeks it continued, followed by 'a pair of Wapeti, or Elks, from the Upper Missouri' along with something called 'the pretended Mermaid'. An 1824 display of Mexican artefacts was replaced the following year by the captured Burmese Imperial State Carriage, studded with some 20,000 gems and displayed rather incongruously alongside a scale model of Switzerland. 'The Musical Sisters', a harpist and pianist aged four and six respectively, topped the bill in 1826, while excitement was generated in 1829 by the Siamese Twins ('two perfect bodies, bound together by an insperable link'). These two eighteen-year-olds, named Chang and Eng, had been brought from Siam to England by a Captain Abel Coffin, who became their manager; they stayed in the country for several years before settling on a farm in America.[25] The first 'Cobra di Capello' (hooded cobra) to be brought alive to Europe thrilled visitors to the Hall in 1831, along with two orangutans and a chimpanzee. A few years later, in 1837, a 'living male child with four hands, four arms, four feet, and two bodies', supposedly born at Stalybridge near Manchester, was on display, and in 1844 the famed American midget 'General' Tom Thumb, proved a huge success, often bringing in as much as £125 a day (paintings by the artist Benjamin Robert Haydon, on display at the same time as Tom Thumb's residency, were by contrast 'scarcely visited by a dozen persons a week').[26]

The following year saw the debut of 'The Eureka', a machine for composing Latin hexameter verse, while the 1846 season featured 'Professor Faber's Euphonia', a speaking automaton, and 'a Mammoth Horse, a Polar Dog, and a dwarf dressed in a bearskin'. This latter curiosity was advertised on a handbill as 'The Wild Man of the Prairies, or What Is It?' The handbill went on to ask, 'Is it Animal? Is it Human? Is it an Extraordinary Freak of Nature?' In fact, it turned out to be a celebrated dwarf called Hervey Leech, who had previously graced the roles of 'Jocko! The Brazilian Ape', 'Bibbo, the Patagonian Ape', and 'the Gnome Fly' at halls run by Barnum and other showmen in the United States during the 1840s.[27]

As this list suggests, the Egyptian Hall was popular, eclectic, and none too highbrow, although it was considered 'respectable' and enjoyed a fashionable location on Piccadilly. It was also one of the main rival venues to the Colosseum, although none of the shows at the Egyptian Hall was technically a panorama in the classic sense of those at the specially constructed rotunda of the Colosseum or the Leicester Square Rotunda. From 1848 to 1850, it was home to Banvard's panorama of the Mississippi (see Chapter 3), and then featured Colonel John C. Fremont's 'Overland Route to Oregon and California', another moving panorama.[28] This lasted until July 1851, before being replaced by a diorama of the Holy Land (with 'Grand and Appropriate Music').[29] Banvard's display was a particularly important precursor to Smith's show because it was probably the first panorama to also feature a narrator, in the shape of Banvard himself. He 'stood beside the panorama and lectured on his voyage as the view unrolled', and after

Banvard's success this became the standard format for future panoramic shows – including, of course, Albert Smith's.[30]

This combination of panoramic views, beautifully painted by Beverley, and the entertaining narration of what became known as the 'cicerone' would prove to be the key factor in the success of 'The Ascent of Mont Blanc' at the Egyptian Hall. There had been panoramas of Mont Blanc as far back as 1826, at the Leicester Square rotunda. But none of them had featured the unique talents of Albert Smith.

14: 'MR ALBERT SMITH'S ASCENT OF MONT BLANC'

Mont Blanc is the Monarch of the Mountains/They crowned him long ago/But who they got to put it on/I don't exactly know. Albert Smith, 'The Ascent of Mont Blanc'

On the stroke of eight o'clock, a door on the right hand side of the Egyptian Hall stage opened, and Albert Smith stepped out. He walked over to a small upright piano, on top of which stood a scale model of a *diligence*, a set of mule bells, an Alpine horn, and a few other objects.

There was no introduction or prefatory remarks. Smith, in evening dress and still sporting the full beard he had grown on his Middle Eastern travels, plunged straight into his narration, a 'rattling and rapid description of the journey from town to Dover; then the run across the channel and the Continent, till in a few minutes he brought the audience to Switzerland itself'.[1] Smith's style was conversational, but authoritative and compelling. This first section of his performance would sometimes include him playing the cornet or the tin fiddle, or singing a 'patter' song.[2]

Once he had reached Geneva, he slowed the pace and began to introduce the various characters who would populate his story: Mrs. Seymour, constantly attempting to track down the box she has mislaid on the journey; Edwards the Engineer, with his *non sequiturs* and his catchphrase, 'What I says is, India isn't England, Mr. Smith'; the three Simmons girls; 'the typical Yankee with his curious new reading of Byron', in whom many detected a resemblance to Barnum; the undecided Mr. Parker, 'whose mind is in as lamentable a state as his voice'; Mr. Brown, with his execrable attempts to speak French; the 'energetic Miss Effingham and the mild Mr. Pringle'; and the two old ladies who always pull down the blinds of their carriage when it approaches a mountain precipice. These characters would become perennial favourites with Egyptian Hall audiences, returning season after season. 'By Jove, if there is not Brown! – his moustache, his French, and his mistaken powers of illustration the same as ever', exclaimed the programme notes to Smith's 1858 season.[3]

The stage itself was carefully and elaborately set up as an Alpine scene. The proscenium facing the audience was designed to look like a two-storey Swiss chalet, with projecting eaves, green shutters, and a carved balcony. Over the front of the chalet was the motto, in German, 'Speak Little, Truth Say; Want Little, Cash

Pay'. Behind it, and off to the right, were rocks with a stream of water cascading down them, powering a small water-wheel and then feeding a miniature lake with lilies and bulrushes on the surface and stocked with live fish, surrounded by Alpine plants. Baskets, knapsacks, alpenstocks, Swiss hats, and other evocative objects were strewn around the balconies, while the rafters and beams of the chalet had vines and creepers running across them. The flags of the various Swiss cantons were displayed around the hall, and the flag of the King of Sardinia (technically also the sovereign of Mont Blanc at this point in history) was draped across the balcony. Near to where the audience entered the auditorium, another fake building had been erected, this one an imitation of an *estaminet*, or small café, with a lamp bearing the sign 'Café Billard' and a pair of crossed billiard cues on the front. Over on the other side of the room was another Swiss-style building, supposed to represent a village shop.

The details of Smith's performance changed over the seven seasons that the show continued, but the basic format was generally the same.[4] The first act would involve Smith describing the journey out to Chamonix, by routes that varied each season. In his first season, the route took in Geneva, the Castle of Chillon on the shores of Lake Geneva, Martigny (a town in the Valais region whose inhabitants Smith described as 'dreadfully afflicted with goitre, cretinism, and agues', and where 'the appearance of decrepitude, deformity, and misery arrests the traveller's attention at every step'), the Convent of St. Bernard with its macabre 'Dead House', and finally the valley and town of Chamonix.[5] As Smith described these stops on the route, the centre of the Swiss chalet would rise out of sight to make way for Beverley's canvases, which during this first half of the show were displayed as separate images on the wall behind Smith. Each season he changed this section of the performance, varying the route to Chamonix to take in stopovers at Paris, Holland, the Rhine, Naples, Pompei and Vesuvius.

Then came the interval, and the appearance of St. Bernard dogs bearing boxes of chocolates for the children of audience members.[6] It was not until the second act that Smith actually got to the business of climbing Mont Blanc. For this section he dropped the comic anecdotes and characters, and 'addressing himself to it, in a tone worthy of the subject, describe[d] with great force, and in a manner equally entertaining and instructive' the perils and thrills of the climb.[7] The audience listened in 'breathless interest' as he narrated the principal stages of the ascent, while Beverley's panoramic illustrations – of the Bossons and Tacconaz glaciers, the Grands Mulets by sunset, the Grand Plateau by moonlight and the ascent of the Mur de la Côte – moved vertically behind him, with dioramic effects to create the impression of sunset over the rocks of the bivouac site, for example.[8] In this second act, rather than separate pictures the images moved in a continuous descending panorama to give the impression of the ascent gradually taking place before the audience's eyes, although the summit and the haphazard descent on steep snow did have their own discrete illustrations.

Having thrilled his audience with this illustrated account of the descent, he might treat them to a brief stop in Paris on the way home, with a hapless English tourist portrayed attempting to order a meal in a restaurant using his phrase book, or Smith the cicerone might take his audience across the Simplon Pass to Italy and a visit to Lago Maggiore. The details changed each season, but the show invariably concluded with a rendition of 'Galignani's Messenger', a comic song in which he poked fun at topical events. *Galignani's Messenger* was a popular English-language newspaper in Paris, established in 1814, which circulated throughout Europe. Smith alluded to it on a number of occasions in his travel writing.[9] He was aided in updating the lyrics by Shirley Brooks, Edward Draper (who in his day job was also Smith's solicitor), and Edmund Yates, each of them 'in the habit of sending down any striking lines that might occur to us to be incorporated into 'Galignani'.[10] 'Beside our press, you must confess, all other sheets are small', went the regular refrain to this song, 'But *Galignani's Messenger*'s the greatest of them all'.[11]

The performance lasted for two hours. By half past ten, Smith was on his way to the Garrick for some refreshment.

'Mr. Albert Smith's Ascent of Mont Blanc' opened on 15 March 1852. The first season did not boast the elaborate stage set described here; that was introduced at the start of the second season. Instead, Smith had simply decorated the stage with Alpine plants, and his narrative began at Geneva, with the first of Beverley's paintings depicting the view towards Mont Blanc. Smith seems to have been unusually tentative on the opening night, asking the audience's indulgence 'for any possible mistake, owing to the newness of material and machinery'.[12] This reticence had not been on display a few weeks earlier, when he showed Henry Vizetelly a rough 'showcard' for the Mont Blanc show, on which Smith's own name appeared in letters twice the size of the words 'Mont Blanc'. When Vizetelly pointed out that, since Mont Blanc was the monarch of the mountains, perhaps it should get the larger billing, Smith reacted angrily: 'it became necessary for him to explain, that he considered his own name of far greater importance than the subject-matter of his lecture'.[13] Nor was Smith's new-found modesty much in evidence at the entrance to the hall, where he had prominently displayed the certificate signed by his guides to attest that he had indeed completed the ascent (ironically, this certificate led some people to doubt that he had made the ascent at all, and to hint that he had bribed the guides to put their names to it).[14]

Illustration of Smith's Mont Blanc show from *Illustrated London News*. Courtesy of
Illustrated London News/Mary Evans Picture Library.

Smith would later recall those early days, when he first arrived at the Egyptian
Hall to set up his show. He found it 'a very dirty place indeed', he told the audience at the end of his third season, in September 1854, full of the detritus
of earlier shows. 'The accumulated rubbish of Laplanders, Egyptian mummies,
overland emigrants to California, Holy Land Bedouins, electro-biologists, and
Ojibbeways' had, he thought, 'something Augean in its magnitude; and the cellars below formed a perfect mausoleum of panoramas. I do not know how many
thousands of miles of countries are lying beneath your feet.'[15] From this rather
inauspicious start, Smith cleaned out the theatre and created a show that would
be performed two thousand times over the following seven seasons.

Reviews were almost uniformly positive from the start. '"Mont Blanc" at once
took the Metropolitan public by storm', recalled Walter Goodman.[16] The *Daily
News*, which had been so disapproving of Smith's antics in Chamonix, was much
more positive when it came to the resulting entertainment. Noting that Beverley's
illustrations were 'executed with considerable correctness and care; and furnish
an excellent opportunity to those who have not travelling tendencies, to place
themselves in communion with nature in its grandest and most terrible aspect', it
praised Smith's narrative as 'even more valuable – genial and amusing always, with
now and then a dash of vigorous truth and nature that is unmistakable'. Although

Smith expressly disclaimed any intention to present a 'comic ascent' of Mont Blanc, he nonetheless 'has so much rollicking fun in his composition,' wrote the paper's theatre critic, 'that he fully succeeded in inspiring his audience with the spirit of indomitable good humour that seems to have enabled him to accomplish this arduous enterprise'.[17]

The *Morning Post* also described Beverley's pictures as being executed 'with perfect fidelity, and yet with all the art which is due to such a lovely or grand subject'. In the second act, the *Post* reported, Beverley's descending panorama was so effective 'that the spectator seems, step by step, to accompany the daring travellers in their hazardous journey, while Mr. Albert Smith, with graphic description, tells every circumstance of the interesting deed'.[18] *Blackwood's*, which had published Smith's account of the climb earlier that year, included Smith's show in a portmanteau review that covered most of the main London theatrical performances that season. 'It is a remarkable combination of talent, humour, lucid narrative, and personal adventure', declared the journal's reviewer, 'which everybody ought to go and hear, and a succession of scenes and paintings which everybody ought to go and see'.[19] The *Illustrated London News*, habitually friendly to Smith, reported that Smith's lecture and Beverley's illustrations were 'to be classed among the few things that turn out better than expected, and are thus more highly valued on acquaintance than before', while *The Times* recalled how Smith's 'Overland Mail' show had succeeded in gratifying 'two classes of visitors – the seekers of instruction and the lovers of a hearty laugh', and was pleased to report that his 'Ascent of Mont Blanc' replicated this success. The first act, *The Times* noted, was enlivened by 'anecdotes of eccentric travellers and two sparkling comic songs', while for the more serious business of climbing Mont Blanc in the second act, 'the lecturer seriously describes the perils of the adventure, which are rendered doubly impressive by the world of snow and granite presented to the spectator by the pencil of the painter'.[20]

Most of the accounts left by individuals who attended Smith's first season were similarly enthusiastic. Thackeray made his excuses for not attending the opening night, claiming a prior engagement, but asked Smith to send him tickets for another night. By August he was writing to his daughters that 'it was so amusing that you don't feel a moment's ennui during the whole performance – a thousand times more amusing than certain lectures and certain novels I know of'.[21] Thackeray's enthusiasm was admittedly short-lived – by the following year, bored and frustrated by the routine of his own lecture tour of the United States, he was wondering 'how I have the courage to keep on delivering them [the public lectures]. What pluck Albert Smith must have not to loathe himself and hang himself after repeating that rubbish of his so many hundred times!'[22] Perhaps he was irritated by Smith's boast to him the previous August that he had already made five thousand pounds from the show.[23] The lawyer and later Conservative MP James Redfoord Bulwer, who tried to climb Mont Blanc that August but was forced to turn back by a storm, had to settle for visiting Smith's show instead. 'Since returning to London I have been to hear Albert Smith's account of his Ascent', he wrote in his journal, 'and the idea he conveys of the whole thing is capital. The views, too, are very good'.[24]

Not everyone was quite so keen. Smith's friend and longstanding collaborator John Leech was reported to have said rather cattily of the show that, 'It's just bad John Parry.'[25] Gideon Algernon Mantell, the country surgeon and amateur geologist who had discovered the fossilized bones of the Iguanadon in the South Downs back in the 1820s, visited the show in its first season, just a few months before his death. The high-minded Mantell was skeptical, going along out of curiosity 'to see and hear the popular tomfoolery', and was unimpressed by Smith's tone of levity. 'I was heartily tired, and chagrined that such a subject should be thus treated', he wrote. 'Had it been a trip to Margate, or the ascent of the hill in Greenwich Park on Easter Monday, it would have been very well: the scenery, the subject, the man, the manner, and the audience, would have been in excellent keeping.' Even he had to admit, though, that 'the moveable transparent scenes were very beautiful', and that 'it was impossible not to laugh heartily at some of the mimickries, and drolleries, and absurdities'.[26]

Mantell's suggestion that not only Smith's delivery but also his audience would have been in keeping with the more conventionally cockney pursuits of a day trip to Margate or a bank holiday excursion to Greenwich points to one of the most intriguing aspects of 'The Ascent of Mont Blanc' – the make-up of its audience. It is impossible to know precisely which social classes the audience for Smith's entertainment came from, but we can make some educated guesses based on ticket prices, anecdotal evidence, and the limited extant records of who actually attended. In later years Smith would perform his show before royalty: Prince Albert visited the show during its second season in 1853, and then Queen Victoria and her children in 1854, after which Smith gave private performances at Osborne House on the Isle of Wight and at Windsor Castle in 1856.[27] Even during his first season, prominent visitors to the Egyptian Hall included the Duchess of Sutherland, the Duke and Duchess of Argyll, and a host of other Marquises, Marchionesses, Dukes, and Lords.[28] Smith cultivated his new royal and aristocratic connections for all they were worth, but the sheer number of people who visited the show meant that his audience could not possibly have been limited to 'the quality'. The price of a ticket – half a guinea for a private box, two shillings for the stalls, and a shilling for the balcony – would have been prohibitive for the genuine working classes, but within the reach of the lower middle classes.[29]

At least some of these lower-middle-class visitors would have been from the section of society often derided as cockneys – clerks, shopkeepers, independent tradespeople. The expansion of the middle classes in the middle of the nineteenth century was widely remarked upon at the time. When the Reverend Nathaniel Woodard published his pamphlet *A Plea for the Middle Classes* in 1848, in an attempt to promote the expansion of public school education to a wider constituency, he acknowledged that the term 'middle class' was now much more compendious than it had been in the past. As well as the 'gentlemen of small incomes, solicitors and surgeons with limited practice, unbeneficed Clergymen, naval and military officers' who had traditionally been considered middle class, Woodard pointed to another, rather less genteel category of tradespeople who were now economically part of the middle classes, too. These included 'persons of very different grades, from the small huckster, who obtains his livelihood by his dealings with the poor, up, step by step, through third and second rate retail shops, publicans, gin-palace keepers, &c, to the highly influential and respectable tradesmen, whose chief dealings are with the higher ranks of society'.[30]

Woodard was restricting his definition to those who could potentially afford to send their children to one of the new public schools, but for a definition of the expanded middle class in the mid-century he could conceivably have cast his net even wider, to cover the very people who populate Smith's novels: what Jerry White describes as 'the clerk, the independent dressmaker or milliner working on her own account, the enterprising shopkeeper, actress, medical man, writer and showman – that whirlpool of energy and mobility up and down that constituted the English lower middle class as it emerged and enlarged'.[31] These people formed a considerable portion of Smith's audience, and were arguably just as important to his success and popularity as the Duchess of Sutherland or the Duke of Argyll. In his turn, he was an important influence on them. Five years after Smith died, Edmund Yates would write about the phenomenon of organized foreign excursions, of the sort that Thomas Cook had pioneered in the early 1860s:

> The trip has a good deal of the cockney element in it, and is mostly composed of very high-spirited people [...] who do Paris, and rush through France, and through Switzerland to Chamounix, compare every place they are taken to with the views which formed part of the exhibition at the Egyptian Hall.[32]

The very fact that these people, whom Yates looked down upon as 'the cockney element', could recall views from the Egyptian Hall indicates that many of them must have visited Smith's show in the preceding decade. In the years that followed, more and more of them would find themselves with the financial resources to travel overseas. That many of them chose to visit the Alps was in no small part due to the influence of Smith's Egyptian Hall show.

This class stratification is an important element in Smith's story. For all that he was derided for his cockney sensibility, the class that Smith was speaking to directly – the emerging middle class – was the most dynamic and influential in its attitudes and behaviour, and was well on its way to becoming the most economically and politically powerful force in society. To have influenced this group was, in effect, to have had an impact on mid-Victorian society as a whole.

Smith now had an overnight success on his hands. 'Judging from the laughter and applause on Monday night, it is safe to predict for *The Ascent of Mont Blanc* a success at least equal to that of its predecessor', wrote the *Daily News*, and as it turned out this new show would far outstrip the success of 'The Overland Mail'. By its second season, *The Times* was remarking that 'the exhibition now seems to be one of the "sights of London" – like St. Paul's and Westminster Abbey and the Monument'.[33]

The sensation caused by the show quickly spread beyond the Egyptian Hall: June 1852 saw the publication of the 'Mont Blanc Quadrilles', written by the prolific composer J. H. Tully, and the 'Chamonix Polka' by C. R. Cooke. These were to be the first in a long line of 'tie-in' products and spin-offs, most of them created and licensed by Smith himself. During Smith's second season, in 1853, a scene in James Robertson Planché's play *Mr. Buckstone's Ascent of Mount Parnassus* at the Haymarket Theatre was staged in a room resembling Smith's Egyptian Hall set, with an actor representing Smith. Always alive to the value of publicity, Smith himself turned up at the Haymarket one evening and took on the role, much to the audience's surprise.[34]

The first season ended on 11 September, whereupon Smith promptly left for Chamonix again, in search of new material and some new props. He was briefly accompanied by William Howard Russell, but the *Times* correspondent was soon called back to report on the funeral of the Duke of Wellington, who died on 14 September and was given a state funeral in November.[35] Smith returned to begin the new season in late November, and created the elaborate new stage setting with mocked up Swiss chalets and other accoutrements, and new views by Beverley of the journey out and the valley of Chamonix itself.

The already considerable speculation about how Smith would keep the show fresh was given added piquancy by a rumour that he had drowned when the Arve flooded during his visit to Chamonix. It is unclear precisely what happened, but evidently his pocket book had been found and it was several days before Smith himself was confirmed safe. He briefly alluded to this incident on the opening night of this second season, 29 November, and the audience 'assured him in a very gratifying manner that they were well pleased to have him safe and sound once more before them'.[36]

The changes were pronounced a success. 'It would have been difficult to increase the popularity of Mr. Albert Smith's clever entertainment of last season – nor did we think it an easy matter to add to its attractions', wrote the reviewer of the *Athenaeum*. 'But the result of Mr. Smith's second visit to Chamouni and its neighbourhood has satisfied us that the journey which he took last autumn was well worth whatever trouble attended it'. Smith's 'Mont Blanc', the reviewer continued, 'is a thing *sui generis*. Available as the subject might be to many, the Valley of Chamouni without his delineations would lack its chief source of dramatic interest.'[37]

Beverley's new illustrations in this second season included views of the Pélerins cascade, the 'dangerous path from the Aiguille du Midi to the upper moraine of the Glacier des Bossons', and a new view of Chamonix itself during the September floods, taken from a sketch by Smith. Both these new images and the redecorated stage found favour with reviewers. 'The room itself is quite an illustration', commented *The Era*, while Smith himself was 'more at his ease than ever, and appears to be edifying and delighting a large party of friends, who relish every word he utters, and admire all he places before them'.[38] The *Illustrated London News* wrote that the effect of the revised staging was 'very novel, and in itself an exhibition; and this tasteful decoration is evidently appreciated. The room is crowded night after night by the most fashionable audiences, and the excitement appears quite equal to that of last season.'[39]

Smith and his brother Arthur did all they could to stoke that excitement. Arthur, who was acting as Smith's stage manager and would go on to become Dickens's manager during the novelist's lecture tours, seems to have been every bit as astute as his older brother when it came to creating publicity. 'Arthur knew all the tricks of the trade as well as Barnum', recalled John Hollingshead, who wrote that Arthur deliberately delayed opening the doors of the Egyptian Hall to the last possible minute in order to block the traffic on Piccadilly and create a minor sensation. 'When complaints were made, he expressed his willingness to pay fifty pounds for another five minutes obstruction.'[40] Arthur Smith's role in his brother's success was considerable; his importance in 'money-taking, check-taking, money-payments, bill-posting, advertising, the comfort of the audience, everything, in fact, save the actual delivery of the lecture and songs' was acknowledged by Albert himself, an acknowledgement which may well have influenced Dickens's decision to take Arthur on as tour manager.[41]

More subtle but equally effective methods of publicizing the show included the various souvenirs, toys, brochures, and other merchandise that Smith produced over the years. Smith was an expert at what would now be called brand build-ing – creating a consistent image across a wide range of media, and constantly reinforcing the message that his Mont Blanc show was the most interesting, en-tertaining, and talked-about entertainment in town. To this end, he created a range of brochures and handbooks, cheaply priced and full of supplementary information about his show, in which more detailed descriptions of each of the destinations were given, along with engravings by Beverley of the various views witnessed onstage. For sixpence, audience members hungry for more information after the show could read about the history of Chamonix, or about the 'Avalanche Dead-House' of the Convent of St. Bernard, where the corpses of unfortunate travellers who died during the crossing of the pass to Italy were stored (Smith made the most of the dramatic possibilities of this particular subject, dwelling on the 'associations connected with death' that the sight produced: 'The vain strug-gling against the fatal drowsiness – the accumulating snow – the roaring bound of the tremendous avalanche, crashing and splitting all before it – and the rending of the mighty glacier.')[42] These handbooks combined the role of travel guide, with recommendations for specific sights and walking routes, with that of souvenir and publicity vehicle.

Other publications were more tangentially relevant but still served to keep Smith's show in the public eye: the 'Mont Blanc Gazette and Illustrated Egyptian Hall Advertiser', which advertised itself as 'Published Occasionally', was full of jokes, cartoons, and anecdotes that complemented the show. It featured fanci-ful images of crowds being transported to the Egyptian Hall on top of trained elephants, and images of some of the characters from the show in peril on Mont Blanc, as well as factual information about the history of the Egyptian Hall or the latest news from the Derby.[43] It often included a digest of the day's events, so that for example on 15 January 1858 it covered 'The Attempt to Assassinate the Emperor Napoleon'.[44]

Smith's brand-building exercises went beyond simply bringing out tie-in pub-lications, however. He created and licensed a whole range of merchandise, from paper fans through to board games, confectionery called *Nougat Glacé de Mont Blanc*, and stereocards, a kind of three-dimensional photo viewer that became popular from the mid-century. He advertised for sale 'the Mont Blanc rose', priced at one shilling and manufactured by the publisher and toy manufacturer Joseph Myers of Leadenhall Street. 'This beautiful little ornament represents on the exte-rior a splendid full-blown rose', ran the blurb in one of Smith's handbooks:

> At first sight the flower seems to be a flat piece of thick cardboard; but by careful-ly introducing the nail between the folds of the paper, it will be found capable of being opened again and again, until it attains a somewhat circular form, which

is covered in beautifully executed Steel Engravings of the interesting localities forming the subjects of Mr. Albert Smith's Entertainment.[45]

Another popular piece of merchandise was the 'Game of Mont Blanc', later rebranded as 'The New Game of Mont Blanc', a board game also produced by Joseph Myers and priced at five shillings and sixpence. This involved the players trying to accumulate a number of counters while advancing across the board. Each player received three dozen counters, and could lose or win further counters depending upon which squares they landed on. So, for example, not feeling sick when crossing the Channel would give a player six more counters, while landing on St. Bernard's Convent would involve giving up six counters to pay the monks for their accommodation. Other counters were forfeited to pay for guides and equipment, and the first player to the summit of Mont Blanc was the winner.[46]

As time went on, Smith brought back not only objects and images from his regular visits to Chamonix but St. Bernard dogs, a pair of chamois, and even a 'trim, obliging Bernese girl' who normally served customers in a woodcraft shop in Chamonix, and who Smith introduced to Queen Victoria at Windsor.[47] Already a multimedia sensation, with his combination of Beverley's moving panoramas and his own monopolylogue, Smith was ensuring that news of his entertainment would branch out to other channels, too.

By the end of his second season, in August 1853, Smith had given 471 performances to an astonishing 193,754 people.[48] He was now one of the most famous men in the country, and his show had become the standard by which all others were judged. Increasingly, new productions were described as being 'in the Albert Smith fashion' or 'similar to the entertainment at the Egyptian Hall'. A 'pictorial, descriptive, and musical show' about California and Australia at the Royal Marionette Theatre, titled 'The Two Lands of Gold', was described in the *Athenaeum* as 'a pleasant entertainment, after the fashion of Mr. Albert Smith', almost as if Smith had invented the format of the pictorial travelogue.[49] Smith returned to Chamonix again in the summer of 1853, attending the opening of the hut at the Grands Mulets in September, but declined to climb Mont Blanc a second time, although a group including John Macgregor (see Chapter 8) did make the ascent. Smith wrote an article for the *Illustrated London News* in which he inevitably claimed that his group had 'the pleasure of forming one of the largest parties of travellers ever assembled on the Grands Mulets', and equally inevitably listed the things he had eaten for breakfast back at the hut while Macgregor and his companions undertook the ascent (tea, cold fowl, bread, wine, and brandy).[50] For his part, Macgregor described Smith's popularity in Chamonix as 'almost romantic', and noted how he had given a celebratory breakfast for the 34 guides who had been engaged in constructing the hut.[51]

Smith was by now a real celebrity in Chamonix, where he was credited with having increased visitor numbers to the area, and back in London his social life was as hectic as ever. He became a member of the Fielding Club, a private members' club whose members met at Offley's tavern in Henrietta Street, off Covent Garden. The Fielding was formed in 1852, primarily as somewhere for Garrick members to move on to when that club closed at midnight. Other members included Thackeray, George Henry Lewes, Tom Taylor, Edmund Yates, William Howard Russell, Shirley Brooks, the Irish MP Morgan John O'Connell, and the sculptor John Edward Jones, and Smith was an enthusiastic member, often writing letters on headed Fielding Club notepaper and using it as a place to relax after his show finished each night.[52] Yates recalled how he would regularly be decanted from the club with Arthur and Albert Smith at about one in the morning into what they called 'the North-Western Mail', a four-wheeled cab that would drop the Smith brothers off at Percy Street, then take Yates on to his home to Gloucester Place.[53]

The Fielding Club was also the site of another often-quoted putdown of Smith by his old adversary Douglas Jerrold. Jerrold was visiting the Fielding one night when Smith arrived from the Egyptian Hall, and was greeted by his fellow club members with the cry, 'Mont Blanc is the Monarch of the Mountains'. 'Yes', commented Jerrold, drily, 'and Albert half-crowned him long ago'.[54] Despite the occasional indignity of this kind, Smith clearly had a ball at the Fielding Club and enjoyed his growing celebrity and respectability. He also assiduously used his contacts there and at the Garrick to promote his show, inviting fellow club members to 'symposiums' at the Egyptian Hall, where they would be plied with 'Oysters from Rules's on Maiden Lane [and] Madame Cliquot and Moets best champage', and where 'the utmost good humour prevailed'.[55] The invitations to these events were printed on fake passports, complete with the words 'Dieu et Mon Droit' over a coat of arms and an illustration of travellers drinking a toast to the Queen on the summit of Mont Blanc. 'Mr. Albert Smith', the text read,

> one of Her Britannic Majesty's Representatives on the Summit of Mont Blanc, Knight of the Most Noble order of the Grands Mulets, Baron Galignani of Piccadilly, Knight of the Grand Crossing from Burlington Arcade to the Egyptian Hall, Member of the Society for the Confusion of Useless Knowledge, Secretary for His Own Affairs, &c, &c [...] requests and requires in the name of His Majesty the Monarch of the Mountains, all those whom it may concern, more especially the Police on the Piccadilly Frontier to allow _____ to pass freely in at the street door of the Eygptian Hall and up stairs to the Mont Blanc Room, on the evening of Saturday December the First, 1855, at 8pm, and to afford him every assistance in the way of oysters, stout, champagne, soda, and brandy, and other aid, of which he may stand in need.[56]

The 'passport' was signed by Albert Smith. This was a classic Smith invention, with its combination of self-parody and self-aggrandizement, conviviality and chutzpah, close attention to detail and relentless promotion of his own show. At some of these events, the guests would be treated to a private view of the show, while oysters, lobsters, crab salad, pale ale, bottled stout, and champagne were consumed. 'It was extremely pleasant', recalled George Augustus Sala.[57] Only a relatively small minority of visitors to the Egyptian Hall would have been invited to these 'symposia', but Smith made sure they were among the most influential and prominent people he could find. 'Of the hundred guests, including myself, ninety-nine were people in some way celebrated, or at least notable', wrote Sala. 'Our host did not care for nobodies.' As well as his fellow club members, Smith would invite peers, members of the Royal Academy, officers from the smarter regiments, 'barristers, and physicians, and surgeons; authors, dramatic critics, journalists and actors. In fact there was a capital gathering of the most prominent lions in London'.[58] Smith fed them, entertained them, and encouraged them to spread the word. 'As you like the show, I hope you'll speak of it', he would enjoin them as they left the Hall.[59]

In the middle of his show's first couple of seasons, Smith also found time to bring out another two books. *Pictures of Life at Home and Abroad*, published by Bentley in 1852, mostly consisted of recycled versions of work already published elsewhere, or variations on themes: a prose version of *Blanche Heriot*, a fictionalized visit to Greenwich Fair, a virtually exact copy of his original account of 'A Rencontre with the Brigands', and so on. The *Athenaeum* was critical of both Smith and his publisher for reprinting so much material available elsewhere, warning that 'meagre collections of the merriest magazine articles will not suffice to keep the ground for a cheap and popular publication – be the line of rail ever so short, and the average passengers travelling upon it ever so miscellaneous in quality'.[60] It did, however, approve of Smith's book-length account of his Mont Blanc climb, *The Story of Mont Blanc*, which Bogue brought out the following year. 'This is as sincere and pleasant a little book as we have lately looked into', wrote its reviewer, 'and it will not surprise us if its popularity keep pace with that of the Exhibition to which it may be called a supplement.'[61]

The Story of Mont Blanc was indeed a success, with two reprints the following year, plus further reprints in 1857 and 1860, and various revised versions after Smith's death.[62] The *Athenaeum* was mistaken, however, in thinking it could match the success of Smith's show. In 1853 'Mr. Albert Smith's Ascent of Mont Blanc' had another five years of life in it, and he could easily have kept it running for longer had he chosen to. Smith's Egyptian Hall show had turned out to be the most successful venture of his adventurous life.

15: 'MONT BLANC MANIA'

The public will never weary of Mr. Smith's Ascent. Illustrated London News, 1855

Why was 'Mr. Albert Smith's Ascent of Mont Blanc' so successful?

After all, Smith's was not the first panorama to deal with Mont Blanc; they had been in existence since at least the 1820s. Nor was he the first to introduce narration over a panorama, since Banvard had already done that with his Mississippi show. Smith's talents as a raconteur and comic singer were considerable but not unique – Charles Mathews and John Parry, to name but two, had already found success in that field, without ever creating the long-running and sensational success of Smith's Egyptian Hall performance.

London in the 1850s was not exactly starved of popular entertainment. Audiences in March 1852, the month Smith's show opened, could instead have chosen to attend Fanny Kemble's readings from *Midsummer Night's Dream* at the St. James Theatre, complete with music composed by Mendelssohn; or visited Michael William Balfe's new opera, *The Sicilian Bride*, at the Theatre Royal, Drury Lane; or gone to see Charles Kean in *King John* at the Royal Princess's Theatre, Oxford Street. They could have visited the Royal Marionette Theatre on Adelaide Street, where a new operetta, *The United Services*, was followed by a 'Neapolitan grotesque Divertissement' called *Arlecchino Fortunato*. The Lyceum was showing G. H. Lewes's successful melodrama *The Game of Speculation* (translated from Balzac's *Mercadet*, and starring Charles Mathews as the swindler Affable Hawk, with the background scenes also painted by Beverley), while the Surrey Theatre was offering an entertainment intriguingly titled *Blue Cap and the King of the Golden Waters, or The Three Kingdoms, Animal Vegetable and Mineral.*[1] The following month, the *Daily News* congratulated the Royal Polytechnic Institution on how well it had survived competition the previous year from the Great Exhibition, and reported that now the Crystal Palace was no longer open, the Institution was 'again resorted to by all who would combine the *utile* with the *dulce* in the occupation of their leisure'. Specifically, it was offering a 'lecture by Mr. Crisp on the various species of rifles and other fire-arms', a talk on the uses of electricity in national defence (by means of electric wire fences), and 'Mr Pepper's lecture on the means of preventing piracy and forgery by the anastatic process'.[2]

Over at the Asiatic Gallery, near Baker Street, a 'diorama of Hindostan' was drawing in the crowds, as was 'the collection of trophies which Mr. Gordon

Cumming has brought home as the result of his five years hunting in South Africa'. This latter exhibition had the added interest of being 'fully described by a young Hottentot, himself not the least curious of the importations, who speaks excellent English'.[3] Wyld's Great Globe at Leicester Square was still in business, while Burford's Panorama in Leicester Square was just about to open a new show devoted to Nineveh, featuring discoveries made by the archaeologist Austen Henry Layard, who had excavated the library of Ashurbanipal in 1851.[4] Meanwhile at the Colosseum in Regents Park, which had just been 'redecorated with the most refined taste and judicious liberality', visitors could marvel at the feathered denizens of the newly reconstructed Gothic aviary, gasp at the 'skeleton of that antediluvian wonder, the mighty mastodon', and admire panoramas of London by Day and Paris by Night.[5]

Smith was competing with all of these, and yet – as the *Daily News* reported in its round-up of 'Easter Amusements' that year – he 'nightly and daily turns more from his doors than he can receive within them – a fact which was especially apparent last evening, although there were many other entertainments to divide the attention of the public'.[6] So what lay behind Smith's unique success, in the face of such intense competition for the public's attention?

Albert Smith's Mont Blanc show stood at the confluence of a number of developments and factors that assured its success. First, his timing was almost perfect. By the early 1850s, the public had been conditioned by the tradition of the sublime and by several decades of Romantic literature to look at mountains in a certain way – forbidding, magnificent, menacing yet glorious. But they were increasingly ready for a change. The aesthetic of the sublime would diminish in power and relevance as the century progressed, and visitors to the Alps and other mountainous regions would increasingly be motivated by the desire for vigorous outdoor exercise, physical challenge, or simply by the impulse to have fun.

As we will see in the next chapter, the growing number of visitors to Chamonix and other Alpine centres, and the rise in the number of people wanting to climb mountains, would soon be facilitated by an improved railway network and a nascent tourist infrastructure, with new hotels and other facilities for visitors. Inevitably this meant that the experience of visiting the Alps was less challenging and certainly less exclusive.

The paradox at work here – that visitors were still attracted by the air of mystery and danger associated with the Alps, while simultaneously enjoying far greater ease of access to Alpine regions, and greatly improved facilities when they got there – was in a sense matched by the paradoxical nature of Smith's own stage show. On the one hand, he continued to present the ascent of Mont Blanc itself as dangerous and daring. On the other, his comedic account of the journey out, his debunking practicality, and his depiction of the eccentricities and follies of British and American tourists on the Continent, served to demystify the experience of travel. Smith's audiences were ready to be 'sold' a version of the Alps which suited their own requirements – exciting, but not too inaccessible; exotic, but capable of being understood and mastered; dramatic, but not too *foreign*. As the *Telegraph* would put it in its obituary of Smith, 'Piccadilly and Mont Blanc became allied, as it were, in the public mind, and it was impossible to think of one without associating it with the other'.[7] To bring Mont Blanc to Piccadilly was to make it accessible to the general public, a commodity that could somehow be purchased for the price of a seat in the stalls at the Egyptian Hall. As the advert for the 'Mont Blanc rose' described in the previous chapter boasted:

> As the inventor of this new "travelling made easy", Mr Albert Smith has become quite a benefactor of mankind. He has surpassed even old Mahomet; for that ancient traveller could never induce the mountain to come to him; while Mr Smith has succeeded in bringing the mountain on a visit to us, and, to crown the miracle, has made the fiery Mount Vesuvius and the icy Mont Blanc repose quietly side by side in Piccadilly.[8]

Other factors were at play, too. As discussed in Chapter 3, Smith's show was being performed in the context of mid-Victorian 'exhibition culture', in an environment where the public appetite for both instruction and entertainment was particularly strong in the wake of the Great Exhibition. Although Smith made no great claims for the educative content of his show, by its very nature it laid claim to a kind of authority and authenticity. The panoramic view of the mountain onstage, accompanied by the omniscient and experienced narrator, and the magisterial view of the journey to and from the Alps, combined to create an all-encompassing world view. Onstage at the Egyptian Hall, Smith was taming and ordering the untamed and disorderly territory of the Alps, just as the wider exhibition culture in which he operated served to impose order and control over the world in general. In the same way that the Great Exhibition or Wyld's Globe attempted to map, list, and categorize the known world for public consumption and amusement, so Smith's 'Ascent of Mont Blanc' attempted to bring the Alps within the purview of the nineteenth-century consumer, at precisely the time when that consumer had the leisure, purchasing power, and inclination to travel there.

So Albert Smith was benefitting from the increased wealth and leisure time enjoyed by the middle classes, while also enjoying the prestige of royal patronage at a time when the royal family was relatively popular (at least in comparison to the monarchy's public image during the reigns of Victoria's predecessors, George

IV and William IV, and the later unpopularity of Victoria during her self-imposed seclusion in the 1860s). He may have been 'selling' the Alps to the Victorian middle classes, but he was fortunate to be doing so at a moment in history when they were very willing buyers.

But Smith was not simply the beneficiary of external forces. He was also the architect of his own good fortune. His innate understanding of visual culture, of the power of spectacle – and the concomitant understanding that 'behind the scenes of a great effect' there is human artifice at work, creating and controlling the scene – helped him to put on a show that could move, awe, amuse, and in places even frighten his audience. He was undoubtedly aided immensely in this by Beverley's talents, but the grand concept for the show was Smith's. As well as his by now considerable experience and understanding of visual spectacle – stretching back to his early tours with his 'Alps in a box', through to his Overland Mail show – Smith brought to bear his own abilities as an entertainer and comic writer on creating the performance.

He also thought carefully about his audience's needs, and went to unusual lengths to satisfy them. This was not just a matter of cleaning out and re-carpeting the Egyptian Hall before his first season began. Smith and his brother Arthur paid attention to every aspect of the audience's experience, from arrival at the venue – where a sensation was produced by the simple expedient of keeping the doors closed until the last minute, blocking Piccadilly with crowds – through to their journey home. Inside the theatre, the audience's experience was deliberately genteel. 'There were no "harpies", as Albert used to call them, catching at fees for cloaks, programmes, or what-not', recalled Edmund Yates approvingly.[9] Instead Smith placed free programmes on the seats before the audience arrived, and gave strict instructions to his staff that no tips were to be solicited or accepted. 'Had I detected one taking anything from anybody, he would have been instantly dismissed', he insisted. The standard one-shilling surcharge for booking tickets in advance was dropped.[10] He started the show promptly on time at eight o'clock in the evening, and finished equally punctually at ten. 'I endeavoured to keep the entertainment within such limits of time that amusement might not gradually flag into bore; and I fixed the time of commencement at an hour possibly better suited to the habits of 1854 than of a century ago. I put a clock before you, that you might be your own timekeepers; and the few minutes of interval between the parts have been most punctually observed', Smith told the audience at the close of his fourth season, in September 1855, reviewing publicly the reasons for his success and congratulating himself on his care for the audience's comfort.[11] Even after the performance was over, Smith's concern for their convenience continued. The free programmes included a list of appropriate omnibus and cab fares from the Egyptian Hall to various parts of London, as well as the main omnibus routes. This latter feature was not unique to Smith's show, but it does hint at a degree of control over the whole experience, from entry to exit and beyond, that went well beyond that of traditional theatrical performance.

In return, the audience was expected to adhere to a code of conduct. Ladies were requested not to wear bonnets during the performance. Smith became openly exasperated if people arrived late, or made a noise during the performance. 'If the unfortunates made much noise in struggling into their place', recalled Yates, 'he would suspend his recitation and remain perfectly silent until they were seated, bestowing on them anything but looks of welcome'.[12] Those who knew Smith were sometimes surprised by his strict enforcement of rules of decorum, which seemed at odds with his disregard for conventional wisdom. 'It was curious', admitted Sala, 'to see one who was ever foremost in demolishing, by frank, downright ridicule, the petty conventionalities of life, so sternly insist upon this trifling observance [ie the removal of bonnets]. But he was determined, although a showman, to make his audience respect him.' Sala thought that Smith wanted to preclude any worse breaches of theatre etiquette: 'Shirt-sleeves in the reserved seats, or cat-calls and beer-cans in the gallery, might have consummated the conversion of liberty into license.'[13]

That certainly did not happen. Douglas Freshfield, one of a number of eminent Victorian mountaineers who saw the show in their childhood, remembered how 'There was no vulgarity in it to frighten away Victorian parents and their children, or even Victoria herself.'[14] Smith discouraged his patrons from bringing young children to the show, pointing out in his handbills that 'there is nothing that can possibly interest or amuse them in its details of travel and sketches of character. The little folk get wearied and restless and are as troublesome to those who bring them as they are annoying to the audience.'[15] However he allowed and even encouraged older children and teenagers, and listed discounted prices for them (for example, the children's price in the stalls was just two shillings at a time when the adult price had risen to three shillings). The novelist Henry James was taken to the show as a boy (James was born in 1843 so could not have been any older than fifteen at the time), and retained a particularly strong memory of one of Smith's 'effects':

> ....the very brief stop and re-departure of the train at Epernay, with the ringing of bells, the bawling of guards, the cries of travellers, the slamming of doors and the tremendous pop as of a colossal champagne-cork, made all simultaneous and vivid by Mr. Smith's mere personal resources and graces.[16]

James's recollection suggests the singular power of Smith's performance. It is impossible now to reconstruct precisely what went on in the Egyptian Hall – we only know from memoirs, programmes, handbills, and a few images of Beverley's pictures (none of the original dioramas has survived) what the show was like. But clearly Smith was able to create something well above the normal run of such entertainments.

As Sala suggested, Smith's insistence on strict standards of decorum sits oddly with his own bohemian, even louche persona. Actually he seems to have become considerably more conventional and perhaps rather choleric as he got older. He wrote to *The Times* in 1855, signing himself 'The London Scoundrel', to complain about 'the swarm of the most obnoxious little vagabonds in London' who infested the area around Leicester Square, begging for money for sweeping away imaginary objects from in front of pedestrians. 'I have watched them now above two years. I have spoken to the policemen, and even given them in charge, and sometimes thrashed them soundly', wrote Smith, complaining that these 'dirty, abusive, un-shocked, unsavoury atoms of humanity' simply moved temporarily to another area. He then turned his attention to an area of pavement between the top of Haymarket and Regent Street – 'a small strip of promenade, but a concentration of all the blackguardism and depravity of London', especially at night:

> I am not an ultra moralist, I do not walk about the streets at night to reclaim fallen virtue or preach religion at obelisks, and I have been long enough fighting the battle of life upon town to be able to stand a great deal unflinchingly, but I do say that this corner of the Haymarket is a cancer in the great heart of the capital and a disgrace to the supervision of any police who may be supposed to have the charge of it [....] I have never witnessed such blatant blackguardism and profligacy as ring along those Piccadilly flagstones at any time after the gas is lighted that you have the ill-luck to traverse them.[17]

Given this area's reputation at the time, the 'blackguardism and profligacy' Smith referred to was probably both male and female prostitution. The point, however, is that his curmudgeonly tone is a striking contrast to the air of raffish bohemianism he had cultivated as a younger man. Smith wrote a couple of days later to a local magistrate, enclosing a copy of the letter and reiterating his strong wish that 'something could be done with the locality'. Alert as always to an opportunity for attracting influential people to his show, he added, 'By the way, I do wish whenever you may feel inclined to bring, or send, anybody to "Mont Blanc", you will let me know.'[18]

Several of Smith's contemporaries noted how he became more conventional and respectable and also grumpier as he got older. Towards the end of his life – only a few years away at this stage – he fell out with several good friends, including Yates and Dickens, and he seems to have become a somewhat blimpish figure.

However, his enforcement of rigid rules at the Egyptian Hall probably stemmed just as much from his calculation that, as Sala put it, 'Give the public an inch and they will take an ell', and from a desire to attract not only the biggest but also the most prestigious and respectable audience possible.[19] Smith was ruthless with anything that he felt might pose a threat to the success of his entertainment, whether rowdy behaviour on the part of the public or the abuse of so-called 'press orders' by the friends of reporters. These were essentially free passes for members of the press, intended to allow theatre critics to attend the show and write their reviews. Smith believed that they were widely abused by, for example, newspapers giving them to advertisers as incentives to gain their business, or reporters selling them on to friends and acquaintances. He made a stand on the issue at the start of his second season, after being infuriated by the number of people bearing press orders for the Egyptian Hall who clearly had no connection with the papers that issued them. Smith drew up a circular and 'sent a copy to every respectable paper', informing them that he was unilaterally withdrawing from the system of press orders. He even went so far as to bring out a booklet on the issue some time later, summarizing the positions of all the main newspapers on the matter. With char- acteristic immodesty, he quoted on the frontispiece the *Globe*'s comment that 'Of this reform Mr. Albert Smith is the Luther.'[20] He later noted that 'all the first-class papers approved of my determination, and admitted that, even to themselves, the distribution of orders had become a nuisance'. Some of the weekly journals, however,

> accused me of discourtesy to the press. This intention I utterly repudiate. Any gentleman connected in any way with the literary or artistic portion of a news- paper has always received my first and best attention; but I would not have the general character of my audience lowered by a quantity of sometimes dirty and doubtful people, into whose hands a press order has been passed, from one to another, until the last possessor has no more to do with the paper he was sup- posed to represent than I have with the woolsack.[21]

The press orders controversy is little more than a footnote in the history of the Mont Blanc show, but it again illustrates Smith's relentlessness in protecting his interests and his attention to every aspect of the show's success.

Another factor in the consistent popularity of Smith's show was the attention he paid to keeping it fresh, incorporating changes each season and responding to what he perceived as changing public expectations. For the third season, Smith's route to Mont Blanc began at the Rhine Bridge at Basle, then took him and his audience through Zurich, up the Rigi, on to Lucerne and Interlaken, and then to the Wengern Alp. After the Mont Blanc ascent, instead of returning to Paris he crossed the Simplon Pass and visited Lago Maggiore. He also added an even more elaborate stage set, designed to look like an Alpine village and 'a vast collection of knick-knackeries, such as model cottages, fans, pictures and carvings of all kinds'.[22] Next season, beginning in December 1854, he changed the route out to take in Rotterdam, some other parts of Holland, and the Rhine. The fifth season retained the Dutch route but added a stopover in Paris, and included new exhibits from the Paris Exhibition, which ran from May to November 1855. For his sixth season, he redecorated the room, and took yet another route out to along the Rhine to Heidelberg and Baden-Baden, then via Basle and Berne to Chamonix, before returning via Chillon, Geneva, Paris, and Boulogne. This season incorporated new views by Beverley, and a panorama of the Rhine.[23]

More significantly, Smith's sixth season saw the Mont Blanc ascent itself relegated to what he called 'a Pictorial Entr'Acte' during the interval. His stated reason for this, given on a handbill for that season, was that with the newly introduced material on the journey out and back, 'the Entertainment might be prolonged to a point when it would cease to be one, in the actual acceptation of the word, and weary the audience instead of amusing them'.[24] However, it seems more likely that he was responding directly to the perception that audiences – and the press – were growing rather bored with Mont Blanc. It is no coincidence that this change occurred just a month after *The Times* had declared in a leading article that 'Mont Blanc has become a positive nuisance', complaining of the frequency with which the mountain was now climbed and the propensity of the young men who climbed it for 'teasing the public with the repetition of a fifty times told tale'.[25] 'At present a perfect Mont Blanc mania pervades the minds of our fellow-countrymen', *The Times* thundered. 'Its majesty is stale, its "diadem of snow" a mere theatrical gimcrack, and its terrors under existing arrangements about as tremendous as the mysteries of the Thames Tunnel.' It mentioned Smith by name as one of the factors that had caused this ennui, by having 'treated the mountain in a comical spirit'. As if to underline the point, on the same day this leader appeared *The Times* carried an account of yet another British ascent of the mountain.[26] Nor was it coincidental that *Bentley's Miscellany* had earlier that year published an article titled 'The Final Ascent of Mont Blanc', with a narrator called Mr. Jolly Green, who is tricked by his guides into believing that he has climbed the mountain.[27]

These were not the first signs of a certain weariness with Smith's presentation of Mont Blanc. As early as 1853, Robert Ferguson was writing that 'There is no exploit from which a man derives such an immediate return for his capital invested as the ascent of Mont Blanc', but pointedly adding that, 'I do not speak of it in the sense in which Mr. Albert Smith has obtained it, but looking at it merely in the light of an exploit.'[28] The following year, *Punch* had run a satirical piece called 'Good News For Cockney Travellers', in which it imagined that 'Mont Blanc has been carpeted as high as the Grands Mulets, Mr. Albert Smith having been requested to bring out with him to Chamouni, carpets of the same pattern as those of the *tapis* in the Council-Room at Osborne, where he recently gave his entertainment.'[29] Mont Blanc – along with the Egyptian desert, the Himalayas, and Niagara Falls – was becoming so tamed and domesticated, suggested *Punch*, that 'we hope speedily to be able to assure the cowardliest and feeblest Cockney, that he may see the world in tolerable safety and comfort'.[30]

There are several layers of irony here. First, Smith had clearly become a victim of his own success. As we shall see in the next chapter, the 'Mont Blanc mania' created by his show led to a massive increase in the number of people visiting the Alps, some to climb Mont Blanc and other peaks, others simply as tourists. Even if, as Darren Bevin points out, satire by *Punch* and others 'centred less on Smith and more on the effect that Smith's shows may have on the landscape as it became commodified by an enthusiastic English public', it is clear that Smith felt the time was right to downgrade the central place of the Monarch of the Mountains.[31] In his final season, he completely transformed the geography of the show to emphasize the Italian part of the journey. He was now returning from Chamonix via the rather improbable route of Naples, Pompei, and Vesuvius, visiting the Blue Grotto at Capri, and the ascent of Mont Blanc was once again relegated to a series of dioramic views during the short interval.[32]

Yet the same year that this final season began, 1857, saw the foundation of the Alpine Club, the organization that would encourage the growth of mountaineering as a hobby for the British middle classes in the decades that followed. Not only mountaineering but also 'cockney' tourism to the Alps were about to become significant cultural phenomena in the wake of Smith's show, and while he was by no means the only reason for these developments, he indubitably made a significant contribution. So just at the point when his show was having its most profound impact, Smith felt that his public were becoming bored with Mont Blanc and required a change.

Smith's willingness to change his show, however, indicates the flexibility and responsiveness that were among the secrets of his success. The programme for his final 1857-58 season gives further evidence of the concern he displayed for the comfort of his audience, for example. The programme begins with the panorama of the Rhine, then moves on to the first view of the Alps, taking in Zurich, the Rigi (where we meet our old friend Mr. Parker), the Jungfrau, and the Convent of the Great St. Bernard, and over the lake to Geneva. In the interval, as well as the views of Mont Blanc, the audience 'may please to look at The Ruins of Paestum (painted by Mr. Beverley), near the Gulf of Salerno'. The second part takes in the

Bay of Naples, the Santa Lucia at Naples, the House of the Tragic Poet at Pompei, and the Blue Grotto at Capri, where Smith halts his audience for a comic song:

> This is the Grotto Azura – a bright home of coral and oyster;
> Ultramarine is the colour that bathes all its wave-fretted cloisters
> Such an abode might the sirens have had, who were 'sold' by Ulysses,
> Not a great way from the grotto – and there became food for the pisces.
> If you would know how they failed to enchant the bold Ithacan roamer,
> Read your Pausanias, Strabo, and Ovid, and Virgil, and Homer.
> In the meantime, as we stop at Sorrento, of Naples the glory,
> List to the Austrian Lloyd's Engineer, and his very dull story.

The programme continues with an ascent of Vesuvius, and finally 'The Eruption of Vesuvius, on the 24th September last (at which Mr. Albert Smith was present), with the lava running down to the Atrio del Cavallo.'[33]

Not content with having reinvented and restructured his show so that it bears little resemblance to its earlier incarnations – and with the supposed raison d'etre, the ascent of Mont Blanc, reduced to a short interval between the main acts – Smith is still making improvements to the audience's experience even in this final season. The programme announces that two new rooms have been opened, 'A comfortable Toilet Room, for Ladies wishing to leave their bonnets; and a general Waiting Room, for the audience, with Newspapers, Books, Pictures, Bradshaw, Punch, Army List, Court Guide, Writing Materials, &c, &c.'[34]

This kind of attention to detail, and willingness to change and adapt in order to avoid boring his audience, was a recurring theme of Smith's Egyptian Hall entertainment. At the final performance of each season, he would tell the audience his plans for travelling during the autumn, enumerate how many performances he had now given, and encourage them to return the following season with 'teasers' about the new material he planned to introduce. So at the end of his fifth season, in September 1856, as well as pointing out that he had now 'had the honour of telling you the same story in the same room 1,482 times, up to this evening', he also tempted his listeners to return next season by letting them know that he would be travelling via the Rhine, and that 'the gambling tables at Baden will occupy my extreme attention; and the still helpless and lamentable state of Brown, everywhere on the Continent, calls for the most earnest measures to alleviate those miseries which cloud his tour, and turn his holiday into a prolonged excursion of imaginary extortion, self-created irritation, disappointed anticipation, and misunderstood behaviour', thus cleverly creating anticipation of fresh scenes alongside the promise of the return of old favourites such as the hopelessly poor traveller Brown.[35]

By now, 'Mr. Albert Smith's Ascent of Mont Blanc' had made him both very famous and very rich. As we have seen, the royal family visited the show several times and Smith also travelled to both Windsor and Osborne House to give special performances. 'Albert Smith gave an entertainment in the White Drawing Room, which was most excellent', wrote Queen Victoria in her diary from Windsor in March 1856, adding that she particularly liked Edwards the Engineer and 'Brown Junior', the young Englishman who is constantly baffled in his attempts to speak and understand French.[36] He had already given a special truncated version of his show at Osborne in August 1854, titled 'Selections of Mr. Albert Smith's Ascent of Mont Blanc, Chiefly Pertaining to the Travelling English and their Autumnal Peculiarities'.[37] Smith was now famous enough to be depicted as a character in fiction. *Marston Lynch*, begun in serial form by the playwright, illustrator, and satirist Robert B. Brough in 1856, is a long biographical novel of London life, which was eventually completed by Sala after Brough's death from alcoholism in 1860. In an echo of the way Smith's own novels had introduced John Parry and other real people as minor characters, Smith himself is spotted at the opening night of a new play, 'nodding to some ladies in the next box'.[38] Smith was not the only real person to feature in *Marston Lynch* (others included Douglas Jerrold and Captain Frederick Marryat, the author of *The Children of the New Forest* and *Mr. Midshipman Easy*), but his presence is a marker of how he had become a household name by the mid-1850s. By 1860, the year of his death, Smith was one of the first two of a 'gallery of living celebrities' to be memorialized in a series of miniature photographic portraits – the other was Dickens, which gives some idea of just how famous Smith had become by this time.[39]

Smith enjoyed his fame and loved to play up his royal connections, although he was rather less forthcoming about the fortune he had made from the show. Speaking at the end of his sixth season, he outlined some of the costs that he had entailed over the course of his time at the Egyptian Hall, in an attempt to allay 'the absurd statements I have seen, both in the English and American papers, of the enormous fortune I have made here'. He claimed to have paid rent for the Hall of six hundred pounds a year, working expenses of seventy-five pounds a week, and said he had never spent less than five hundred on each season's alteration to the set and other programme changes.[40] He did not, however, clarify how much profit he made after these outgoings. It is impossible to know exactly how much Smith did make. We do know, however, that an astonishing number of people visited the show over the course of its life. Since Smith gave two thousand performances, and the Egyptian Hall held roughly 430 people, even a conservative estimate – taking into account many repeat visitors and a large number bearing press orders or other passes allowing free entry – would put the number of people who saw the show at around eight hundred thousand.

To attempt to put this into perspective, we might compare Smith's show with a modern theatrical sensation, the musical *Les Misérables*. This show has been seen by around seventy million people since it began in 1985. But that number has been spread over nearly three decades, and has involved multiple productions in over forty countries, and translation into more than twenty different languages.[41] *Les Misérables* has been performed an astonishing forty-eight thousand times around the world to achieve that audience figure. Perhaps a fairer comparison would be with *The Mousetrap*, which holds the Guinness World Record for the longest continuous run of any show. *The Mousetrap* celebrated its sixtieth anniversary in 2012, at which time the producers estimated that it had been seen by ten million people.[42] Seen in that light, Smith's audience of eight hundred thousand (and potentially as many as eight hundred and sixty thousand) from a show that ran in a single London venue for just seven seasons is truly phenomenal.

The 'Ascent of Mont Blanc' was a theatrical juggernaut. It left even the indefatigable Smith with little time or energy to pursue other activities, although he did manage to bring out an 1855 pamphlet – *The English Hotel Nuisance* – in which he complained about the poor standard of service and accommodation in Britain. Describing the custom of having to tip individual staff members for service instead of paying a standard charge as 'inn-fluenza', he goes on to describe the system on Continental Europe as superior. The list of hotels he uses to make this point illustrates just how grandly cosmopolitan Smith had become by this stage in his career. They include 'the *Grand Laboreur* at Antwerp, the *Baur* at Zurich, or the *Schweitzer Hof* at Lucerne – Bairr's at Milan – the *Colonies* at Marseille – the *Ville de Paris* at Strasbourg – the *Trois Couronnes* at Vevay – the *Couronne* at Bern', and so on. 'We have not a house in all England to compare with them', he complains.[43] Smith also found time during this period to raise a public subscription after a fire in July 1855 destroyed one Chamonix hotel and badly damaged two others. He responded to an appeal in *The Times*, saying he would be happy to receive subscriptions. He contributed twenty pounds himself, as did the philanthropist Angela Burdett-Coutts. Dickens contributed one pound, writing to Smith, 'Chamouni shall have my sovereign, willingly, and you shall come down here to "collect it"; whenever you feel disposed for a quiet Sunday rest, write and tell me so.'[44]

The correspondence with Dickens indicates how their friendship had progressed during the 1850s. Dickens wrote to Bradbury and Evans in 1854, asking for presentation copies of *Hard Times*, published that year, to be sent to Smith, as well as to Shirley Brooks and Lady John Russell.[45] The same year, Dickens wrote in self-referential terms to Smith, inviting him to dine at Tavistock House. 'We have no party of an Easterly or bleak nature – no flavour of genteel company – only half a dozen people whom you know very well', he wrote, in a clear reference to John Jarndyce in *Bleak House*.[46] A year earlier he had read and evidently enjoyed Smith's *Story of Mont Blanc* while visiting Chamonix himself. Staying at the Hôtel de Londres, probably on Smith's recommendation, he wrote to Catherine Dickens that he found the book 'extremely well and unaffectedly done'.[47] The friendship would be cemented by Dickens's employment of Arthur Smith to organize his reading tours in 1858 and 1861, but severely strained over Dickens's relationship with Ellen Ternan and Smith's response to it. For now, however, Dickens evidently esteemed Smith's friendship and was happy to write him a letter of recommendation to Timothy Yeats Brown, British Consul at Genoa, when Smith visited Italy in 1857 to prepare for his revamped Egyptian Hall show. 'All the world knows Mr. Albert Smith', Dickens wrote to Yeats Brown,

> Innumerable people who know nothing of Mont Blanc itself, perhaps know more about it of him than they have ever known of their own fathers and mothers [...] He is an intimate friend of mine, for whom I have a great regard, and in whose prosperity in all ways, I am much interested.[48]

Smith's relations to Thackeray continued to be rather more fraught, as we shall see later. Nonetheless, this period of his life seems to have been generally successful and contented, if rather complicated. Still unmarried, he was continuing his long-standing relationship with his future wife, Mary Keeley, while conducting another affair with his mistress Pattie Oliver. In 1857 he moved two doors down to number 12 Percy Street, where his parents, sister, and aunt occupied the first floor and several bedrooms while he kept the ground floor for himself. According to some accounts, Arthur Smith also lived in the same building during this period – he had certainly shared number 14 with Albert before the move.[49]

The 'Ascent of Mont Blanc' continued playing to packed houses until July 1858. At the end of each season, Smith would take off to Europe in search of fresh material. In addition to his travels and his daily performances, he was also closely involved in the writing, production and performance of an amateur production of the pantomime *Harlequin Guy Fawkes*, performed to raise money for Angus Reach. Reach, Smith's erstwhile colleague on *The Man in the Moon*, had suffered a mental breakdown in 1854, from which he never fully recovered. He was to die in 1856. Reach's friends at the Fielding Club, Smith and Edmund Yates prominent among them, put on the pantomime at the Olympic Theatre in March 1855, to great fanfare. Prices for stalls tickets were reported to have reached ten pounds.[50] Dickens, who was in the audience, wrote afterwards to Wilkie Collins that it 'was amazingly good, and it really was a comfortable thing to see all conventional dignity so outrageously set at naught. It was astonishingly well done, and extremely funny'.[51]

A second performance was given in front of Queen Victoria at Drury Lane in May that year (despite Dickens's warning to Arthur Smith, who was also involved, that the venue would be too big) this time to raise funds for the establishment of Wellington College, a charitable institution in Berkshire for the orphans of army officers.[52] Victoria wrote in her diary that the pantomime was a 'wonderful idea and very cleverly carried out', and described Smith – in the role of the gunpowder plotter Catesby – as 'inimitable'.[53]

It was a succinct and accurate description. However, in the years to come many people *would* attempt to imitate Smith's feat, stepping out from the tightly controlled space of the Egyptian Hall into the real, uncontrollable Alpine land-scape. Many of them would do so under the auspices of the Alpine Club. At the centre of things as usual, Smith would be one of its founding members.

16: 'TORMENTED BY COCKNEYS'

*Probably no event in England has awakened so keen an interest in the Alps,
as the entertainment which the late Albert Smith gave in the Egyptian Hall.*
C.D. Cunningham & W. de W. Abney, *The Pioneers of the Alps* (1887).

It would fair to say that Albert Smith was not a representative member of the Alpine Club.

Formed in 1857, the Alpine Club was the single most important organization in promoting and developing British climbing throughout the nineteenth century and into the first part of the twentieth. For the most part it was the home of upper-middle-class men, often scientists, lawyers, or clergymen; women were not allowed to join until the late twentieth century, although there were many active female climbers from the earliest days of recreational mountaineering. Some of its members were part of the Victorian 'intellectual aristocracy', among them the author and first editor of the *Dictionary of National Biography* Leslie Stephen, the scientist John Tyndall, and the critic and poet Matthew Arnold, but others were civil servants, bankers, schoolmasters, Oxford and Cambridge dons, physicians, businessmen, and industrialists.

As an analysis of the Club's membership rolls by Peter Hansen has shown, its members were 'drawn overwhelmingly from the professional middle classes'.[1] In this respect, it represented a rather narrower swathe of Victorian society than the audiences who had flocked to see Smith's show at the Egyptian Hall. Smith himself was certainly atypical – in fact, of the various clubs he belonged to, the Alpine Club was the one where he must have felt least at home. Smith's only experience of mountaineering, apart from strolling up the Rigi or Montenvers, was his single Mont Blanc ascent, and his ebullient personal style was clearly far removed from the patrician, ascetic ethos of men like Stephen. Nonetheless, he met the requirements for membership simply by virtue of having climbed Mont Blanc.[2] His entry in the official Alpine Club Register lists him as having made 'the earliest ascent of Mont Blanc [...] by any (future) member of the A.C.', and further notes that his Egyptian Hall show was 'immensely popular and successful, and contributed not a little to the interest in mountaineering which was growing up during these years'.[3]

Smith was one of the twenty-eight members who met at Ashley's Hotel in Covent Garden in December 1857 for the Club's inaugural meeting. He had been approached as a potential member by Edward Shirley Kennedy, an adventurous traveller of independent means who had already established himself as a pioneering Alpine climber. Kennedy had discussed the idea of a mountaineering association with the Reverend Fenton John Anthony Hort, and later talked it over with Birmingham land agent William Mathews during their ascent of the Finsteraarhorn in Switzerland in the summer of 1857. Kennedy wrote to a number of potential members that autumn, and Smith was among the first to respond. He cheekily claimed in his reply that he and John Auldjo had already discussed the idea 'long ago' but had been too busy to pursue it.[4]

Unsurprisingly, not everyone welcomed the idea of Smith as a fellow member. Mathews wrote to Kennedy from Birmingham that 'I cannot say that I see the inclusion of Albert Smith's name with feelings of great satisfaction', and there seems little doubt that some members shared his misgivings.[5] Others were more philosophical about the mixed blessing of having the great showman join their club. The Anglican clergyman Isaac Taylor accepted his own invitation to join by suggesting that 'Albert Smith should give us all free tickets in return for the benefit of our experience.'[6]

The fact that Smith, perhaps the least typical mountaineer of the mid-Victorian period, should have been one of the founding members of the organization that most typified mountaineering in this era is far from the only irony in this part of his story.[7] For although Smith undoubtedly did have some impact on the history of mountaineering – the statistics for ascents of Mont Blanc before and after his show bear that out, as do the testimonies of climbers who attended the Egyptian Hall – his real influence was not on the serious-minded, committed mountaineers who forged the so-called 'Golden Age' of Alpinism in the period up to 1865. Rather it was on the lower-middle-class tourists who began to arrive in the Alps in ever-greater numbers – the very people who Alpine Club members would often complain about in the years ahead. Albert Smith did not need to sell the Alps to his fellow Alpine Club members – they were already convinced of the attractions of mountain climbing. Instead, his packaging of his Mont Blanc experiences into an aspirational form convinced many non-mountaineers that the Alps were an appealing holiday destination, and in some cases that they, too, should attempt to climb mountains.

Nonetheless, Smith's show clearly did influence mountaineers as well as tourists. Criticism of his show may have started early, but so did accounts by climbers of having been to see it, and suggestions that it had inspired some of them. Douglas Freshfield has already been mentioned as one of the future mountaineers who attended. The eighteen-year-old Edward Whymper, later to become famous as the first person to climb the Matterhorn, recorded in his diary that he attended the final season of Smith's show. 'People often go to these sort of things with exorbitant expectations raised by previous descriptions which have been told them', he noted. 'I however found myself quite satisfied and more.'[8] Writing later in the century Whymper noted the growing popularity of Mont Blanc ascents in the period after Smith's show, and while pointing out that this was in part due to the increased accessibility of Chamonix by rail, he concluded that,

> it is due to Albert Smith to say that his influence extended much beyond Chamonix and Mont Blanc. Many persons date their first craving for the Alps from the time when they heard this able lecturer and genial showman, and amongst others, I think, some of those who made the first ascent of Mont Blanc "without guides".[9]

Whymper was referring here to Smith's fellow Alpine Club members Kennedy and the Reverend Charles Hudson, who in 1855 made the first guideless ascent of Mont Blanc and on their return to Britain published an account with the breezy title *Where There's a Will There's a Way*.[10] Charles Edward Mathews, younger brother of William and the man who would roundly mock Smith's hyperbolic account of climbing the Mur de la Côte, acknowledged that 'scores of men who afterwards distinguished themselves in the exploration of the great Alps first had their imagination fired by listening to the interesting story told at the Egyptian Hall'.[11]

Even those mountaineering writers who disapproved of Smith conceded that his influence had been extensive and not wholly malign. As late as 1898 (by which time Smith had been largely forgotten by the general public) a review in the *Climbers' Club Journal* of Mathews' book *The Annals of Mont Blanc* commented that, 'We smile at Albert Smith's version of his own ascent, and all but the most equable and good-humoured readers, such as Mr. Mathews himself, feel disgusted at the man and his bare-faced means of making money out of his mountaineering by grotesque misrepresentation and belated discovery of the "humour" of it', but went on to concede that 'Albert Smith, caricature of a mountaineer though he was, did more than any other to bring people to the Alps.'[12]

The question, though, was 'which people?'

Mountain climbing as an end in itself was a relatively new activity in the early 1850s. Most ascents of Alpine peaks in the past had been made for purposes of scientific research – for example, by the pioneering Scottish glaciologist James David Forbes in the 1820s and 1830s – or by adventurous eccentrics. For those travellers who did choose to climb without a scientific motive, the usual goal was Mont Blanc, climbed simply because it was the highest peak in western Europe. From around the early 1850s, as the mountaineering historian W.A.B. Coolidge put it, 'Englishmen were waking up to the fact that "mountaineering" is a pastime that combines many advantages, and is worth pursuing as an end in itself, without any regard to the thought of the advancement of natural science.'[13] Thus began what later came to be known as the 'Golden Age' of Alpine mountaineering, a period usually considered to begin with Alfred Wills' 1854 ascent of the Wetterhorn and to end with the mingled triumph and tragedy of Edward Whymper's 1865 Matterhorn ascent.

Wills climbed the 3,692-metre Wetterhorn in Switzerland during his honeymoon, and his feat is often cited in support of the claim that British visitors 'invented' mountaineering in this period. In fact, there had already been plenty of ascents of Alpine peaks before this by Continental European climbers – Wills wasn't even the first to climb the Wetterhorn – and even if the British were the first to attribute 'sporting' motives to the activity of climbing mountains, other nationalities were not slow to catch up.[14] Mountaineering associations soon sprang up in other countries; an Alpine Club was formed in the United States in 1863, and by the end of the century there were counterparts in most of the western European nations as well as in New Zealand and South Africa.[15] Nonetheless, in its early years mountaineering was considered a characteristically British activity, and it was mostly British climbers who systematically worked their way through the unclimbed peaks of the Alps during the Golden Age – a process that culminated in the 1865 Matterhorn climb, in which four of Edward Whymper's companions were killed by a fall during the descent. By 1862, the author of a *Cornhill* magazine article on 'The Art of Alpine Travel', could confidently open with the assertion that mountaineering 'is now firmly established as one of our national sports', a claim that could not reasonably have been made even a decade earlier.[16]

The reasons for the growth of this new activity were many and varied – ranging from the growing wealth and self-confidence of the middle classes, the cultural influence of imperialism, the ethos of 'manliness' in the public school system, and even changing attitudes to risk in a rapidly urbanizing industrial society, not to mention the improved ease of access to mountainous regions – and a full exploration of the phenomenon is outside of the scope of this book.[17] What is fairly certain, however, is that mountaineering would have taken off without the influence of Albert Smith's show. Seeing his thrilling performance at the Egyptian Hall may have stimulated the imaginations of a few individuals who would later go on to become serious mountaineers, but Smith's overall impact on the development of mountaineering was limited. His real influence was not on his fellow Alpine Club members but on the wider development of Alpine tourism.

As Smith's own ascent shows, it was not only dedicated, committed mountaineers who climbed Mont Blanc. Even in the first half of the century it had been climbed by the curious and the adventurous, and those who simply wanted to say they had been there. It was seen as a physical challenge, and climbed by people who – like Smith himself – would never climb any other peaks. Just as many people today will undertake the Three Peaks Challenge or perhaps a sponsored ascent of Kilimanjaro, in the same spirit they would enter a marathon or try bungee-jumping, without necessarily considering themselves mountaineers, so in the nineteenth century there were plenty of potential Mont Blanc climbers who were not Alpine Club members and did not consider themselves serious climbers. What is clear is that the number of such people skyrocketed in the years immediately after Smith's show became successful.

Only thirty-nine ascents had been made before Smith's group reached the top in 1851. After that, the mountain was climbed an astonishing eighty-eight times in just five years.[18] In 1851, the year of Smith's climb, only one other successful attempt was made on the mountain, and there were two failed attempts (including that of the Irishman who had briefly joined Smith's party at the Grands Mulets). During the 1854 season, there were sixteen successful ascents and an unknown number of failed attempts.[19]

Tracing the advice given to tourists about Mont Blanc in *Murray's Handbook* gives some idea of how rapidly and comprehensively attitudes changed after Smith's ascent and show. The *Handbook* was still claiming as late as 1854 that Mont Blanc climbers were frequently 'persons of unsound mind', but by 1856 it had changed the emphasis, claiming only that '*several* of those who have made this ascent have been persons of unsound mind', and acknowledging that the ascent 'is now become very common in favourable weather, especially since that of Albert Smith, in 1851, has effectually popularized the enterprise'.[20] By 1858 *Murray's* had dropped its reference to 'unsound minds' altogether, and by 1867 had changed its tune completely, noting that 'The ascent of Mont Blanc is now frequently made when the weather is favourable for the expedition. The mountain is now so well known, and the proper precautions so thoroughly understood, that little serious risk is incurred.'[21] Unfortunately, *Murray's* newly blasé advice would turn out to be ill-timed. In 1870 eleven climbers died on the mountain in a blizzard, and later that year the Harrow schoolmaster and keen mountaineer John Stogdon gave a paper to the Alpine Club in which he tried to draw some lessons from the tragedy. Mont Blanc, he warned his fellow climbers – and by extension the tourists who were now increasingly drawn to the mountain – was too often underestimated. 'If Mont Blanc has been the scene of many successful expeditions', said Stogdon, 'he has, on the other hand, more blood on those white snows of his than, I think, we may say, all the other Alpine peaks put together.'[22]

Even by the mid-1850s, however, the growing popularity of Mont Blanc in the wake of Smith's show meant that the normal route up from Chamonix was being eschewed by more ambitious mountaineers in favour of attempts to forge new routes to the summit, as well as to climb other peaks in the wider Mont Blanc massif. Hudson and Kennedy's guideless 1855 ascent, for example, was from St. Gervais, the first successful ascent by this new route. But the majority of Mont Blanc climbers were less concerned with forging new, more challenging routes to the summit than in simply being able to say they had been up the mountain. As Leslie Stephen put it, 'Whilst [Hudson and Kennedy] were the esoteric prophets of the new creed, whose followers had not yet organized themselves into a distinct set, Albert Smith was preaching to the populace.'[23]

Most people who climbed Mont Blanc did not die, of course, and most of the people who visited the Alps did not climb Mont Blanc or any other peak, except perhaps the Rigi or the Montenvers – and after 1871, when the first Alpine funicular railway opened to the summit of the Rigi they did not even need to do that any longer.[24] Funicular railways were just one sign of the growing popularity of the Alps. The cult of the sublime and the influence of Romantic literature had encouraged tourism to the region since at least the late eighteenth century, but in the middle of the nineteenth the rising affluence of the lower middle classes – the same group who had flocked to the Egyptian Hall to see Smith's show – allowed them to seriously consider taking foreign holidays. The growing rail network made this feasible, bringing the Alps within the scope of a relatively short holiday; as Douglas Freshfield pointed out, Smith was fortunate to have launched his show 'just at the psychological moment when railways across France brought the Alps within the Englishman's long vacation'.[25] Perhaps just as importantly, the invention of package tourism by Thomas Cook meant that even the most timid could feel confident about travelling to a country where they did not understand the language and were unfamiliar with the customs. Thomas Cook had been arranging excursions within Britain since 1841, using the newly expanded railways to conduct groups from his Leicester base to Snowdonia, Scotland, and other locations. In 1855 he took his first party to Europe, and in 1863 he began organizing tours to Switzerland, motivated at least in part by the lingering interest in the Alps after Smith's show.[26] The cost of the Swiss trip – nine pounds for a two week tour – opened up the Alps to a whole new constituency of lower-middle-class travellers who could never have contemplated the expense of hiring mountain guides and equipment to climb Mont Blanc or other peaks, but who could now visit the Mer de Glace.[27] Nine pounds would barely have covered the cost of a single Alpine climbing trip, but it did allow Cook's clients to see the Alps in reasonable comfort, staying at hotels which catered to the tastes and requirements of British visitors and guided by an experienced cicerone in the person of Cook himself or later one of his employees.

Part of Cook's success, according to the travel sociologist John Urry, lay in his 'almost infinite capacity for taking trouble, his acute sense of the needs of his clients' – a formula that sounds very similar to that of Albert Smith's at the Egyptian Hall, catering to his audience's needs and organizing their experience from entrance to departure.[28] Cook, in a sense, was the inheritor of Smith's role: one of them provided the packaged Alpine spectacle for the audience in England; the other provided an almost equally packaged version in the Alps themselves. A considerable proportion of Cook's early clients were women travellers, who took advantage of what was effectively a chaperone system. However, the reported comment of one of Cook's female clients that, 'We would venture anywhere with such a guide and guardian as Mr. Cook' could apply just as easily to his male clients.[29] Cook was guide and guardian, allowing his clients to experience a version of the Alps which was contained and commodified, just as Smith's audiences at the Egyptian Hall had experienced 'Mont Blanc and Piccadilly' brought together in an exciting but ultimately unthreatening domestic alliance. Those travellers who, as Edmund Yates put it, were inclined to 'compare every place they are taken to with the views which formed part of the exhibition at the Egyptian Hall' were able to at least partly reproduce that experience by keeping their Alpine adventure within certain limits.[30]

The mountaineers of the Alpine Club tended to regard this as an anaemic and attenuated experience of the Alps, and it was not long before complaints about the 'Cookites' were being aired in the pages of the *Alpine Journal* and in other climbing publications. Complaints about 'cockney' trippers in the Alps were not new. As early as 1833, the writer William Brockedon was complaining in print about an English family who stayed in the hospice on the St. Bernard Pass (an institution that featured in several of Smith's novels and in his travel writing) and recording his disbelief that 'such vulgarity could have reached the Great St. Bernard'.[31] Brockedon was astonished that 'such persons' would even have contemplated an Alpine journey, and he admitted that 'I had no idea that the gentilities of Wapping had ever extended so far from the Thames.'[32] But whereas 'such persons' were the exception in 1833, even by the early 1850s the number of members of the lower middle classes who were able to travel to the Alps – and abroad in general – had greatly increased. In an odd twist, Albert Smith himself was complaining about this in an article written just a year after his own influential Mont Blanc climb. 'Even we ourselves, when abroad with the rest, are completely paralysed with the sight of the mobs of English that are running about over every habitable corner of the Continent', he wrote. He continued in language strangely similar to that which would be used later in the century to condemn the very visitors who he himself had inspired:

We pass over Paris and Baden-Baden, for they have become almost portions of our own country, whatever opinion to the contrary may be held by Louis Philippe and the Grand Duke. But we will go further abroad – again, the same crowd of our countrymen awaits us. They climb the snowy mountains, and traverse the clear blue lakes of Switzerland; they swelter in the noontide sunshine of the smoothly-paved cities of Italy; they plunge into the bowels of the great pyramids of Egypt, or turn dizzy on the summits of the minarets of Constantinople; whilst their travelling wants transport bottled porter to Athens and Windsor soap to Calabria. Doubtless, before another year has passed, an English hotel and tea-gardens will be established in the heart of Canton.[33]

By the 1860s the number of people visiting the Alps who could be designated as 'cockneys' had risen enormously. Mass tourism became the engine of its own expansion – as more and more people began to visit the Alps, so the infrastructure to feed, accommodate, and transport them around grew, in turn attracting more and more tourists. New hotels sprung up in formerly remote Alpine villages; the funicular railway to the summit of the Rigi had by the end of the century been joined by others to the top of the Gotthard Pass, and to the summits of Mount Pilatus, Wengern Alp, and Gornergrat;[34] regional railway lines extended more and more into Alpine valleys; and a growing number of local people were employed in the burgeoning tourist economy. Albert Smith may not have been wholly or even mainly responsible for this, but he was certainly considered by many commentators at the time to be one of the prime factors in this process. As early as 1856, Herman Merivale was writing in the *Edinburgh Review* that the Swiss township of Zermatt had 'become a second Chamouni; but with nothing, yet, of the Cockneyism, the Albert Smithery, the fun, frolic and vulgarity of that unique place of resort'.[35]

The phrases 'Cookite', 'tripper', and 'Cockney' increasingly featured in writing about Alpine travel during this period. The 'cockney' visitor became such a recognized social archetype that by 1874, Henry and Athol Mayhew's play, *Mont Blanc* (Theatre Royal, Haymarket) could introduce a character called Chirpy, who intends to create publicity for his pickle business by climbing the mountain.[36] Perhaps nowhere was it more insistently repeated, though, than in the pages of mountaineering literature. Writing the chapter on Alpine climbing in Anthony Trollope's *British Sports and Pastimes* (1868), for example, Leslie Stephen suggested that the 'true' mountaineer who ascends the high Alps 'bears away indelible impressions such as are hidden from the traveller confined to the valleys, and tormented by cockneys and inn-keepers'.[37] Stephen would go on to describe a particular inn at Chamonix as 'an oasis in a desert of cockneydom', while in *The Playground of Europe* (also published in 1871) he claimed that 'the bases of the mountains are immersed in a deluge of cockneyism', and in a paper given to his fellow Alpine Club members in 1874 he described the Montenvers as one of 'the most cockney-ridden of all the well-known points of view' in the Alps.[38]

Leslie Stephen clearly had something of an obsession with the spectre of the cockney tripper, but he was far from alone in his characterization of lower-middle-class tourists. Rather, his distinction between the pure, unalloyed experience of the high mountains and the touristic hell experienced – and created – by the undiscerning cockneys down in the valleys was to become a recurrent theme of mountaineering literature in the second half of the century. There was a sense that the 'trippers' did not and could not enjoy access to the same quality of experience as the mountaineers and that by their very presence they were polluting and diluting the experience for everyone. By the middle of the 1870s, when Douglas Freshfield was writing about his experiences in the Italian Alps, the 'incursion of cockneydom' had become such a commonplace of mountaineering writing that the author could mention it virtually in passing.[39]

Some of this was simple class enmity and snobbery – as when, for example, Stephen's wife Minnie Thackeray wrote to her sister during her 1867 honeymoon to complain that their Zermatt hotel was 'swarming with the most alarming kind of vermin, including commercial travellers'. Zermatt, Minnie wrote, 'used to be a little heaven here below (especially last year) & now it is going to be inundated with beings of the most contemptible shopkeeper order'.[40] But many other complaints about mass tourism were fed by a growing understanding that the Alps were a fragile environment, increasingly threatened by the spread of railways and other tourist infrastructure.

This latter concern would turn out to be prescient. By the end of the century, the rise of what we now call winter sports had put the finishing touches to the commodification of Alpine travel. This, of course, was long after his death, but it was the culmination of a process that Smith had helped put in motion back in the 1850s. Smith's legacy consisted not only of cockney trippers and Cook's tourists, but eventually of cable cars, ski lifts, pylons, and the whole infrastructure of skiing that developed and expanded in the twentieth century – development that has altered the Alpine environment permanently.

Albert Smith had 'sold' the Alps to a wider public than ever before. The relatively small elite who could afford to visit areas like the valley of Chamonix, inspired by its depiction in the pages of Romantic literature, or who could undertake lengthy and expensive mountaineering expeditions to unclimbed peaks, were now joined by the type of person whose parents and grandparents had probably never left their home country.

As a result, the profile of visitors to the Alps, and the reasons they came, were far less homogenous than in the past. In the early years of the nineteenth century the characteristic image of the Alpine visitor had probably been that of Caspar David Friedrich's 1818 painting, *The Wanderer above the Sea of Fog*, in which a masterful figure stands on a mountain precipice, gazing down over the sublime landscape. By the late nineteenth century this image still had some cultural currency, but it had been joined by a host of others. What *was* the typical image of the Alpine traveller in the second half of the century? Was it Albert Smith and his companions, drinking toasts in champagne on the Grands Mulets and then sliding their empty bottles down the glacier for the sheer hell of it? Or the tall, austere figure of Leslie Stephen making the first ascent of the Schreckhorn in 1861? Or was it the hapless 'Doctor of Laws' on his first Alpine climbing trip being rescued by his guides from his undignified position 'deep down in a crevasse' as described by John Hill Burton in 1864?[41] Or the self-reliant figure of Albert Mummery, dispensing with guides to pioneer some of the most challenging routes in the Alps before his death on one of the first Himalayan climbing expeditions in 1895? Or was it the 'trippers' who crowded the slopes of the Montenvers and the Rigi, or who chose to catch a funicular to the top of an Alpine pass rather than get there under their own steam? The sheer variety of mountain experiences in the years after Smith's Mont Blanc show defies easy categorizations, and even within the relatively small and esoteric world of serious mountaineers – in the pages of the *Alpine Journal* and the other climbing club journals that began later in the century – there were debates about the meaning, ethos, and direction of mountain climbing. But to some degree or other, all these different visitors to the Alps in the second half of the century were Smith's descendants – the people to whom he had sold the Alps as a desirable and aspirational landscape in which to climb, explore, or simply have fun.

17: 'NO 1 SING-SONG PIGEON MAN'

The Chinese were greatly puzzled by what to make of Mr. Albert Smith. Hong Kong Daily Press, 1858.

'The time has come – I can scarcely believe it – for me to say "Goodbye" to Mont Blanc', Smith told his audience on 5 July 1858, the final performance of the 'Ascent'.

'An hour before the doors opened the foot-traffic of Piccadilly was impeded by the crowd stretching into the roadway' reported the *Daily News*, 'and such shouts of laughter and applause welcomed each joke and song that a provincial visitor might have imagined he was attending the inauguration rather than the departure of this popular favourite.' Smith took leave of his audience with the simple declaration that, 'Having had the honour of telling you the same story in this same room two thousand times up to this evening, I will not venture to refer to it, for you must know it almost as well as I do.' He proceeded to tell them about his plans to visit China, and promised that when his new show resumed he would endeavour to make the hall even more comfortable and to improve the layout of the hall to provide 'clear, comfortable view of everything that is going on'. He finished with a flourish: 'I now release you from your flattering attention until December.'[1] Three days later he was on his way to China.

Smith was by now one of the most famous men in the country. His connections were enviable, although there were still those (notably among his fellow Garrick and Fielding club members) who sneered at his bouncing cockney style. In particular, his relationship with Thackeray – always fraught, although never as straightforwardly hostile as it had been with Jerrold, who died in 1857 – was to go through a series of minor crises. In 1857, a mutual friend called Joe Robbins got into financial difficulties through an unrealistic ambition to become a professional actor: 'giving up his job for a career on the boards, he quickly ruined himself', as Thackeray biographer D. J. Taylor puts it.[2] A subscription was raised to help him, and Thackeray heard and took seriously a rumour that Smith had declined to contribute. Thackeray circulated a caricature, in which 'Robbins was represented wounded by thieves and being assisted by some good Samaritan, also portrayed, while Albert Smith, the Pharisee of the parable, was passing scornfully on the other side'.[3] Smith had in fact been quietly giving Robbins financial assistance before the fund was set up. His own reaction is not recorded, but Thackeray seems to have been genuinely contrite when he realized his mistake, writing to Dickens that he had been 'egregiously wrong and Smith's conduct has been quite right and generous'.[4]

Not long before Smith left for China, he became tangentially involved in what became known as the Garrick Club Affair – a storm in a clubland teacup whose only real significance was in the fault lines it exposed between various eminent Garrick members, Thackeray and Dickens prominent among them. The story has been told numerous times, most recently by Barbara Black in her 2012 study of Victorian clubland, *A Room of His Own*, but in short it erupted when Thackeray accused Edmund Yates, at this stage still an eager young journalist, of betraying private conversations (or what he referred to in *Cornhill to Cairo* as 'the sacred confidence of the mahogany') in the Club by repeating them in print. Yates had written an unflattering profile of Thackeray, published in 1858 in a new publication called *Town Talk*, and the resulting furore drew in Dickens and various other Garrick luminaries.[5] Smith sided with Yates and Dickens, but the general meeting of the club which was called to resolve the matter took place on 10 July, by which time he had already left the country.

Smith's relationship with Thackeray is interesting because it underlines his still ambiguous class position. Broadly speaking, Thackeray was associated with an older and more aristocratic set at the Garrick (although he was only five years older than Smith), and most accounts suggest that he barely tolerated Smith, considering him a vulgar upstart, while Smith seems to have hankered for the social cachet that acceptance by Thackeray would have bestowed upon him. He wrote to Dickens from Paris in October 1855, angling for an invitation to a dinner in Thackeray's honour at which Dickens was to preside. Smith had read about it, appropriately enough, in *Galignani's Messenger,* and wrote somewhat forlornly, 'I should very much like to be there. Will you oblige me with one line, telling me when it is, and I will run over.'[6] For Smith, then at the height of his fame and popularity, to be reduced to this undignified attempt to gatecrash a private event suggests how badly he craved Thackeray's approval.

Yet whatever his private feelings, Thackeray was generally civil to Smith in public, seems to have been genuinely remorseful over the 'Pharisee' cartoon, and in 1860 – just a month before Smith's death – he gave an address to the Garrick in which he referred to Smith as 'the mighty traveller and industrious Companion of our order we all know and admire'. There may have been an element of sarcasm here – in the same speech he referred to Smith as 'Sir Albert of Waltham', and he was known to refer to him ironically as 'Albert the Great'.[7] But Thackeray's references to Smith, both in public and in his correspondence, are ambiguous enough to suggest that his feelings towards him were more complex than the simple contempt that has sometimes been assumed.

'Albert Smith starts for Hong Kong, via Marseilles, tomorrow night, a hot and weary journey for a man of his figure', wrote Dickens to William Howard Russell on 7 July. Dickens added that he had recommended to Smith 'Sheridan's advice as to saying he saw it, and not putting himself out of the way to go to see it' (the playwright Richard Brinsley Sheridan had supposedly responded with this remark when his son proposed going down a coal mine 'for the pleasure of saying he had done so').[8] Smith ignored this, just as he had ignored those who said he was too old and unfit to climb Mont Blanc, and his voyage to China was to provide him with a wealth of new experiences and material for another show, as well as a large collection of Chinese memorabilia. Arguably it also broke his health permanently, leading to his death just eighteen months after his return to Britain.

Smith's journey to China took over six weeks. He took the overland route from Alexandria to Suez, then by boat through the Red Sea to Aden, and on to Ceylon, Penang (off the west coast of Malaysia), and Singapore, finally arriving at Hong Kong on 21 August.

It was a hot, gruelling, and on occasion dangerous voyage, with dubious fellow passengers, bad food, and long periods of boredom. Despite this, his diary of the trip still makes for entertaining reading. From entering the harbour of Alexandria, 'piloted in by an Arab, grubbily resplendent with the dirty finery that characterizes the Eastern races generally', whereupon 'a crowd of swarthy beings still dirtier swarmed up the sides and about the deck and lower rigging, climbing, squabbling, and jabbering like so many apes', through to being awarded the title 'No. 1 Sing-Song Pigeon Man' after a performance of his Mont Blanc show at Hong Kong, Smith's account is full of the bracing humour, sweeping racial generalizations, blithe disregard for conventionality, and contempt for danger that characterized his earlier travel writing. Warned at Alexandria that Bedouin rebels are 'coming up the Red Sea, in forty boats, to take Suez, and that it was also their intention to plunder the mail and murder the passengers', he mildly notes in his diary that 'This was unpleasant news, and we all naturally felt rather anxious', then promptly sets off for Suez anyway.[9] At a railway buffet en route to the Red Sea port, he remarks, 'Here was another large refreshment barrack, with more nasty things to repress one's appetite.'

At Suez he joined a vessel called the *Bentinck*, with a crew composed of 'Lascars, Sepoys, Cingalese, Malays, "Simale-boys", "Seedy-boys", Ethiopians, and Chinese. The latter were out and away the cleanest and most industrious', he noted. 'The row these creatures made, when the mails and baggage were being embarked – the native swearing, chattering, fighting, and jabbering – was awful.'[10] From here on,

Smith's diary gives the sense of an almost trance-like boredom and lassitude in the numbing heat of a sea voyage ('All the passengers complaining more or less – very seedy, and unable to eat. Dozed through the greater part of the day'), interspersed with the odd incongruous or alarming incident. At Galle, the fortified city on the southwestern coast of Ceylon, he was gratified to find copies of *Ledbury* and *Christopher Tadpole* for sale, while a few days later, in the middle of the Bay of Bengal, he reveals in passing, and without comment, that the *Bentinck's* cargo is opium, destined for the lucrative Chinese market: 'Some of the people say that the smell of the opium cargo, which is very strong, makes them drowsy.' Although he does not mention it in his diary, Smith was travelling during the period of the Second Opium War (1856-60), when Britain and France attempted to force the opening up of China to their merchants and the legalization of the opium trade.

Smith mentions a number of times in his diary how incurious he finds his fellow passengers. Many of them had lived for years in China, but had nothing interesting or useful to tell him about it. 'The other passengers did not read, or do anything; they would sit for hours looking at the sea, or trimming their nails with penknives, or talking mercantile, about freights, and exchanges, and dollars.' Smith, with his lively, enquiring mind and his boundless energy, clearly found the enforced inactivity of the voyage a trial, rendered worse by the bovine indifference of his fellow passengers. He himself proved to be as good an observer as ever. In Singapore, for example, he wrote about local fruit and plants, the printing presses of the *Straits Times*, Buddhist temples, the way barbers shave customers with rice-water instead of lather, and, of course, about the food.

Arriving in Hong Kong, he tasted sharks-fin soup and frog curry, and again remarked on the incurious habits of many British residents. 'From the majority it was difficult to get any practical hints respecting the native habits of the people themselves – those small prominent traits about which the public most care.' This was Smith the showman thinking in advance about material for his next performance. Later on in his journey he would again express his frustration at,

> the almost remarkable ignorance of every feature and phase of Chinese life, pe-
> culiar to the "Commercials" out here. The Almighty Dollar, in its relations to
> tea, silk, and opium, is the only study, or source of thought, with them; and
> what they can possibly do, when left to themselves, to get through the day,
> beyond smoking and tea-tasting, is to me a matter of the most marvellous
> incomprehensibility.

Despite this, Smith seems to have enjoyed social success among the expat community in Hong Kong. He gave a charity performance of 'Mr Albert Smith's Entertainment, Chiefly Relating to the Travelling English, and their Autumnal Peculiarities on the Continent', with characters including 'Mr. Muff, a London

Swell, who is bored' and of course Edwards the Engineer (this appears to have been broadly the same show that he performed for Victoria at Osborne House). 'I never had so good an audience, and literally everybody was there, from Sir John Bowring [Governor of Hong Kong, 1854-9] and Sir Michael Seymour [Commander-in-Chief of the East Indies and China stations during the Second Opium War] downwards', he wrote, clearly gratified.

> Some of my attacks on the routine of conventional society appeared to startle them a little at first, and they looked at one another with that expression, which I know so well with my London morning audiences from the suburbs, of 'Good gracious! What will he say next? Ought we to laugh at this or not?' But I evidently had a few old Piccadilly friends in the room, to tell them it was all right and perfectly well received at this Hall; and then, of course, they entered into it.[11]

A cutting from the *Hong Kong Daily Press*, reproduced by Smith in the handbook to the 'Mont Blanc to China' show he staged on his return, gives an idea of the impression he made (although Smith was naturally selective in the local press reports he used). The colony's main English-language paper recorded that

> The Chinese were greatly puzzled by what to make of Mr. Albert Smith. He mixed with them as much as he possibly could, and tickled them amazingly with his drollery. They saw he was a celebrity among his countrymen, and they came to the conclusion he was something between a sage and a funny devil.[12]

Upon his departure from Hong Kong, he was awarded a hero's send-off, with a sedan chair to transport him from the club where he was staying to the wharf where he joined his P&O vessel home, music, fire crackers, and numerous gifts of presents and trinkets, many of which would end up in the Egyptian Hall. Smith had already spent a good deal of time during his visit seeking out what he called 'properties' – memorabilia and decorations that could be used upon his return to the stage. Noting a sign in a Hong Kong restaurant that the proprietors would not be responsible for anything stolen, for example, he promptly copied it for the Egyptian Hall.

Smith was gratified by his reception in Hong Kong, and lost no opportunity to let his audience in London know how well he had been received there. But he was also clearly bored by the dull provincialism and bad manners he perceived around him in the colony, and even more so on the voyage home when he shared a vessel with a group of Anglo-Indians on their way 'home' to England.[13] 'I am finishing up my diary, in my room, in the costume of an ancient statue', he wrote in Hong Kong, 'the crickets wearing themselves out with creaking, and the click of the billiard balls, and the perpetual cries of "Boy" sounding all over the club'. Never the most racially enlightened of men, even by the standards of his time, he nonetheless seems to have found attitudes to local servants troubling, or at least unnecessarily rude. He particularly disliked the colonial habit of shouting 'Boy' to attract the attention of waiters and other servants, and remarked on it a number of times. In an appendix to his diary, he published a section called *Of Indian Snobs,* which begins, 'Sometimes I meet people who irritate me very much, and I wish it was allowable, in polite society, to throw something at their heads; but I was most made so continuously angry by a lot of people I met coming home from India in one of the Peninsular and Oriental Boats.' He continued:

> You would have thought that India was the world, and England some small province, somewhere or another, used for brewing beer and preserving provisions [...] The manner of all these people towards the servants of the ship was most atrocious. They looked upon them as so many niggers, to be driven and ordered about as occasion required; and not a word of civility or acknowledgement ever passed their lips towards their inferiors. They were all helplessly, hopelessly, idle; and could not even move a cushion from one chair to another without calling their 'Boy!' whom they would afterwards keep tugging the punkahs for hours, until his arms must have been ready to drop off.

His animosity towards this kind of colonial boorishness did not diminish after his return. Writing to William Howard Russell, who had evidently sent him a manuscript version of his Indian diaries (they were published in two volumes in 1860 as *My Diary in India*), Smith pronounced himself delighted with the book. Russell had fearlessly described some of the atrocities perpetrated by both sides during and after the Rebellion of 1857, but he was equally merciless in detailing the overweening arrogance of many colonial administrators when dealing with Indian officials. 'The smallest English official treats their prejudices with contempt, and thinks he has a right to visit them [local rulers] just as he would call on a gamekeeper in his cottage', Russell had complained, describing 'the insolence and rudeness of some of the civilians to the sirdars and chiefs in the north-west after the old war'.[14] This was clearly grist to Smith's mill, and he wrote a magnificently splenetic note to 'Billy', congratulating him on

> the view you have taken of the windbag snobbish conventionality of all the stuck-up dry-winded sweaty Anglo-Indians believing they are somebodies over there, instead of being a set of currie-brained, chutney-boweled, Parsee-writing, chow-chow bloated, 'boy'-bawling sons of prickly-heated bitches and be damned to them. You will see from the latest song I enclose from my diary ("Handbook Sixpence!") what I thought of them.[15]

The song Smith refers to comes at the end of the *Indian Snobs* section of his own published diary, and is called 'Great Failure in the East'. It includes a succinct skewering of the 'fishing fleet' that brought unmarried British women out to

India to look for husbands: 'Worst of all, each steamer brings/Some lovely English girls/Here to be sold, for wedding rings/To Chutney-livered churls.'

With the exception of stops at Ceylon on the voyage out and back, Smith never actually visited the Indian subcontinent. Perhaps it was just as well.

Smith arrived back in Britain in mid-November 1858. It had been an exhausting and unhealthy journey, and friends who met him on his return noted that he seemed changed. 'He who had never known a finger-ache was constantly complaining', remembered Yates. 'The heat in China had played the deuce with him, he said; he had travelled too quickly; he wished he had contented himself with his Swiss holiday, and left the Eastern trip for another year.'[16]

Smith was not only in poor health. He had also become, as Yates put it, 'brusque and almost brutal'. Smith had always been slightly intolerant of strangers, Yates knew, but now he 'decidedly refused to make the acquaintance of anyone whom a common friend might wish to present. "Who is he?" "What has he done?" "I don't want to know him – I hate all strangers" – these were his frequent cries', recalled Yates, 'and one had constantly to bear in mind what an excellent fellow he really was, and what a valuable friend he had been, to keep the proper seal on one's lips under his irritation'.[17] He quarrelled with a mutual friend, then fell out with Yates when the friend was invited to a dinner party. Yates and Smith were later reconciled, but Yates realized with sadness that 'he was a changed man; the hard work, the late hours, and free living, spread over a long series of years, were beginning to show their effect'.

'Mr. Albert Smith's Mont Blanc to China' opened at the Egyptian Hall in late December 1858. The stage was set up to represent a flower-garden pavilion, part of a Cantonese shop, a pagoda, and other atmospherically Chinese scenes. There was no moving panorama this time – instead, in the background, there was a huge willow-pattern plate, although the show did feature static illustrations by Beverley. Around the hall Smith had hung scrolls with inscriptions translated into English from Chinese, 'of the kind ordinarily hung on the walls of Chinese apartments'. These included such supposed pearls of Oriental wisdom as, 'Good laughs make the best physic'; 'There is no crowd but you find a thief'; 'Oil quiets waves, smiles calm anger'; 'Dull books are foes to study'; and 'The back hair betrays the care'.

The first section of the show was partly an amalgam of the Mont Blanc and Overland Mail shows – although the ascent of Mont Blanc itself no longer played a huge part, Smith clearly felt it had become an important brand, a kind of shorthand for his own attractions as a narrator and showman. In his first season, views of the Mont Blanc ascent appeared in a kind of pre-show introduction that melded the familiar Mont Blanc material with a promise of new horizons. So

Part One was divided into two parts: in the first, 'The Deck of a Peninsular and Oriental Steamer, on the Mediterranean. Night. Where takes place a dream of the past, illustrating as in a vision, The Ascent of Mont Blanc.'

Smith then appeared on stage and described the voyage out; some of this material was adapted from 'The Overland Mail', but some – such as the voyage from Suez to Hong Kong – was brand new. Views by Beverley, painted from photos brought back by Smith, included Shepheard's Hotel in Cairo, Cairo street scenes, the desert and railway, and Singapore. The second part of the show was devoted to China and Hong Kong (Smith had travelled to Canton – now Guangdong – on the mainland during his visit, although most of his time had been spent on Hong Kong). The 'City and Harbour of Victoria, Hong Kong, then a Waterside Bazaar, Hong Kong, then the Bogue Forts on the Canton River' were among the scenes. This was followed by a 'Pre-Raphaelite Pictorial Panorama (by a Native Artist)', and finally 'Howqua's Gardens, near Canton'. Smith's narration during this second part included 'amusing gossip about pigtails and little feet, and Chinese barbers and tailors [and] specimens of Canton or "Pigeon English"'.[18] The programme ended with 'A Chinese song leading to a Well-Known View in China, where the latest day's events will be reviewed in *Galignani's Messenger*'.[19]

As well as new material, Smith had once again thought about the wider audience experience, and was as concerned as ever to enforce a certain minimum standard of behaviour. A 'New and Elegant Chinese Waiting Room has been opened for their accomodation [sic]', and patrons were 'asked not to leave their seats until the conclusion of the entertainment, as much annoyance and confusion is sometimes caused among the audience by persons moving in front of them a few minutes before the last scene'. There was also the usual Smith memorabilia for sale: willow pattern plates bearing Smith's image could be purchased for one shilling each (these quickly became collectible after Smith's death, when they changed hands for up to three guineas each).[20] There were also copies of Smith's *To China and Back* for 6d, or a shilling edition of the same book 'with Coloured Frontispiece, and Considerable Additions, Songs, &c, by Albert Smith'. Chinese fans made of palm leaf could also be purchased from the attendants, while copies of 'The China Times' ('circulates in Canton, Hammersmith, Amoy, Camberwell, Macao, Hackney, Hongkong, Camden Town, Pekin, Brixton, and all the Midland Counties', ran the masthead) replaced the 'Mont Blanc Gazette'. Like its predecessor, the 'China Times' was full of poems, jokes, riddles, as well as factual material to supplement the show. A copy from March, 1860 – which must have been one of the last produced, since Smith died not long afterwards – includes a short account of seeing captured Chinese pirates on the quayside at Canton, and a list of supposed Chinese proverbs which include 'When the tree falls the monkeys go away quickly', and 'A talkative schemer is one who climbs a tree to catch a fish.' These pamphlets, as usual, were liberally dotted with adverts for Smith's novels, and for the book version of his China diaries, published in 1859.[21]

Image of a commemorative plate created for Smith's 'Mont Blanc to China' show. Courtesy of Bill Douglas Cinema Museum, University of Exeter

If Smith was attentive to the comforts and behaviour of his audience, and their interest in buying souvenirs of the show, he was also fully aware of the interest that could be generated by macabre stories and objects. To this end, he had brought back and displayed what he claimed were the wooden crosses on which people were cut to pieces during a recent uprising. His accompanying leaflet to the show includes a particularly gruesome description of these 'instruments to which the victims were tied who were condemned to the special torture of being sliced to death':

> Upon one of these the wife of a rebel general was stretched, and her flesh was cut from her body [...] Her breasts were first cut off, then her forehead was slashed and the skin torn down over her face, then the fleshy parts of the body were sliced away. There are Englishmen still alive who saw this done.[22]

Somewhat incongruously, this grisly account is followed by the announcement that 'A Ladies' Toilet Room, with a female attendant, has been placed at their disposal.' It is not clear if this story formed part of Smith's actual narration – it seems unlikely, since it was not mentioned in the reviews. These were generally positive, as was the response of audiences. Smith was 'received with enthusiastic acclamations by a brilliant and numerous audience' on his first night, according to the *Morning Post,* while the *Standard* announced that the 'spectator is transported at once into China, and receives almost as many impressions on his senses of Chinese life as though he had accompanied the architect of the substantial vision before him on his formidable pilgrimage'.[23] According to the *Era,* 'Mr. Smith has never been more felicitous or happy in what he has performed' – its reviewer predicted that 'there can be no doubt that Mr. Albert Smith's "China" will be fully as popular as "Mont Blanc" and its predecessors'.[24] The suffragist and birth control campaigner Kate Stanley, who would later become Viscountess Amberley and mother to the philosopher Bertrand Russell, attended the show at the age of sixteen (in between visits to Thomas and Jane Carlyle and a ball at the home of the Duc d'Aumule). She wrote to her brother that she 'found it very amusing indeed though very vulgar & he really tells one nothing about China that one did not know before'. Her sister Blanche was irritated by the show, but Blanche's husband David Ogilvie and his friend Augustus Fox 'split almost with laughter – I think he would amuse you, he is such a good mimic'.[25]

The China show was certainly successful while it lasted, but somehow it never quite reached the same heights of popularity and acclaim as Smith's Mont Blanc entertainment. Even Yates, one of Smith's most consistent champions, admitted that while 'the experiment was a success, it never had the vitality or "go" of the old one'.[26] Nor did Smith. He finally married Mary Keeley in August 1859, and after a honeymoon in Chamonix the couple moved from Percy Street to a large house in Walham Green, Fulham, called North End Lodge, complete with stables, entrance lodge and carriage drive. But just before Christmas that year Smith suffered what was probably a stroke (it was variously described at the time as a 'convulsive seizure' and 'a partly epileptic, partly apoplectic stroke'), and from here onwards his health deteriorated rapidly.[27] He was confined to his house for three weeks, but insisted on resuming performances in January, repeatedly protesting that 'I have never felt better in my life; I am only surprised that I have not lost strength.'[28]

In February 1860 Smith invited Dickens to North End Lodge for dinner, at the same time inviting Helen Hogarth, his sister-in-law. Dickens, in the wake of his affair with Ellen Ternan and his rejection of his wife Catherine, had fallen out badly with Helen and her mother, who had taken Catherine's side and who he believed had urged her to file for divorce. He had bullied them into signing a formal statement repudiating 'certain statements' he believed had been made about him (essentially that he was having what would legally amount to an incestuous affair with his sister-in-law), and was still furious with them. Arthur Smith had already been involved in what became known as the 'Violated Letter' affair, when a statement issued by Dickens justifying his behaviour towards Catherine was leaked to the American press, although this does not seem to have affected relations between Dickens and Arthur.[29]

Whatever one thinks of Dickens's behavior towards his wife and the Hogarths, which was clearly appalling, it seems a strange move on Smith's part to have invited him to the same dinner party as Helen. Perhaps Smith was not fully aware of all the circumstances surrounding the affair, although that seems unlikely; perhaps the stroke had clouded his judgement; perhaps he simply felt that since Helen Hogarth had done nothing wrong, there was no reason not to invite her to his home. Whatever the reason, Dickens unsurprisingly declined the dinner invitation, writing to Smith, 'It is really painful to me to be unable to accept your invitation. Pray let it be understood between us, that this makes no difference in our friendship. But I can not be a guest at any house where Mrs. Hogarth's youngest daughter is received in the same capacity.'[30] Smith's reply is not recorded, but it was clearly hostile. Dickens wrote back the following day: 'I think you will find on reconsideration that you have not written me quite a good natured little letter.'[31] They never spoke again, and three months later Smith was dead.

During all this period, Smith was still performing at the Egyptian Hall. On 12 May he walked through the rain to the Garrick after his evening performance, arriving soaked, and soon contracted bronchitis. He had to cut the songs from his subsequent performances, and by 21 May his doctors had forbidden him to perform at all. Notices were put up at the Egyptian Hall apologizing for his absence – it was the first time he had ever missed a performance. Three different doctors attended him on the evening of the 22nd, but at half-past eight on the morning of 23 May, 1860, Smith died in the presence of his wife, Mary and his brother, Arthur. He was just one day short of his forty-fourth birthday.

For one of his era's most famous showmen, Albert Smith had requested a very modest funeral. He stipulated in his will that no more than twenty-five pounds (and preferably no more than twenty) be spent on the ceremony, and there were only a handful of mourners.[32] He was interred in the same grave at Brompton Cemetery, not far from his North End Lodge home, where his father had been buried three years before him, and where his brother Arthur would join him within a year. As well as his wife and blood relatives, the chief mourners included his father-in-law Robert Keeley, his executor Arthur Pratt-Barlow, and his solicitor Edward Lane.

Edmund Yates was there, too. Yates would later write of his friendship with Albert Smith that, 'I owe much of my life's happiness, amongst other items of it my wife' to him.[33] The last time they had spoken, Smith had been at North End Lodge, standing on the lawn. 'When you come down next week', Smith had told him, 'this place will be lovely, for the pink may will then all be out.' The may blossom in fact appeared on the day Smith died.[34]

Albert Smith. Courtesy of Bill Douglas Cinema Museum, University of Exeter

CONCLUSION

I step outside the hut at half-past-midnight, the high peaks around me visible in silhouette under the starlight. From somewhere up above I can hear the slither of an avalanche and the rumble of falling rocks.

Stuart and I are the first pair of climbers to leave the hut. By the light of our head torches we tie in to either end of the rope, strap on crampons, and begin to climb up the Glacier du Dôme to the point where we will join the ridge to the summit of Mont Blanc.

I visited Chamonix in the summer of 2014 to compare the experience of climbing Mont Blanc today with that described by Albert Smith over one hundred and sixty years earlier. Alpine mountaineering, however, is an activity that begins and ends early in the day, before the heat of the sun starts to melt snow and ice, increasing the risk of rockfall and generally making climbing conditions less favourable. As a result, I found myself with plenty of time in the late afternoons and evenings to poke around the town for evidence of Albert Smith's time there.

I wonder if Smith's legacy will be any more visible here than in his home country. The traces of his life and career vanished remarkably quickly after his death in 1860. His brother Arthur died in 1861, and Smith's widow Mary soon put the palatial North End Lodge property up for auction; Mary herself would die of consumption in 1870. Of the other people who were closest to Smith, his mistress, Pattie Oliver, continued to act professionally and became manager of the Royalty Theatre in Soho in the late 1860s, but died of cancer at the age of 46.[1] His old friend Edmund Yates went on to a successful career as a journalist, novelist, and dramatist. As mentioned earlier, Yates turned down the chance to write his old friend's biography in the early 1890s, deciding Smith was simply too obscure to be of interest to the reading public.

Even at the Egyptian Hall, Smith's legacy was not to last for long. By the mid-1860s his show already seems to have been considered something of an anachronism, ripe for parody by the American entertainer Artemis Ward, who began a comic lecture and panorama at the Hall in 1866 in which he parodied Smith's boasts about improvements and the pains he took for his audience. 'During the Vacation the Hall has been carefully swept out, and a new Door Knob has been added to the Door', Ward announced, offering to 'call on the Citizens of

London, at their residences, and explain any jokes in his narratives which they may not understand'.[2] Other shows at the Hall after Smith's death included exhibitions of electro-biology and phrenology; 'The Highways and Byways of Song', a performance of popular songs by Mr. Frederic Pena; and an appearance by M. Robin, the Original French Wizard, and his Soirées Fantastiques, as well as exhibitions more directly influenced by Smith's, such as Hamilton's Excursions to the Continent. In this show, which ran from the early 1870s, a diorama of various European scenes, including the Mer de Glace from Montenvers and Mont Blanc itself, was introduced by Mr. Leicester Buckingham and 'accompanied by appropriate National Music'.[3] Smith's influence was still evident even in the style of the handbills for this performance, but the entertainment world had moved on and the Egyptian Hall was soon to become one of the earliest venues in London for showing animated pictures. By the late nineteenth century it was primarily given over to conjuring acts, with the renowned magician John Nevil Maskelyne making it his 'Home of Mystery' for many years. It was finally demolished in either 1904 or 1905, and with it the last trace of Albert Smith's extraordinary career seemed to have disappeared forever.[4]

At first glance, Smith seems equally absent from the valley he called 'the nicest place in Europe'. The history of mountaineering is, of course, visible everywhere in the commune of Chamonix-Mont Blanc, to give it its full title. From the town centre statues of Mont Blanc's first climbers, Balmat and Paccard, and their sponsor Saussure, to the names of the streets and the natural features in the surrounding hills, the legacy of climbing in the development of this town from small, impoverished hamlet to prosperous, multinational tourist resort is inescapable. A Promenade Marie Paradis and a Route Henrietta d'Angeville commemorate the first two women to reach the summit of Mont Blanc. Other streets are named after prominent local mountain guides; the Chemin de Francis Devouassoux, the Avenue Michel Croz, the Chemin Gabriel Loppé, and the Rue Joseph Vallot, not to mention the Espace Tairraz exhibition hall. The Britons who forged the Golden Age are commemorated, too. Chamonix boasts a Rue Mummery and a Rue Whymper, and the surrounding mountains have features named Signal Forbes, Pointe Whymper, and Col Freshfield. The grave of Edward Whymper can be found in the town's cemetery, along with memorials to generations of local guides.[5] John Ruskin, arch-critic of mountaineers but lover of mountains, is also commemorated by the Pierre à Ruskin, and a street of the same name that leads to it.

Albert Smith – the man who did so much to popularize Chamonix and Mont Blanc in the 1850s, and who helped pave the way for the popularity of Alpine tourism in the second half of the nineteenth century – appears missing from these public memorials. Scratch the surface, though, and traces of Smith's presence remain. The building owned by Victor Tairraz, where Smith stayed on his first visit to Chamonix in 1838 and on all his subsequent visits, stands on the edge of Place Balmat in the town centre. Known as the Hôtel de Londres when Smith was here, it later became the Hôtel de Londres et Angleterre, and although it no longer functions as a hotel – its ground floor is now given over to a bank and a florist, while the upper storeys are residential – the structure is essentially the same as when Smith stayed here. Its residents can now look down from their balconies at the statue of Saussure and Balmat, depicting the peasant guide pointing out the route to the summit of Mont Blanc to his Genevan sponsor and client. Across the River Arve – near the train station where a cog railway still carries tourists up to Montenvers and what Smith derided as the 'ploughed field' of the Mer de Glace – Chamonix's small Anglican church has a plaque to Smith above its doorway, erected by Arthur after his brother's death. Arthur himself is commemorated by another plaque on the same wall, placed there 'by friends to whom he was very dear' after his own death in October 1861. Back on the eastern side of the Arve, the headquarters of the Compagnie des Guides can still be found in the same building from where Smith's mammoth troupe of guides would have been hired. Nearby, a temporary street exhibition on the 'Histoires au Mont Blanc' mentions Smith's contribution to 'la notoriété du Mont Blanc'

For such a colourful, noisy character, Albert Smith's legacy in Chamonix is surprisingly low-key, but it lingers nonetheless and is likely to become more prominent. In the summer of 2015, the town plans to commemorate the sesquicentennial anniversary of the conquest of the Matterhorn and the end of the Alpine Golden Age. A variety of events – lectures, exhibitions, and commemorative climbs – are scheduled, and there are even plans to reissue Albert Smith's board game, the 'New Game of Mont Blanc' as a souvenir. Suddenly, after being virtually forgotten for years, it seems that Albert Smith's name is once again being heard in Chamonix.

* * *

The Gonella hut stands on the Italian side of Mont Blanc, some 3,070 metres above sea level. To reach it, we had spent much of the previous day trekking from Italy's Val Veni up the vast, debris-strewn Miage glacier, then on to a dramatic mountain path whose upper reaches are equipped with fixed ropes. Mountain refuges can be spartan but the Gonella hut, rebuilt in 2011, is clean and comfortable, its young guardians provide delicious Italian food, and the views in every direction are breathtaking. Sixteen climbers, mostly French and Italian, are staying here in preparation for an early morning ascent of Mont Blanc – or rather Monte Bianco, since we are approaching the mountain from Italy. We eat dinner in the early evening and retire to bed until midnight, waking for a snatched breakfast then out into the night to begin climbing.

Albert Smith's route up Mont Blanc via the Grand Mulets is no longer navigable at this time of year; a patchwork of crevasses, and giant seracs that could topple over at any moment, make it too dangerous for a summer ascent, although it can still be navigated on skis in the winter. Our approach from the Gonella hut is much less well-known and thus less crowded than the usual routes from the French side of the mountain. Stuart, my guide, has climbed Mont Blanc roughly thirty times before, but this is his first time on this particular route. Known as the Voie Normale or Italian Normal Route, it is sometimes also known as the Pope Route, as it was first used (as a descent route) in 1890 by a climbing party that included the future Pope Pius XI, Achille Ratti.

I have climbed fairly extensively in Britain but this week has been my introduction to the new skills of Alpine mountaineering, and I do not cover myself in glory during the early stages of the ascent. Befuddled and nervous, within half an hour of leaving the hut I have managed to fall into a crevasse – fortunately only a small one, but deep enough to trap my right foot, threatening the loss of my crampons. I expand valuable energy attempting to dig myself out with my ice axe, until Stuart is forced to climb back down the glacier to help me. Suffering fools gladly is not one of Stuart's many strengths, and he offers some choice words of advice while extricating me.

We continue up to the Piton des Italiens, the point where the Dôme glacier meets the ridge leading up to the summit of Mont Blanc. Conditions on the glacier had been calm and benign, but the wind up here is ferocious and the sense of exposure intimidating. The knife-edge ridge falls away on either side in steep snow slopes, and we move in single file at a steady uphill pace, roped together more closely than on the glacier. The lights of settlements far below add to the sense of immense elevation and isolation. The climbing is technically straightforward, but I am all too aware that without the skill and experience of a professional guide I would now be in a terrifying and dangerous position. Stuart, a Chamonix mountain guide who has climbed everywhere from Alaska to Antarctica, with ascents of Everest and other Himalayan summits thrown in, exudes calmness and competence. He walks in front and I try to move at a pace that keeps the rope between us neither too tight nor too slack.

Occasionally I glance back down towards the glacier to see the head torches of the climbers who have left the hut behind us strung out along the route. The sun comes up around half-past-five, bathing the summit ridge in an orange glow, and we stop near the Vallot hut – originally the site of a scientific observatory built in the nineteenth century, but now a rudimentary bivouac shelter – to briefly rest and eat. We have now joined the main route to the summit from Chamonix, over the north-western flank of the Dôme du Goûter, and I become aware that we are also joining a stream of other climbers. Most are still on their way up to the summit, although some are already descending. I have spent several days acclimatizing, sleeping in mountain huts at high altitude and climbing other peaks in the Mont Blanc massif, but once we reach the Vallot hut – which sits at over 4,300 metres – I begin to struggle. Even walking on a flat surface at this altitude is challenging, and as we move uphill across the Bosses Ridge towards the summit I feel as though a plastic bag has been placed over my head. The pace slows, and I am forced to make frequent stops to catch my breath.

Finally, seven-and-a-half hours after leaving the refuge, we are on top of Mont Blanc. One hundred and sixty three years earlier Albert Smith had stood on this same spot and reflected thus:

> We had laboured with all the nerve and energy we could command to achieve a work of downright unceasing danger and difficulty, which not more than one-half of those who try are able to accomplish, and the triumph of which is, even now, shared but by a comparative handful of travellers – and we had succeeded![6]

The contrast between then and now could hardly be more striking. By my estimate there are at least two hundred, perhaps three hundred other climbers moving up and down the mountain this morning. In the few minutes we spend on the summit, I hear French, Japanese, German, and English spoken. As we begin the long, arduous, knee-crunching descent to Chamonix, which we will finally reach some six hours later, more and more climbers are coming up behind us. On the narrower sections of the ridge we have to stop and wait for people coming uphill to pass us. The mountain is almost farcically overcrowded and it's impossible to retain the sense of remoteness and wildness I had felt in the early hours of this morning, as we attained the Piton des Italiens. Estimates of the number of people who attempt to climb Mont Blanc every year vary between 20,000 and 30,000, many of them, like me, dilettante climbers with no real Alpine experience or skill. If Albert Smith's legacy is still faint in the town of Chamonix, up here it is perhaps all too evident.

The next day, too exhausted to climb, I take a cable car up to the Brévent, a 2,500-metre peak on the other side of the valley from Mont Blanc. I walk a short distance from the crowded terrace of the cable car station and look across at the mountain. From here I can trace the details of Albert Smith's route to the summit, as well as my own line of descent from the day before. The Brévent has the same polyglot mix of visitors as the town of Chamonix below it and the summit of Mont Blanc across the valley.

A day later I join another local guide, Mark, on the 6.30am cable car to the Aiguille du Midi, one of the great granite needles that tower above the valley of Chamonix. This first transport is crowded with alpinists, along with a sprinkling of Japanese tourists, eager to see the fabled Chamonix Aiguilles before heading off on the next stage of their whistle-stop tour of the Alps. Mark and I emerge from the tunnel of the cable car station onto a narrow arête of snow, then descend to below the south face of the Aiguille du Midi. We climb a relatively short but exhilarating route called the Cosmiques Arête, finishing by clambering up a wobbly metal ladder onto the cable car station, to an audience of startled tourists. We were lucky to be the first climbers on the ridge. It is one of the most popular routes in the area, and by the time we head back down to Chamonix groups are starting to queue at the base.

This, too, is part of Smith's legacy – the crowds, the queues, the jostling for position on popular climbing routes, the tourists ticking off one breathtaking sight before rushing on to the next. It is the culmination of a process he helped to put in motion back in the 1850s, and which nowadays arguably brings as many problems as benefits to this region. I wonder what Smith would have made of it. Would he have been horrified by the commercialization and the 'mobs of English' – not to mention just about every other nationality – who now flock to the valley and its surrounding peaks, or would he have felt proud of the bustling prosperity of the town he loved and promoted?

I suspect Smith might have been more relaxed about the whole business than some of the British visitors who came after him. It's not hard to imagine the reaction of Leslie Stephen, for example, to the overcrowded peaks and the modern, globalized equivalent of the 'cockneys' he resented so much.[7] But sharing a cable car up to the Brévent with a young Polish woman who is spending her summer working in a mountain hut before taking up a place at the University of Grenoble, or watching families of tourists tracing the route of Balmat and Paccard's first Mont Blanc ascent on the multilingual information boards, I am reminded that Smith was always suspicious of anyone who believed the 'good old days' were better than the present, and remained profoundly interested in new technology and modes of transport and communication. He would, I imagine, have been delighted with the cable car that whisked me up here, and I think he might have welcomed the more democratic access to this stunning landscape enjoyed by twenty-first century visitors.

Or perhaps not. It is also entirely possible that Smith would have been horrified, and would have written about the 'jabbering' of foreign tongues and the overcrowding of his beloved mountain. George Orwell's biographer, Bernard Crick, once wrote about his suspicion of what he called the 'speculative teleology' of biography – in other words the temptation for biographers to wonder about their subjects' possible other lives: 'What would he have done had he lived differently or longer, the logic of the "real" character, not the grossly empirical course of the actual life.'[8] This is a temptation when writing about Smith, too: to ask what he would have made of modern mountaineering, of organized winter sports, of mass tourism; what he would have done next had he lived longer; or if he'd ever made it to America? Crick was making the point that such speculation is futile. It's impossible to know whether Albert Smith would have loved or hated present-day Chamonix. It is probably equally pointless to speculate in the other direction – to wonder how Alpine tourism would have developed if Smith's Mont Blanc show had never taken place. The biographer can only work with the facts of a life, and those of Smith's life are well-documented in some areas and remarkably thin in others.

Back in Britain I visit Brompton Cemetery, where Smith was buried. Opened in 1840, Brompton was one of a group of large, modern cemeteries sometimes referred to as the 'Magnificent Seven' that were built in this period to take the strain off inner city churchyards, as the urban population expanded and the question of how to dispose of the dead became a major concern. It is strangely beautiful in a gloomy, Gothic fashion, full of ornate gravestones, mausolea, and carved angels, and while some parts are groomed and manicured other sections are overgrown and wild, as though nature were reclaiming it at the edges. Many of Smith's fellow Victorian celebrities are buried here, including his friend William Howard Russell, suffragette Emmeline Pankhurst, medical pioneer John Snow, and Samuel Smiles, of *Self-Help* fame. The riot of ferns, bushes, and grass makes it difficult to locate some gravestones in the untended sections, and those that can be seen through the undergrowth are often faded beyond legibility.

Albert Smith's grave is close to the path, but only the top section of his headstone remains above ground and the original inscription is now illegible. However, at some point since his brother Arthur's death a small stone plaque has been added to this upper section of the headstone. Its inscription is quite clear, and it remains the only physical memorial to either brother in this country. The plaque eschews any grand theories about his legacy, his significance, or his place in history, in favour of a bald statement of fact. It reads simply:

Albert Smith

Arthur Smith

Mont Blanc

Egyptian Hall

1852-1860

ENDNOTES

INTRODUCTION

1   The Magic Circle, founded in the same year the Egyptian Hall was demolished, has placed a plaque in the hallway of Egyptian House, commemorating the Hall's importance as a venue for stage magicians in the late nineteenth century.

2   P. D. Edwards, *Dickens' 'Young Men': George Augustus Sala, Edmund Yates and the World of Victorian Journalism* (Aldershot: Ashgate, 1997), p. 194.

3   George Eliot recorded this request in her journal for 8 January, 1858; *The Yale Edition of the George Eliot Letters*, 6 vols, ed. by Gordon S. Haight (London: Oxford University Press; New Haven, CN: Yale University Press, 1954), II, 1852-1858, 418.

4   This anecdote crops up in a number of memoirs of the period, but the original source was probably Jerrold's grandson, Walter. See Walter Jerrold, *Douglas Jerrold and 'Punch'* (London: Macmillan, 1910), p. 35.

5   J. Monroe Thorington, *Mont Blanc Sideshow: The Life and Times of Albert Smith* (Philadelphia: John C. Winston Company, 1934), p. xi.

6   Peter Hansen, 'Albert Smith, The Alpine Club, and the Invention of Mountaineering in Mid-Victorian Britain', *Journal of British Studies*, 34 (1995), 300-324 (p. 300).

7   C. D. Cunningham and W. de W. Abney, *The Pioneers of the Alps* (London: Sampson Low, Marston, Searle, and Rivington, 1887), p. 20.

8   The phrase is from Leslie Stephen's best-selling mountaineering memoir of 1871, *The Playground of Europe*. Stephen's book was arguably as influential as Smith's show on a later generation of visitors to the Alps, although his tone and ethos were very far removed from that of Smith.

CHAPTER 1

1   Albert Smith, 'Theatrical Ashes', *Household Words*, 13 (1856), 217-20 (p. 217). This was actually the second time in its history that the theatre, which had a long and illustrious history, had burnt to the ground. The building that Smith knew had been rebuilt in 1809 after a fire the previous year destroyed the original 1732 structure.

2   One of these tiny oak-bound volumes survives in the Victoria and Albert Museum's Theatre and Performance Archive: PN 2596.L7 C8. 'Covent Garden, March 5 1856, Souvenir of the Burning of Covent Garden'. I am grateful to Simon Sladen of the V&A for drawing my attention to this item.

3   'Theatrical Ashes', p. 219. It seems likely that Albert attended the 1822 production of *Cherry and Fair Star* at Covent Garden, which would have made him six years old. This production was reviewed in *The Rambler's Magazine, Or, Fashionable Emporium of Polite Literature*, 1 (1822), p. 226.

4   Owen Manning and William Bray, *The History and Antiquities of the County of Surrey*

(London: John Nichols & Son, 1804-1814), p. 205.

5   The remark was attributed to Smith by Chertsey historian Lucy Wheeler in her 1905 book, *The Existence of the Past* (London: Wells Gardner, Darton & Co., 1905).

6   Claremont, a Palladian mansion just outside Esher, was purchased by Act of Parliament in the year of Smith's birth to become a residence for Princess Charlotte, daughter of George IV, and her husband Prince Leopold of Saxe-Coburg.

7   Charles Dickens, *Oliver Twist* (London: Richard Bentley, 1838), Book the First, Chapter 22; Book the Second, Chapters 7-12. There is no evidence to suggest that Smith met Dickens during his Chertsey visit, and in fact Smith was probably living in London at the time. They came to be on friendly term in later years, and Smith was regularly invited to dine at Dickens's London home. A real mansion near Chertsey, called Pycroft House, has been suggested as the original for the Maylie's house: see David Paroissien, *The Companion to Oliver Twist* (Edinburgh: Edinburgh University Press, 1992), p. 177; Percy Hetherington Fitzgerald, *Bozland: Dickens' Places and People* (London: Downey & Co., 1895),   p. 76.

8   For an account of Elizabeth's Armistead's career and her Chertsey funeral, see Katie Hickman, *Courtesans* (London: Harper, 2011) and I. M. Davis, *The Harlot and the Statesman: The Story of Elizabeth Armistead and Charles James Fox* (Bourne End, Buckinghamshire: The Kensal Press, 1986).

9   Unpublished manuscript by Lucy Wheeler, c. 1905, item CHYMS 0094/1 in Chertsey Museum.

10 The scope and impact of the Apothecaries' Act and other pieces of legislation was disputed at the time and remains the topic of debate among medical historians. Smith himself facetiously described an Apothecaries' Company diploma as 'a licence to kill human game by powder and ball, in the shape of calomel and bolus, which every person regularly qualified for that art must possess' (*Ledbury*, p. 170). However, there is no doubt that the period from around 1780 to the middle of the nineteenth century was, as Andrew Wear and Roger French put it, 'the Age of Reform, in medicine as in politics'. See Wear and French, eds., *British Medicine in an Age of Reform* (London and New York: Routledge, 1991). Further reform and reorganization of the profession would come in 1858, with the passing of the Medical Act, but by this time Richard Smith had been dead for a year and Albert had long since ceased to practice medicine. See M. Jeanne Peterson, *The Medical Profession in Mid-Victorian London* (Berkeley, CA: University of California Press, 1978).

11 Charles Dickens, *The Pickwick Papers* (London: Chapman and Hall, 1836-37), Chapter 30.

12 Albert Smith, *The Natural History of the Flirt* (London: David Bogue, 1848), p. 70.

13 Albert Smith, *The Adventures of Mr. Ledbury and His Friend Jack Johnson* (London: Richard Bentley, 1844), p. 127.

14 Quoted in John Black Atkins, *The Life of Sir William Howard Russell, C.V.O., LL.D., The First Special Correspondent*, 2 vols (London: John Murray, 1911), I, 112.

15 The only source I can find for Dickens's fishing trips comes in the *Surrey Archaeological Collections, Relating to the History and Antiquities of the County*, published by The Surrey Archaeological Society, Volume 30, (1917), p. 36.

16 Warwick Wroth, *The London Pleasure Gardens of the Eighteenth Century* (London: Macmillan, 1896), p. 318.

17 Albert Smith, 'An English Masquerade', in *Comic Sketches from the Wassail-Bowl*

(London: Richard Bentley, 1848), p. 36.

18 Albert Smith, 'Vauxhall', in *Gavarni in London: Sketches of Life and Character* (London: David Bogue, 1849), p. 92. The rather obscure phrase presumably means that he was head boy during a particular school year and retained the title when he moved into the fourth form. Smith attended the Merchant Taylors' School from 1826 to 1831 (the spelling of the name was changed from Tailor's to Taylors during his time there), and visited Vauxhall in 1827. David Coke and Alan Borg, in their monumental history of the Vauxhall Gardens, note that a Juvenile Fete took place on 14 July that year, but argue that Smith could not have witnessed the Waterloo reenactment on that occasion since it was cancelled to avoid frightening the young visitors: David Coke and Alan Borg, *Vauxhall Gardens: A History* (New Haven, CT and London: Yale University Press, 2011), p. 313 fn.

19 Smith, 'Vauxhall', p. 92.

20 Albert Smith, 'A Go-Ahead Day with Barnum', in *Bentley's Miscellany*, 21 (1847), 522-27 and 623-28 (p. 522).

21 Albert Smith, *A Pottle of Strawberries, to Beguile a Short Journey, or a Long Half Hour* (London: David Bogue, 1848), p. 9.

22 He also had something of a soft spot for Cairo and for Smyrna, was impressed by his first sight of Constantinople, and (as we shall see in Chapter 2) was immediately captivated by Chamonix. However, he was even disappointed in the famed Mer de Glace, the so-called 'Sea of Ice' glacier on the northern flank of Mont Blanc, remarking that it looked less like a frozen sea than a ploughed field: See Smith, 'Recollections of a Cheap Tour', *Bentley's Miscellany*, 24 (1848), 408-16. Darren Bevin points out that this tendency was not confined to Smith's non-fiction prose; his novels, too, 'are thematically concerned with the collision between expectation and reality': Darren Bevin, *Cultural Climbs: John Ruskin, Albert Smith and the Alpine Aesthetic* (Saarbrucken: VDM, 2010), p. 55.

23 Smith, 'Vauxhall', p. 91.

24 Smith, 'A Little Talk about Science and the Show-Folks', in *Wassail-Bowl*, p. 49.

25 Smith, 'An English Masquerade', p. 33.

26 Albert Smith, *To China and Back: Being a Diary Kept, Out and Home* (London: Chapman and Hall, 1859), p. 17 and p. 63.

27 John Timbs, *Anecdote Lives of the Later Wits and Humourists*, 2 vols (London: Richard Bentley, 1874), II, 110. Timbs had been editor of the *Mirror of Literature, Amusement, and Instruction* where Smith had work published early in his career: see Chapter 2 for more on this publication.

28 Albert Smith, *The Story of Mont Blanc* (London: David Bogue, 1853), p. 28.

29 Smith, *Mont Blanc*, p. 30.

30 *Story of Mont Blanc,* p. 1.

31 John Auldjo, *Narrative of an Ascent to the Summit of Mont Blanc, on the eighth and ninth of August, 1827* 3rd edition (1828; London: Longman, Green, Brown, and Longmans, 1856), p. 23. Many years later, in the Preface to the third edition of his book in 1856, Auldjo would pay his respects to 'my friend Albert Smith' who 'has drawn all classes, from royalty downwards, to hear the details of his ascent': Auldjo, *Narrative*, p. vii.

32 Auldjo, p. 2.

33 *The Peasants of Chamouni: Containing an Attempt to Reach the Summit of Mont Blanc, and a Delineation of the Scenery Among the Alps* (London: Baldwin, Cradock, and Joy, 1823), p. 15. The mountaineer Edward Whymper described it as 'a little twadly book,

which was published for the delectation of children': Edward Whymper, *Chamonix and the Range of Mont Blanc* (London: John Murray, 1896), p. 43.

34 The motives of Dr. Joseph Hamel, a Russian courtier and scientist, for attempting to climb Mont Blanc were typical of ascents made in the early part of the nineteenth century. Hamel wanted to carry out scientific experiments, including studying the oxygen content of air and blood at altitude on the summit. In the event, his party never made it to the summit, three guides being killed by an avalanche during the ascent. See Elisabeth Simons and Oswald Oelz, 'Mont Blanc with Oxygen: The First Rotters', in *High Altitude Medicine and Biology*, 2 (2001), 545-9.

35 *Peasants of Chamouni*, p. 158.

36 See Fergus Fleming, *Killing Dragons: The Conquest of the Alps* (London: Granta, 2000).

37 As Simon Schama points out, Saussure's *Voyages* had a similarly seductive effect on the fifteen-year-old John Ruskin, establishing a life-long interest in mountains. Ruskin's approach, however, could not have been more different from that of Smith. See Simon Schama, *Landscape and Memory* (New York: Alfred A. Knopf, 1995), p. 491.

CHAPTER 2

1 Merchant Taylors' School Register, 1561-1934, edited by Mrs. E. P. Hart. I am grateful to Sally Gilbert, Merchant Taylors' School Archivist, for tracking down this record.

2 See Anthony Trollope, *An Autobiography* (London: William Blackwood, 1883). Trollope also records in his autobiography meeting Smith for the first time in 1860, at a dinner for contributors given by George Smith, publisher of the *Cornhill Magazine* and *Pall Mall Gazette*, at which Thackeray, G. H. Lewes, John Everett Millais, and William Howard Russell were also present: see Trollope, p. 65.

3 The piece appears in *Bentley's Miscellany*, 24 (1848), 603-608. What Smith refers to as 'Lord Mayor's Day' is now more commonly known as the 'Lord Mayor's Show', or officially as 'The Presentation of the Lord Mayor at the Royal Courts of Justice', and during the period he was writing about it took place on 9 November each year.

4 Smith, 'Lord Mayor's Day', p. 604.

5 Smith, 'Theatrical Ashes'.

6 Fanny Kemble appeared in 'Romeo and Juliet' in the autumn of 1829, saving Covent Garden Theatre (managed by her father, the actor and impresario Charles Kemble) from bankruptcy. Edward Fitzball's stage version of Edward Bulwer-Lytton's 1830 Newgate novel *Paul Clifford* (the book that introduced the phrase 'It was a dark and stormy night' to the English language) was staged at Covent Garden in 1835. See Jane Moody, *Illegitimate Theatre in London, 1770-1840* (Cambridge: Cambridge University Press, 2007), p. 112.

7 Albert Smith, *A Month At Constantinople* (London: David Bogue, 1850), p. 24.

8 Albert Smith, *The London Medical Student* (London: Routledge, 1860), p. 120. First published as *The London Medical Student and Curiosities of Medical Experience* (London: Carey and Hart, 1845). Smith reiterated his point that a good command of French was of far greater use to the traveller than knowledge of classical tongues, in the Introduction to his book about climbing Mont Blanc: 'The Channel once crossed, there is no comparison between the positions of one traveller who can chat with the *conducteur*, or the foreigner by his side in the *banquette* or at the *table d'hôte*, and of another who can put "Old Dan Tucker" into marvellous Latin or Greek verses, but stumbles in his inquiries as to roads,

food, time, or expenses'. Smith, *Story of Mont Blanc*, p. x.

9   H. Campbell Thomson, *The Story of the Middlesex Hospital Medical School, 1835-1935* (London: John Murray, 1935), p. 44. Edmund Yates claimed that Smith was awarded a midwifery prize while a student at Middlesex, but no record of this award survives. I am indebted to Annie Lindsay, Trust Archivist and Records Manager at UCLH NHS Foundation Trust for checking the archives for details of Smith's training and employment at Middlesex. See Edmund Yates, 'Bygone Shows', *Fortnightly Review*, 39 (Jan-June, 1886), 633-47.

10 Smith, 'Lord Mayor's Day', p. 604. The execution was probably that of James Greenacre, who was hanged on 2 May, 1837 for murdering and dismembering his fiancé. See Camden Pelham, *The Chronicles of Crime, or The New Newgate Calendar* (London: Thomas Tegg, 1841), Vol. 2, pp. 428-53.

11 *The Mirror of Literature, Amusement, and Instruction*, 30 (1838), p. 298. The review actually appeared in 1837; this volume was a compendium of the previous year's fortnightly issues.

12 *The Phrenological Journal and Magazine of Moral Science, for the year 1838* (London: Simpkin, Marshall, and Co., 1838), p. 62.

13 *The London Medical Student and Curiosities of Medical Experience* (London: Carey & Hart, 1845), p. 96.

14 Albert Smith, 'Curiosities of Medical Experience', *Punch, or The London Charivari*, 2 (January-June, 1842), 145-146 (p. 145).

15 Smith, *Ledbury*, p. 36.

16 Smith, 'An English Masquerade', p. 34. A *débardeur* was a stevedore. Although Smith eschewed costumes for his stage show – Yates recalled that he had 'a horror of what he called the "ducking down business"' (in which a lecturer would duck beneath the lecture table and reappear in a wig and costume change) – he appears to have quite enjoyed dressing up offstage. He would often bemuse visitors to his Percy Street home by wearing a French *ouvrier*'s top (similar in appearance to an artist's or Cornish fisherman's smock) around the house.

17 'English Masquerade', p. 34. The Opera Comique was one of the most popular Parisian theatres, founded in the early eighteenth century.

18 See, for example, 'The Grisette: A Story of Paris', in *Comic Sketches from the Wassail-Bowl*, pp. 142-57, and his references in *Ledbury* to the superiority of French working-class females to their British counterparts, p. 44.

19 *Ledbury*, p. 28.

20 Smith, *A Month At Constantinople*, p.155.

21 The prolific editor and writer John Timbs, who edited the *Mirror* between 1827 and 1838, confirmed that Smith had contributed to the publication in that year. See Timbs, *Anecdote Lives*, p. 110. According to Smith's obituary in the *Athenaeum*, he was paid half a crown per column for his *Mirror* articles: see 'Mr. Albert Smith' *Athenaeum*, 1700 (26 May, 1860), 719.

22 Smith would later have one of the characters in his final novel define a *diligence* as follows: 'Divide an omnibus into three parts [...] and turn the middle one sideways, making such doors as occasion may require. Place an old private cab on the top, and cover with a tarpaulin. Finish with a crust of gypsum-dust and rain water': *The Pottleton Legacy: A Story of Town and Country Life* (London: David Bogue, 1849), p. 295.

23 'Recollections of a Cheap Tour', p. 408. Equally typical was the fact that Smith later recycled the whole account to pad out his 1853 book *The Story of Mont Blanc*. Subsequent references are from this later version.

24 Smith, *To China and Back,* p. 21.

25 Smith, *To China and Back,* p. 17.

26 Albert Smith, *The English Hotel Nuisance* (London: David Bryce, 1855), p. 15.

27 Goitres, a form of thyroid swelling, were common in the Alps up to the end of the nineteenth century as a result of iodine deficiency, and were frequently remarked on by visitors, as was the related condition known as cretinism. See Fleming, *Killing Dragons*, p.84.

28 *Ledbury*, p. 327.

29 For an account of Windham and Pococke's visit to the Mer de Glace, and the wider context of eighteenth-century travel to the Alps, see Schama, pp. 463-6.

30 *Murray's Handbook for Travellers to Switzerland* (London: John Murray, 1838), p. 291. Murray's *Handbook* – and the very idea of guidebooks for travellers – was itself a product of the Romantic movement, as Jack Simmons points out (see his Introduction to the 1970 reprint of *Murray's Handbook* by Leicester University Press). John Murray had set out for the Continent in 1829 at the age of 21, and was struck by the difficulty of getting logistical information on hotels, transport, etc, as well as cultural information about the countries he visited. He began to take detailed notes, and upon his return suggested to his father (already one of the country's leading publishers) that he produce a 'Handbook' – the first coinage of the word in English. Less than half a century later Albert Smith would use the same word, 'handbook', to describe some of his own publicity materials to accompany his Mont Blanc show.

31 It is worth bearing in mind that Smith's recollections were not always reliable, and his accounts of the same event in different publications sometimes contradicted each other. In his 1852 essay, 'The Album at Chamonix', for example, he claims that the first time he visited the town it rained constantly and he scarcely left the Hotel de Londres, never catching a glimpse of Mont Blanc. Clearly both versions of his first visit to Chamonix cannot be true, but the version recounted in *The Story of Mont Blanc* was the one he repeated most often. See 'The Album at Chamonix', in *Pictures of Life at Home and Abroad* (London: Richard Bentley, 1852), p. 4.

32 When Smith's next season at the Egyptian Hall opened in December, 1855, he included illustrations of the fire damage. A handbill for his 1855 season announces that during the five-minute interval between the two acts there will be a 'View of Chamouni After the Fire of July 17th, 1855, from a sketch taken on the spot by Mr. Albert Smith'.

CHAPTER 3

1   Smith, *Story of Mont Blanc*, p. 28. I have continued to quote from the later work, but this advice to travellers was originally contained in his 1848 *Bentley's* article.

2   The first was Maria Paradis in 1809. See Walt Unsworth, *Savage Snows: The Story of Mont Blanc* (London: Hodder & Stoughton, 1986), p. 36.

3   Erkki Huhtamo has recently argued that Smith's account of his early career here 'fits a little too neatly into the context' of the immense popularity of moving panoramas in the mid-century. He suggests that Smith may have been 'a self-serving propagandist promoting his commercial entertainment' by reshaping the facts, since 'conjuring moving

panoramas transformed an opportunist into a pioneer'. In the absence of other evidence to the contrary, however, I regard Smith's account as being as reliable as anything else he wrote – which is to say, not always trustworthy. In any case, as Huhtamo points out, 'whether Smith's reminiscences were factual or imaginary, they reveal a showman's mind-set'. See Erkki Huhtamo, *Illusions in Motion: Media Archaeology of the Moving Panorama and Related Spectacles* (Cambridge, MA: M.I.T. Books, 2013), p. 221.

4   Smith, *Story of Mont Blanc*, p. 32.

5   Smith, *Story of Mont Blanc*, p. 32. It is worth pointing out that what Smith took to the various institutions was not a magic lantern show, as has occasionally been claimed. As the historian of magic lantern culture Mike Simkin points out, Smith's early show involved 'simple cut-outs and an illuminated candle', not the mechanical slides associated with magic lanterns. Nor were Albert and Arthur using the limelight that was the standard way to make magic lantern images brighter from the 1820s onwards. Simkin records one occasion in the 1850s when Albert Smith did use a magic lantern, to illustrate a version of his Mont Blanc lecture at the Royal Polytechnic Institution. See Mike Simkin, 'Albert Smith: A Nineteenth-Century Showman', *New Magic Lantern Journal*, 4 (1986), 68-71. Erkki Huhtamo also notes that when Smith's Mont Blanc show at the Egyptian Hall became successful, it was quickly copied by magic lantern showmen, who simply copied William Beverley's designs and turned them into painted lantern slides. See Huhtamo, p. 234.

6   He may also have taken his show to the Marylebone Literary and Scientific Institution in Edward Street, Portman Square, although Smith himself does not record this. See Timbs, *Anecdote Lives*, p. 110. However, this was a grander and more prestigious institution than the small provincial societies that Smith mentions in his own account, with over 100 members and a hall that could seat 600, and it seems uncharacteristically modest of Smith to omit an appearance at such an impressive venue. See *The Mechanics Magazine, Museum, Register, Journal, and Gazette*, 20 (1833-34), 240.

7   *Ledbury*, p. 198.

8   Like Smith, Christopher Tadpole bases his lecture show (on 'Ancient Sports and Pastimes of the People of England') on some old pictures he finds a book. See Albert Smith, *The Struggles and Adventures of Christopher Tadpole* (London: Richard Bentley, 1848), p. 451.

9   Lionel Lambourne, *Victorian Painting* (London: Phaidon, 1999), p. 151.

10   Lambourne suggests that the panorama, channelled through Cole's paintings such as *The Oxbow* (1836), was a formative influence on the Hudson River school of American painting. See Lambourne, p. 152.

11   Bernard Comment, *The Panorama* (London: Reaktion Books, 1999). Ralph Hyde points out that this venue remained open for business until 1863, by which time a total of 126 different panoramas had been exhibited there: See Ralph Hyde, *Panoramania: The Art and Entertainment of the 'All-Embracing' View* (London: Trefoil Publications/Barbican Art Gallery, 1998), p. 58.

12   Albert Smith, 'The Panoramania', *Illustrated London News*, 25 May, 1850,

p. 363.

13   Lambourne, p. 154.

14   Lambourne, p. 154.

15   See Hyde, p. 109.

16   Daguerre used the proceeds from his successful dioramas to finance the experiments

that led to the 1839 invention of the daguerreotype. See Lambourne, p. 155.

17 Lambourne, p. 156.

18 Hyde, p. 109.

19 Alison and Helmut Gernsheim, *L. J. M. Daguerre: The History of the Diorama and the Daguerrotype* (New York: Dover Publications, 1968), p. 33.

20 Gernsheim, p. 43.

21 Hyde, p. 131.

22 Lambourne, p. 154.

23 Hyde, p. 133.

24 Hyde, p. 133.

25 The descriptions of Smith's voice are by, respectively, William Howard Russell, George Augustus Sala, Henry Vizetelly, and Edmund Yates. See Black Atkins, p. 112; George Augustus Sala, *The Life and Adventures of George Augustus Sala, Written by Himself*, 2 vols (London: Cassell, 1895), I, 196; Henry Vizetelly, *Glances Back Through Seventy Years*, 2 vols (London: Kegan Paul, 1893), I, 319; Edmund Yates, 'Bygone Shows, *Fortnightly Review*, 39, New Series (Jan-June, 1886), 633-47 (p. 640).

26 Martin Meisel, *Realisations: Narrative, Pictorial and Theatrical Arts in Nineteenth-Century England* (Princeton, NJ: Princeton University Press, 1983), p. 33.

27 Albert Smith, 'A Little Talk about Science and the Show-Folks', in Comic Sketches from the Wassail Bowl (London: Richard Bentley, 1848), p. 43. This book was originally published by Bentley in 1843, in two volumes.

28 'A Little Talk', p. 43. Adelaide Gallery – or, to give it its proper title, the National Gallery of Practical Science, Blending Instruction with Amusement – stood in the Lowther Arcade on the Strand, and contained scientific machines and models, including a steam gun, pocket thermometer, and daguerrotypes.

29 'Transactions of the Geological Society of Hookham-cum-Snivey', *Punch, or The London Charivari*, 1 (1840), 141.

30 'A Handbook of Mr. Albert Smith's Ascent of Mont Blanc', 1856, British Library collection, BL 10196 aa.12.

31 Malcolm Andrews, *Landscape and Western Art* (Oxford: Oxford University Press, 1999), p. 141.

32 Andrews, p. 141.

33 Paul Young, *Globalization and the Great Exhibition: The Victorian New World Order* (Basingstoke: Palgrave Macmillan, 2009), p. 71.

34 Liza Picard, *Victorian London: The Life of a City, 1840-1870* (London: Weidenfeld & Nicolson, 2006), p. 257.

35 Young, p. 71.

36 For Smith's connection to *Cosmorama*, see George Hodder, *Memories of my Time* (London: Tinsley Brothers, 1870), p. 88. Hodder went on to work with Smith at *Punch*, and described him as 'a most frank and agreeable companion' – a view with which not everyone at the magazine concurred.

37 St. Peter's Church in Chertsey still possesses the original 'curfew bell', dating back to 1830, that gave rise to the Blanche Heriot legend. The American poet Rosa Hartwick Thorpe later adapted the story for her 1867 poem, *Curfew Must Not Ring Tonight*, which

relocated the tale to the period of the English Civil War.

CHAPTER 4

1   Hodder, *Memories*, p. 92.

2   Jerry White, 'Unsentimental Traveller: The London Novels of Albert Smith', *The London Journal*, Vol. 32, No. 1 (March, 2007), 29-51. White notes that the 1851 census showed '21 artists of one sort or another in Percy Street, 14 music professional and seven medical men' (p. 46). Further testimony to the atmosphere of the area can be found in the *Post Office London Directory* for 1841, the year Smith moved in to Percy Street, which shows that the previous occupant of Number 14 was a cabinet maker, while an artist called Henry P. Bone lived at Number 12, where Smith would later move (p. 201).

3   Albert Smith, 'Music in the Streets', in *Gavarni in London: Sketches of Life and Character*, ed. by Albert Smith (London: David Bogue, 1849), p. 21.

4   *Ledbury* p. 340.

5   Edmund Yates, *Fifty Years of London Life* (New York: Harper & Brothers, 1885), p. 201.

6   Sala, *Life and Adventures*, I, 196; Henry Vizetelly, *Glances Back Through Seventy Years*, 2 vols (London: Kegan Paul, 1893), I, 315. Smith gives a detailed – and unusually sombre and restrained – description of an execution by guillotine in *Ledbury*, but there is no evidence that he witnessed such an event during his time in Paris.

7   Albert Smith, 'Physiology of the London Idler', *Punch*, 3 (July-December 1842), p.5. Smith re-used this paragraph in the Introduction to his book *Natural History of the Idler upon the Town* (London: David Bogue, 1848).

8   *Bentley's Miscellany* was launched by publisher Richard Bentley, with the first volume appearing in January 1837 under the editorship of Charles Dickens. William H. Ainsworth took over as editor when Dickens resigned in 1841, and some sources suggest Smith himself briefly served as editor when Ainsworth resigned: *The New Cambridge Bibliography of English Literature*, for instance, lists Smith as one of the editors, although the dates it gives are anomalous. In any case, Smith would become the most frequently serialized novelist in *Bentley's* after Dickens's departure through to 1849. See *British Literary Magazines: The Victorian and Edwardian Age, 1837-1913*, ed. by Alvin Sullivan (Westport, CN & London: Greenwood Press, 1984), p. 37; *The New Cambridge Bibliography of English Literature*, ed. by George Watson, 5 vols (Cambridge: Cambridge University Press, 1969), III, Column 1846.

9   Albert Smith, 'A Rencontre with the Brigands', *Bentley's Miscellany*, 9 (1841), 375-381 (p. 375). A posting carriage was a horse and carriage used to transport the mail, which sometimes took along paying passengers, as opposed to a scheduled *diligence* passenger service.

10 For Smith's memories of this highwayman play, see Chapter 2, Footnote 6.

11 Simon Schama points out that 'desolate mountainscapes where brigands set upon unfortunate travellers' actually comprised only a small portion of Rosa's work, but that these scenes were disproportionately influential on later paintings by English artists such as Joseph Groupy, whose *Robbers* (1740) in turn influenced Walpole and his Alpine travelling companion Thomas Gray. In an interesting parallel to Smith's later career, Walpole and Gray were important in encouraging the taste for wild, rugged mountain scenery that would eventually lead to the popularity of mountain climbing in the following century. See Schama, Chapter 8.

12 James William Wallack (1794-1864) was an Anglo-American actor-manager at various London and US theatres, among whose notable roles was the lead in *The Brigand*. See 'Wallack, James William', in *Appleton's Cyclopaedia of American Biography*, ed. by James Grant Wilson and John Fiske, 6 vols. (New York: D. Appleton, 1889), VI, 336.

13 Smith, *Tadpole*, Chapter 28. Smith's description of Venice in the same novel suggests he was underwhelmed by his time there. He warns his readers not to be misled by the exaggerations of poets about the city, claiming that the approach from Mestre ('which is to Venice what Twickenham is to Eel Pie Island') is 'not exactly like the dioramas and descriptions you have formed your notions from. In fact in commonplace minds it may suggest unfavourable comparisons with Wapping': *Tadpole*, p. 256.

14 The 'silver fork' novel was a short-lived but wildly popular genre, flourishing from around 1825 to the early 1840s. Bulwer Lytton and Benjamin Disraeli both wrote novels in this style in their early careers. See Edward Copeland, *The Silver Fork Novel: Fashionable Fiction in the Age of Reform* (Cambridge: Cambridge University Press, 2012).

15 See Patrick Leary and Andrew Nash, 'Authorship', in *The Cambridge History of the Book in Britain* (vol. 6, 1830-1914), ed. by David McKitterick, 6 vols. (Cambridge: Cambridge University Press, 2009).

16 Walter Besant, *Fifty Years Ago* (London: Chatto & Windus, 1888), p. 195.

17 Quoted in Leary and Nash, p. 174.

18 *Le Charivari* was a French satirical publication started in 1832 by Charles Philipon.

19 Patrick Leary, *The Punch Brotherhood: Table Talk and Print Culture in Mid-Victorian London* (London: British Library, 2010), p. 2.

20 Brian Maidment, 'The *Illuminated Magazine* and the Triumph of Wood Engraving', in *The Lure of Illustration in the Nineteenth Century*, ed. by Laurel Brake and Marysa Damoor (Basingstoke: Palgrave Macmillan, 2009), pp. 17-39 (p. 20).

21 Leary, *Punch Brotherhood*, p. 1.

22 M. H. Spielmann, *The History of Punch* (London: Cassell & Company, 1895), p. 305.

23 Since contributions to *Punch* were unsigned, I am grateful for the invaluable 'Punch Contributor Ledgers', digitised as part of the Liverpool John Moores University's Digital Collections, which I have used to identify some of Smith's work for the magazine.

24 'The Physiology of London Evening Parties', *Punch*, 2 (1842).

25 'Underlying all the *Physiologies* was the sense that modern city life had become both infinitely interesting and mysterious, as well as decidedly ridiculous and bathetic': Brian Rigby, 'Physiologies', in *The New Oxford Companion to Literature in French*, ed. by Peter France (Oxford: Oxford University Press, 1995), p. 622-23.

26 'Brighton', in '*Punch*'s Guide to the Watering Places', *Punch*, 3 (1843), p. 50.

27 'Tower Hill', in 'Handbooks for Holidays Spent in and about London', *Punch*, 5 (1843), p. 53.

28 'Tower Hill', p. 53.

29 *The Revolt of Bruges* was performed at the Olympic Theatre in 1842. Blanchard was a prolific playwright who later became well known for his pantomimes at Drury Lane.

30 *Blanche Heriot, or The Chertsey Curfew: A Domestic and Historical Drama in Two Acts* (Royal Surrey Theatre, 1842). The Surrey Theatre was on Blackfriars Road between 1782 and 1934, existing under a variety of names during its life; it had been known as the Royal Circus and Equestrian Philharmonic Academy from 1782, but burnt down in 1803 and

was rebuilt by Rudolph Cabonel (the architect of the Old Vic) as the Surrey.

31 *Illustrated London News*, 1 October, 1842, p. 334. Reviews of Smith's work in the *Illustrated London News* need to be treated with caution, as he later became a theatre critic on the paper and was not above using his connections there to promote his own shows. However, this review appeared before Smith began working for it. The paper had only begun publication earlier that year, founded by Herbert Ingram, and quickly acquired a high circulation, largely due to its innovative use of illustrations. See M. Oliphant, *The Victorian Age of English Literature*, 2 vols (London: Percival & Co., 1892), II, 334.

32 Albert Smith, 'The Armourer of Paris: A Romance of the Fifteenth Century', *London Saturday Journal*, 2 (1842).

33 *The Adventures of Mr. Ledbury and His Friend Jack Johnson* was serialized in *Bentley's Miscellany* between September 1842 and December 1843. It was then published in book form by Bentley in three volumes from January 1844. Smith continued to write for Parry (1810-1879) over the next few years, and briefly introduced him as a character in both *Ledbury*, when Titus Ledbury is invited backstage at Her Majesty's Theatre (which at this point was still home to the opera company that would move to the Theatre Royal, Covent Garden in 1847), and in *Christopher Tadpole*, when Parry is invited to sing at Sir Frederick Arden's house party.

34 Albert Smith, *Comic Sketches from the Wassail Bowl* (London: Richard Bentley, 1848), p. 8. This is essentially the same book that appeared in two volumes five years earlier as *The Wassail Bowl*, reissued by Bentley in one volume with an amended title.

35 *Wassail Bowl*, p. 15.

36 *Wassail Bowl*, p. 17.

37 *Brother Jonathan*, 5 (1843), p. 446. Just to confuse matters, the same play is also cited as a source for Donizetti's opera: see Emanuele Senici, *Landscape and Gender in Italian Opera: The Alpine Virgin from Bellini to Puccini* (Cambridge: Cambridge University Press, 1995), p. 95.

CHAPTER 5

1 'Letter to Edward Fitzgerald, March-May 1848', in *The Letters and Private Papers of William Makepeace Thackeray*, 4 vols, ed. Gordon N. Ray (London: Oxford University Press, 1945-46), 11, 366. Fitzgerald was a poet best known for his translations into English of *The Rubaiyat of Omar Khayyam*.

2 This and subsequent definitions of the word are taken from the *Oxford English Dictionary*. Jerry White provides another useful and succinct definition of the word in this context as 'a low class social climber': White, p. 32.

3 Albert Smith, *The Natural History of Stuck-Up People* (London: David Bogue, 1847), p. 2.

4 Albert Smith, *The Natural History of the Gent* (London: David Bogue, 1847), p. 2. Both the *Gent* and *Stuck-Up People* natural histories were published in emulation of the French *physiologies* discussed in the previous chapter.

5 Gareth Stedman Jones, 'The 'cockney' and the nation, 1780-1988', in *Metropolis London: Histories and Representations since 1800*, ed. by David Feldman and Gareth Stedman Jones (London and New York: Routledge, 1989), pp. 271-324 (p. 289).

6 Stedman Jones, p. 288.

7 Quoted in Atkins, I, 111.

8   Alan Hankinson, *Man of Wars: William Howard Russell of the* Times (London: Heinemann, 1982), p. 113.

9   Gaston Rebuffat, *Mont Blanc: Jardin féerique* (Paris: Denoël, 1987), p. 52; Rana Kabbani, *Imperial Fictions: Europe's Myths of the Orient* (London: Pandora, 1988), p. 164.

10 In fairness to Venables (a distinguished climber who among other achievements was the first Briton to reach the summit of Everest without supplementary oxygen) he was simply pointing out that Smith's show had helped to inspire Edward Whymper, who by contrast was a committed and pioneering mountaineer. But his comment does belong to a tradition of using words like 'flashy' about Smith which has remained extraordinarily consistent: Stephen Venables, 'Foreword', in Peter Berg, *Whymper's Scrambles with a Camera: A Victorian Magic Lantern Show* (London: The Alpine Club, 2011).

11 Landseer had not yet become Sir Edwin – he was knighted in 1850. For more on the *Punch* Club see Walter Jerrold, *Douglas Jerrold and 'Punch'* (London: Macmillan, 1910), written by Douglas Jerrold's grandson.

12 Accounts of this episode can be found in Spielmann, p. 304, and Athol Mayhew, *A Jorum of 'Punch'* (London: Downey & Co., 1895), p. 108, the latter written by Henry Mayhew's son.

13 For invaluable portraits of Jerrold and other contributors to *Punch*, see Laurel Brake and Marysa Demoor, eds., *Dictionary of Nineteenth-Century Journalism in Great Britain and Ireland* (Gent & London: Academia Press & British Library, 2009).

14 Smith and Jerrold seem to have been reconciled later in life. Smith was one of the mourners at his funeral in 1857, and was involved in the attempts of Dickens's 'Amateurs' acting troupe to raise money for his widow by public performances – attempts which backfired rather embarrassingly when Jerrold's son protested at the assumption his father had left the family destitute. See Nigel Cross, *The Common Writer: Life in Nineteenth-Century Grub Street* (Cambridge: Cambridge University Press, 1985) p. 70.

15 H. Sutherland Edwards, *Personal Recollections* (London: Cassell, 1900), p. 53.

16 Walter Jerrold, p. 35. The anecdote about Smith's initials has subsequently been reported with Jerrold referring to Albert Richard Smith's three initials, A.R.S. See for example, George Band, *Summit: 150 Years of the Alpine Club* (London: HarperCollins, 2006). However, Smith signed his articles as 'A.S.', and the 'two-thirds' remark only makes sense if Jerrold was referring to the word 'ass' rather than 'arse'.

17 Vizetelly, I, 319.

18 Sutherland Edwards, p. 187.

19 A. A. Adrian, *Mark Lemon, The First Editor of Punch* (London: Oxford University Press, 1966), p. 106. Sutherland Edwards attributed this rhyme to 'Father Prout', the pen name of the Irish humourist Francis Sylvester Mahoney: Sutherland Edwards, p. 189.

20 Walter Jerrold, p. 36.

21 Sutherland Edwards, p. 187.

22 Sutherland Edwards, p. 189.

23 Vizetelly, p. 320.

24 Arthur William à Beckett, *The à Becketts of Punch* (London: Archibald Constable, 1903), p. 257.

25 Leary, *The* Punch *Brotherhood*, p. 13.

26 Brake & Demoor, p. 71.

27 Bodleian Library Special Collections, Oxford. MS Eng Lett d. 398/1 (book 3). Letters to Bradbury and Evans. Albert Smith to Bradbury and Evans, 1 July 1844.

28 Bodleian, Letters to Bradbury and Evans, Smith to Bradbury and Evans, 4 July 1844.

29 Bodleian, Letters to Bradbury and Evans, Smith to Bradbury and Evans, 15 July 1844.

30 J. W. T. Ley, *The Dickens Circle* (London: Chapman & Hall, 1918), p. 329.

31 Darryll Grantley, *Historical Dictionary of British Theatre: Early Period* (Plymouth: Scarecrow Press, 2013), p. 409. This appears to have been an unauthorized version of the novel, although Smith's next involvement with Dickens was in the authorized adaption of *The Cricket on the Hearth* the following year.

32 S. J. Adair Fitzgerald, *Dickens and the Drama* (London: Chapman & Hall, 1910), p. 183.

33 *Mirror of Literature, Amusement, and Instruction*, New Series, 5 (1844), p. 43.

34 Albert Smith, *The Fortunes of the Scattergood Family* (London: Richard Bentley, 1845), p. 262-3. The play was *Hop-O'-My-Thumb, or The Seven League Boots: A Romance of Nursery History*, and was performed at the Lyceum in 1846.

35 Smith, 'A Go-Ahead Day', p. 522.

36 'Go-Ahead Day', p. 522.

37 The only real source for Smith's alleged dislike for Shakespeare is Vizetelly, who as we have seen was scarcely a disinterested source. Even in his 1848 pamphlet on *Why Our Theatres are Not Supported* Smith has little – positive or negative – to say about Shakespeare, and the few references to the bard in his novels are generally comic or at least ironic. A travelling hawker in *Ledbury*, talking about the distinction between high and low art, proclaims, 'Shakespeare's all very well in his way; but he couldn't do the doll-trick. What's Macbeth to the pancake done in the hat, or the money in the sugar-basin? Answer me that now – what's Macbeth to them?' *Ledbury*, p. 398.

38 P. T. Barnum, *The Life of P. T. Barnum, Written By Himself*, ed. Terence Whalen (1855: Urbana & Chicago: University of Illinois Press, 2000), p. 281.

39 Smith, *Scattergood Family*, p. 258.

CHAPTER 6

1 *Pottleton* actually began life as a serial in the short-lived *London Telegraph*, but was published in stand-alone format when that paper folded. The *Telegraph* was founded by Herbert Ingram, founder of the *Illustrated London News*, but failed to match that publication's success and only ran from February to July 1848. See Edmund Yates, 'Biographical Sketch of Albert Smith', in *The Struggles and Adventures of Christopher Tadpole* (London: Downey & Co., 1897), Brake & Demoor, *Dictionary of Nineteenth-Century Journalism*, p. 307.

2 These dramatizations of Dickens's novels were done with the writer's approval, unlike the adaption of *Martin Chuzzlewit* for which Smith had written the prologue.

3 Albert Smith, 'Anecdotes of Dr. Johnson', in *A Bowl of Punch* (London: David Bogue, 1848), p. 93-4.

4 Leary & Nash, 'Authorship', p. 184.

5 Sutherland Edwards, p. 188.

6 *Ledbury*, p. 12.

7 *Ledbury*, p. 319.

8 *Ledbury*, p. 158.

9 *Ledbury*, p. 171.

10 White, 'Unsentimental Traveller', p. 29.

11 *Ledbury*, p. 11.

12 *Ledbury*, p. 51.

13 *Ledbury*, p. 107.

14 *Christopher Tadpole*, p. 261.

15 *Ledbury*, p. 289.

16 *Ledbury*, p. 21; p. 271.

17 Yates, 'Biographical Sketch'.

18 John Hollingshead, *My Lifetime* (London: Sampson Low, Marston & Company, 1895), p. 142; 'Christmas Books', *Athenaeum*, 1054 (8 January 1848), 37-38.

19 The advert appears in 'A Handbook of Mr. Albert Smith's Ascent of Mont Blanc', 1858, Guildhall Library, PAM 8473.

20 Quoted in Sutherland Edwards, p. 187. Oxenford (1812-1877) translated Goethe into English and introduced Schopenhauer to the British reading public.

21 'Letter to Albert Smith', 2 January 1844, in *The Letters of Charles Dickens*, The Pilgrim Edition, ed. by Madeline House, Graham Storey, Kathleen Tillotson, 12 vols (Oxford: Clarendon Press, 1965-2002), IV, 8; 'Letter to Douglas Jerrold', 24 October 1846, in *Letters of Charles Dickens*, IV, 642-645 (643). Smith's advert had been written in the form of an 'Act for the Establishment of a New Periodical Story called "Christopher Tadpole"', a parody of an Act of Parliament which Smith was fond of using – he employed the same format for his *Social Parliament* article of 1848. Later in his career, Smith would regularly mock up passports, royal warrants, legal documents and other official-looking papers to act as marketing gimmicks for his Mont Blanc show.

22 Ley, p. 329.

23 *The Spectator*, 27 December 1845, p. 10.

24 Quoted in Raymund Fitzsimons, *The Baron of Piccadilly* (London: Geoffrey Bles, 1967), p. 46.

25 There would have been no legal barrier to their beginning a sexual relationship immediately, although there is no evidence that this did happen. The age of consent was not raised to 16 until the Criminal Law Amendment Act of 1885.

26 G. S. Layard, *A Great Punch Editor: Being the Life, Letters, and Diaries of Shirley Brooks* (London: Sir Isaac Pitman & Sons, 1907), p. 407.

27 Montagu Williams, *Leaves of a Life*, 2 vols (London: Macmillan, 1890), I, 62.

28 Portraits of both Mary and Smith's mistress Pattie Oliver (the former a print by photographer George Herbert Watkins) exist in London's National Portrait Gallery.

29 Albert Smith, *The Fortunes of the Scattergood Family* (London: Richard Bentley, 1845), p. 57.

30 *Scattergood*, p. 60.

31 *Scattergood*, p. 170.

32 *Scattergood*, p. 89.

33 Dumas' book was not translated into English until the 1890s, and Melville's poem was written in 1891: See Alexandre Dumas, *Celebrated Crimes*, 8 vols, translated by I. G. Burnham (London: H. S. Nichols, 1896), VII; Robert L. Gale, *A Herman Melville Encyclopedia* (Westport, CT: Greenwood Publishing, 1995), p. 54.

34 *The Marchioness of Brinvilliers: The Poisoner of the Seventeenth Century. A Romance of Old Paris* (London: Richard Bentley, 1846), p. 118.

35 British Library, Add MS 46,614 'Bentley Papers', Vol. 5, *ff.* 328-329.

36 Translating historical sums into present-day equivalents is not an exact science and can be misleading. I have used the Retail Price Index as the best measure for past earnings. See www.measuringworth.com

37 Albert Smith, 'Preface to the New Edition', *Christopher Tadpole* (London: Willoughby & Co., 1854).

38 *Christopher Tadpole*, p. 218.

39 *Christopher Tadpole*, p. 163.

40 *Christopher Tadpole*, pp. 357-9.

41 *Christopher Tadpole*, p. 36. A cresset is a metal container mounted on a pole, containing burning oil or coal for illumination.

42 *Christopher Tadpole*, p. 118.

43 *Christopher Tadpole*, p. 192.

44 Letters from Albert Smith to John Leech, LUL MS. 45 (120326) Liverpool Sydney Moore Library, Special Collections and Archives; LUL MS. 45.1 'Liverpool, June 1851'; Letters from Albert Smith to John Blackwood, National Library of Scotland, Blackwood Papers Vol. 11 (MSS. 4001-4940), 1851 letters, MS 4095, 'Teignmouth, Devon, October 1851'.

45 Vizetelly, p. 316.

46 See Fitzsimons, p. 64; Hollingshead, p. 142; Edmund Yates, 'Biographical Sketch'.

47 *Natural History of the Gent*, p. 3.

48 *Natural History of the Gent*, p. 99.

49 *Natural History of the Gent*, p. 3.

50 *Natural History of the Flirt*, p. 25.

51 *Natural History of Stuck-Up People*, p. 13.

CHAPTER 7

1 *Tadpole*, p. 399. Astley's Ampitheatre was a famous venue for live performances, mentioned by Dickens in several of his novels and by Jane Austen in *Emma* (1815). It continued to operate under various names until 1893.

2 Albert Smith, *The Pottleton Legacy: A Story of Town and Country Life* (London: David Bogue, 1849), p. 437.

3 *Pottleton*, p. 438.

4 *Pottleton*, p. 441.

5 'Ascent of Mr. Green's Balloon from Cremorne Gardens', *Illustrated London News*, 12 June 1847, p. 379. Smith was not actually listed as the author of this article, but he alludes to having written it in his account of the second, near-disastrous balloon ride. It is not

clear why he dropped his usual insistence on a byline in this instance.

6 Albert Smith, 'An Adventure in a Balloon', *The Town and Country Miscellany*, 5 (August 1850), 192-202 (p. 196). Smith edited this publication from its first volume in 1850.

7 'Adventure in a Balloon', p. 197. The Lord's Chamber was completed in 1847, the year of Smith's flight, although full rebuilding of the Palace of Westminster was not completed until 1870.

8 'Adventure in a Balloon', p. 198.

9 'Ascent of Mr. Green's Balloon'.

10 'Ascent of Mr. Green's Balloon'.

11 Albert Smith, 'Perilous Descent of Mr. Gypson's Balloon, on Tuesday Night', *Illustrated London News*, 10 July 1847, p. 29.

12 'Adventure in a Balloon', p. 199.

13 'Perilous Descent'.

14 'Adventure in a Balloon', p. 201.

15 'Adventure in a Balloon', p. 202.

16 Alfred Bunn, *A Word with Punch* (November 1847).

17 Mayhew, *A Jorum of Punch*, p. 128.

18 Layard, p. 43.

19 *The Man in the Moon*, 2 (1848), p. 282.

20 Cross, *Common Writer*, p. 107.

21 *The Man in the Moon*, 5 (1849), p. 96.

22 *The Man in the Moon*, 5 (1849), p. 31.

23 Layard, p. 43; *The Man in the Moon*, 1 (1847), p. 359.

24 *The Man in the Moon*, 5 (1849), p. 356.

25 *The Man in the Moon*, 1 (1847), p. 87. The first public demonstration of the use of ether in anaesthesia had taken place in Boston in 1846, although it had been used in Britain in conjunction with opium since the early 1840s.

26 The actual causes, background, and details of the Monte Cristo riots are considerably more complex than can be explained here. A good account, which mentions Smith, can be found in Jim Davis and Victor Emeljanow, *Reflecting the Audience: London Theatregoing, 1840-1880* (Hatfield: University of Hertfordshire Press, 2001), pp. 194-196.

27 Thorington, p. 56.

28 *The Social Parliament* (London: David Bogue, 1848).

29 Vizetelly, p. 320.

30 Hodder, *Memories of my Time*, p. 91.

31 Hodder, *Memories of my Time*, p. 91.

32 Albert Smith, 'The Crossing-Sweeper', in *Gavarni in London: Sketches of Life and Character*, ed. by Albert Smith (London: David Bogue, 1849), pp. 33-36 (p. 34).

33 Smith, 'Acrobats', in *Gavarni in London*, n.p. (frontispiece).

34 Wendy Kolmar, 'Review of Albert Smith, editor, *Gavarni in London: Sketches of Life and Character with Illustrative Essays by Popular Writers* (1849). Edited with an Introduction by Stephen Banks', *The Literary London Journal*, 10 (Spring 2013). Online at www.

literarylondon.org/london-journal/spring 2012/kolmar.html Accessed on 14/8/2014.

35 The railway network had grown from just 471 miles of track in England and Ireland in 1835, to 13,411 miles by the middle of the century, and this process was continuing to accelerate. See James Walvin, *Leisure and Society, 1820-1950* (London: Longman, 1978), p. 21.

36 *Pottleton*, p. 172.

37 *Pottleton*, p. 471.

38 *Pottleton*, p. 132.

39 *Pottleton*, p. 459.

40 *Pottleton*, p. 259.

41 *Pottleton*, p. 263.

42 Charles Dickens, *Bleak House* (1853: London: Penguin, 1996), p. 53.

43 *Pottleton*, p. 416.

44 *Pottleton*, p. 214.

45 Ian Anstruther, *The Scandal of the Andover Workhouse* (London: Bles, 1973).

46 Margaret Crowther, *The Workhouse System, 1834-1929* (London: Batsford, 1981), p. 198.

47 *Pottleton*, p. 433.

48 Edmund Yates, *His Recollections and Experiences*, 2 vols (London: Richard Bentley, 1885), I, 236.

49 *Pottleton*, p. 336.

50 The full title of Egan's journal was *Life in London, or the Day and Night Scenes of Jerry Hawthorn, esq., and his elegant friend, Corinthian Tom, accompanied by Bob Logic, the Oxonian, in their rambles and sprees through the Metropolis.* The series continued until 1828.

51 Oliphant, I, 318.

52 'Mr. Albert Smith', *Athenaeum*, 1700 (26 May 1860) p. 719.

CHAPTER 8

1 Yates, 'Bygone Shows', p. 640.

2 Edmund Yates, *Fifty Years of London Life* (New York: Harper & Brothers, 1885), p. 148.

3 P. D. Edwards, *Dickens' "Young Men": George Augustus Sala, Edmund Yates and the World of Victorian Journalism* (Aldershot: Ashgate, 1997), p. 28.

4 *Month At Constantinople*, p. 190.

5 *Month At Constantinople*, p. 119.

6 *To China and Back*, p. 6.

7 *To China and Back*, p. 8.

8 *Christopher Tadpole*, p. 595.

9 *Christopher Tadpole*, p. 527.

10 *To China and Back,* p. 54.

11 *Pottleton*, p. 415; *Scattergood Family*, p. 172.

12 Henry James, *A Small Boy and Others: Memoirs* (1924: London: Gibson Square Books, 2001), p. 165.

13 Vizetelly, p. 321.

14 Quoted in Atkins, I, 111; William Ballantine, *Some Experiences of a Barrister's Life* (London: Richard Bentley, 1882), p. 141.

15 The recollection is from a *New York Times* column by 'Belgravia', dated 25th October 1874. I am grateful to Jerry White for drawing my attention to this cutting in his private collection of Albert Smith material.

16 'Belgravia', *New York Times*.

17 Yates, *Recollections and Experiences*, I, 152; George Hodder, *Memories of My Time* (London: Tinsley Brothers, 1870), p. 88; Edwin Hodder, *John Macgregor, "Rob Roy"* (London: Hodder Brothers, 1894), p. 139.

18 Sullivan Edwards, p. 188.

19 G. N. Ray, *Thackeray: The Age of Wisdom, 1847-1863* (London: Oxford University Press, 1958), p. 349.

20 Yates's tribute comes in the foreword to an illustrated children's version of Smith's Mont Blanc book, *A Boy's Ascent of Mont Blanc*, published in London by Ward, Lock, and Tyler. The date of publication is unknown, but is clearly after Smith's death. A copy of the book exists in the Bill Douglas Cinema Museum at Exeter University, EXEBD46178.

21 Henry Silver joined *Punch* in 1857, becoming its youngest staff writer: Leary, Punch *Brotherhood*, p. 27.

22 'Henry Silver's diary', British Library Add MS 88937/2/13.

23 Lord William Pitt Lennox, *Celebrities I Have Known*, 2 vols (London: Hurst and Blackett, 1877), II, 5.

24 Lennox, 7.

25 Mayhew, *Jorum of Punch*, p. 128.

26 'Letter to Emile de la Rue', 23 October 1857, Dickens, *Letters*, Vol. 8, 472.

27 Charles Dickens, *The Speeches of Charles Dickens* (London: Michael Joseph, 1937), p. 166.

28 *Pottleton*, p. 413.

29 *Pottleton*, p. 157; *Christopher Tadpole*, p. 13.

30 *Ledbury*, p. 345.

31 *Christopher Tadpole*, p. 103.

32 Timbs, *Anecdote Lives*, p. 110.

33 Timbs, *Anecdote Lives*, p. 114.

34 *Tadpole*, p. 580.

35 *Tadpole*, p. 129.

36 Albert Smith, 'An English Holiday', *The Month: A View of Passing Subjects and Manners, Home and Foreign, Social and General*, 1 (July 1851), 30-8 (p. 30).

37 'An English Holiday', p. 31. Smith's distaste for Greenwich Fair was evidently shared by the authorities, since it was abolished in 1857, part of a process of suppressing traditional fairs that continued from the mid-eighteenth to mid-nineteenth century as national holidays were gradually standardized and the long-established leisure activities of

the working classes were discouraged: see Judith Flanders, *Consuming Passions: Leisure and Pleasure in Victorian Britain* (London: Harper Press, 2006), p. 209.

38 'An English Holiday', p. 32.

39 National Library of Scotland (NLS), Blackwood papers Vol. II (MSS. 4001-4940 letters from Albert Smith to Blackwood), 1854 letters to Blackwood MS 4107.

40 *Month At Constantinople*, p. 21.

41 J. W. Cross, ed. *George Eliot's Life, As Related in Her Letters and Journals*, 3 vols (Edinburgh and London: William Blackwood, 1886), I, 347. Smith would not, of course, have been aware at this stage that 'George Eliot' was a woman. The story was submitted to Blackwood by G. H. Lewes on behalf of an anonymous 'friend'. Nor was he alone in his response: Blackwood wrote that Smith's fellow members of the Garrick Club 'seem to have mingled their tears with their tumblers over the death bed of Milly'.

42 Albert Smith, 'How I Got Away from Paris After the Rebellion in June', *Bentley's Miscellany*, 24 (1848), 210-16 (p. 210).

43 *Month At Constantinople*, p. 10.

44 *Month At Constantinople*, p. 31.

CHAPTER 9

1   Geoffrey P. Nash, *Travellers to the Middle East from Burckhardt to Thesiger: An Anthology* (London: Anthem Press, 2011), p. 17; Richard D. Altick, *The Shows of London* (Cambridge, MA. & London: Belknap Press of Harvard University Press, 1978), p. 474. Warburton's book is rather more conventional and less facetious in tone than the other two, but its author is certainly given to magisterial generalities about the countries he visits: 'The Turk is vain, ignorant, presumptuous, and authoritative', he proclaims, 'yet in society he is courteous, affable, and gentlemanlike': Eliot Warburton, *The Crescent and the Cross: or, Romance and Realities of Eastern Travel* (London: Henry Colburn, 1845), p. 123.

2   Nash, p. 12.

3   Alexander William Kinglake, *Eothen, or, Traces of Travel Brought Home from the East* (London: John Ollivier, 1844), p. 31.

4   'I swear solemnly that I would rather have two hundred a year in Fleet Street, than be King of the Greeks', wrote Thackeray, in the guise of the pseudonymous A. M. Titmarsh, *Notes of a Journey from Cornhill to Grand Cairo* (London: Chapman and Hall, 1846), p. 72.

5   *Month At Constantinople*, p. v.

6   *Blackwood's Magazine*, 67 (1850), p 680.

7   *Month At Constantinople*, 2nd edition (London: David Bogue, 1850), p. vii.

8   *Month At Constantinople*, p. 3.

9   *Month At Constantinople*, p. 41.

10 'Mr. Albert Smith', *Athenaeum*, p. 720.

11 *Month At Constantinople*, p. 44.

12 *Month At Constantinople*, p. 48. It is interesting to compare Thackeray's impressions of an almost identical introduction to the city; Thackeray was reminded of one of Clarkson Stanfield's theatrical scenes at Drury Lane, but continued to be impressed as he was taken through the streets of Pera: *Cornhill to Grand Cairo*, p. 98.

13 *Month At Constantinople*, p. 80. The Cricketers was a pub on the Chertsey side of the bridge, which apparently survived into the early 1990s, but has now been demolished.

14 *Month At Constantinople*, p. 108.

15 *Month At Constantinople*, p. 141.

16 Reinhold Schiffer, *Oriental Panorama: British Travellers in 19th Century Turkey* (Amsterdam: Rodopi, 1999), p. 200.

17 'Slaves Sold to the Turk', *New York Times*, 28 March 1886.

18 *Month At Constantinople*, p. 37.

19 Carl Plasa and Betty J. Ring, *The Discourse of Slavery: Aphra Behn to Toni Morrison* (London: Routledge, 1994), p. xiv.

20 Quoted in Graham Storey, *Dickens: Bleak House* (Cambridge: Cambridge University Press, 1987), p. 8.

21 *Month At Constantinople*, p. 111.

22 *Month At Constantinople*, p. 130.

23 Warburton, p. 85.

24 'Letter to Dr. John Brown', 25 March 1853, *Letters and Private Papers of Thackeray*, I, 553.

25 *Month At Constantinople*, p.130.

26 Goodman, p. 249. Admittedly Keeley expressed his sentiments after visiting slave sales 'to see what they were like'.

27 *Month At Constantinople*, p. 236.

28 I have not been able to establish when Smith was blackballed, but William Pitt Lennox's account of meeting Smith makes it clear that it did happen. Smith thus joins the theatrical knight Sir Henry Irving and the broadcaster Jeremy Paxman in having been initially blackballed and later allowed to join the Club.

29 Yates, *Recollections and Experiences*, p. 49.

30 For a fascinating discussion of this trend see Christopher Oldstone-Moore, 'The Beard Movement in Victorian Britain', *Victorian Studies*, 48 (Autumn 2005), 7-34.

CHAPTER 10

1 Willis's Rooms had formerly been known as Almack's after their founder William Almack, who opened assembly rooms on the site in 1765. According to some accounts the name did not formally change until the 1870s, but the assembly rooms were commonly known as Willis's Rooms for much of the nineteenth century, and contemporary accounts of Smith's performance certainly refer to it as taking place in Willis's Rooms, not Almack's.

2 See John K. Sidebottom, *The Overland Mail: A Postal Historical Study of the Mail Route to India* (London: Postal History Society, 1948). Waghorn's own account of his journeys in the days before the way-stations were established gives some idea of the difficulties of the journey: Thomas Waghorn, *Particulars of an overland journey from London to Bombay* (London: Parbury, Allen & Co., 1831).

3 The distinction between the two was not always made clear at the time. Richard Altick confirms that not long after their introduction, the terms panorama and diorama 'came to mean whatever exhibitors wanted them to mean, irrespective of the actual nature of the entertainment in question': Altick, p. 173.

4   Yates, 'Bygone Shows', p. 633.

5   Altick, p. 474.

6   'Mr. Albert Smith's *Overland Mail', Illustrated London News*, 1 June 1850, p. 390.

7   The Atfeh locks separate the Mahmoudieh canal from the Nile. The Frank Square – variously known as the Grand Square, Place Muhammad Ali, and nowadays Midan al-Tahrir, or 'Liberation Square' – was the largest square and one of the principal 'sights' of Alexandria. See Anthony Sattin, *Lifting the Veil: Two Centuries of Travellers, Traders and Tourists in Egypt* (London and New York: Tauris, 2011), p. 155. The reference to the Middle Station is to one of the eight buildings erected by Waghorn on the route between Suez and Cairo, which offered travellers stabling and bedrooms. In one of the 'handbooks' that accompanied this show, Smith described in detail how 'the *cuisine* is very tolerable for the locality, and the prices are not out of the way. Dinner is charged four shillings and breakfast two. Port is five shillings a bottle, and stout ale, and porter, about one and tenpence'. 'A Handbook to Mr. Albert Smith's Entertainment entitled *The Overland Mail*', 3rd edition, 1850, Item 36923, Bill Douglas Cinema Museum, Exeter.

8   'Mr. Albert Smith's Entertainment', *The Times*, 29 May 1850, p. 5.

9   Quoted in Edward Ziter, *The Orient on the Victorian Stage* (Cambridge: Cambridge University Press, 2003), p. 52.

10 'Mr. Albert Smith's Entertainment'.

11 Handbook for 'Mr. Albert Smith's Entertainment The Overland Mail', Item 36923, Bill Douglas Cinema Museum.

12 Item 36923, Bill Douglas Cinema Museum.

13 Egyptian Hall file 1845-1873, V&A Theatre and Performance Archive.

14 Altick, p. 207.

15 Fitzsimons, p. 104. Ironically, later in the 1850s Albert Smith was one of the characters who Woodin would imitate in this fashion: see Jacky Bratton, *The Making of the West End Stage: Marriage, Management, and the Mapping of Gender in London, 1830-1870* (Cambridge: Cambridge University Press, 2011), p. 66.

16 Yates, 'Bygone Shows', p. 640.

17 'Mr. Albert Smith's *Overland Mail', Illustrated London News*.

18 Flanders, p. 274.

19 Ballantine, p. 174.

20 'Mr. Albert Smith's *Overland Mail', Illustrated London News*.

21 MS. 45/4, in 'Letters from Albert Smith to John Leech', LUL MS. 45 (120326) Liverpool University Sydney Moore Library, Special Collections and Archives.

22 'Letter to John Blackwood from Torquay, Devon', December 1851, MS. 4095 1851 Letters to Blackwood, NLS. I am grateful to Mike Simkin for allowing me to consult his private collection of flyers and other publicity material for 'The Overland Mail', which includes valuable information about its regional touring schedule. Smith's schedule changed several times during this tour, so that the programme shown on some early flyers is different to that of later publicity material.

23 Bodleian, Letters to Bradbury and Evans, Smith to Bradbury and Evans, n.d. but presumably July 1851.

24 'Nursery Rhymes of the Great Exhibition', *The Month*, 1 (July 1851), p. 46. The Koh-i-noor Diamond was one of the most popular attractions of the Exhibition, displayed in

a shadowed case to allow the sunlight to catch its edges, but there were complaints that it literally 'failed to sparkle'.

25 'London Labour and the London Rich', *The Month*, 1, p. 4.

26 'The Drama's Last Kick', *The Month* (December 1851).

27 The correspondence is in C.56, Alpine Club Archive, London.

28 MS. 45/4, 'Letters from Albert Smith to John Leech', Sydney Moore Library.

29 MS. 45/11, 'Letters from Albert Smith to John Leech', Sydney Moore Library.

30 Bodleian, Letters to Bradbury & Evans, Smith to Bradbury & Evans, n.d.

31 This letter is in Mike Simkin's private collection.

CHAPTER 11

1 Albert Smith, 'Mont Blanc', *Blackwood's Edinburgh Magazine*, 71 (Jan 1852), 35-55 (p. 37). Subsequent quotations are from this account – the first to be published of Smith's ascent – or from his 1853 book *The Story of Mont Blanc*, unless otherwise stated.

2 Hodder, p. 95.

3 The official *Alpine Club Register* gives the lower figures: A. L. Mumm, *The Alpine Club Register, 1857-1863* (London: Edward Arnold, 1923), p. 294. An earlier historian of Mont Blanc climbs, Charles Edward Mathews, suggests that fifty-two people were successful in the years between the first ascent and 1850: C. E. Mathews, *The Annals of Mont Blanc* (London: T. Fisher Unwin, 1898), p. 175. Edward Whymper claimed there were fifty-seven ascents up to the end of 1850: Whymper, *Chamonix*, p. 44. The anomalies may be partly caused by some historians counting successful climbs by parties, others counting up the number of individuals that successfully reached the summit. For the purposes of this book, I have chosen to follow the very detailed appendix given by Gavin DeBeer and Thomas Graham Brown in their *The First Ascent of Mont Blanc* (London: Oxford University Press, 1957). Brown and DeBeer list both the failed and successful ascents of the mountain between 1762 and 1854, and according to this list Smith's party was the 40th to reach the summit: Appendix LXXVII, p. 433-442.

4 For a good general overview of the early history of Mont Blanc climbing, see Fleming, *Killing Dragons*; Walt Unsworth, *Savage Snows: The Story of Mont Blanc* (London: Hodder & Stoughton, 1986); and Jim Ring: *How the English Made the Alps* (London: John Murray, 2000). Peter H. Hansen's *The Summits of Modern Man: Mountaineering after the Enlightenment* (Cambridge, MA & London: Harvard University Press, 2013) is an interdisciplinary study of the links between mountain climbing and modernity, which includes a detailed examination of the cultural and intellectual milieu of eighteenth-century Geneva in which de Saussure came to develop his interest in Mont Blanc, and the Alps in general.

5 It is difficult to be certain of statistics from the first half of the nineteenth century, before the Alpine Club and other organisations began systematically collecting data on mountaineering accidents. However, as far as I can ascertain the next *fatal* accident on Mont Blanc did not take place until 1864. After that Mont Blanc began to make regular appearances in the 'Alpine Accidents' section of the *Alpine Journal*. See C. E. Mathews, 'The Alpine Obituary', *Alpine Journal*, 11 (1882-84), 78-89. A particularly bad accident in 1870 saw eleven climbers die on the mountain after being caught in bad weather. See J. Stogdon, 'The Late Accident on Mont Blanc', *Alpine Journal*, 5 (1870-72), 194-99.

6 Whymper, *Chamonix*, p. 43.

7   Quoted in R. L. G. Irving, *A History of British Mountaineering* (London: B. T. Batsford, 1955), p. 52.

8   The first quotation is from Mary Wollstonecraft Shelley's *History of a six week's tour through a part of France, Switzerland, Germany, and Holland: with letters descriptive of a sail round the Lake of Geneva, and of the glaciers of Chamouni* (London: T. Hookham, 1817), p. 156. The second is from her *Frankenstein or, The Modern Prometheus* (1818; London: Penguin, 2013), p. 100. The Mer de Glace was at its maximum size in the nineteenth century, extending all the way down to the hamlet of Les Bois in the Chamonix valley. At the time Mary Shelley was writing it was generally referred to as the Glacier de Montenvers, but by Smith's day it had become known as the Mer de Glace.

9   *Murray's Handbook for Travellers in Switzerland, Savoy, and Piedmont* (London: John Murray, 1843), p. 332.

10   *Murray's* (1843), p. 298.

11   *Murray's Handbook for Travellers in Switzerland, Savoy, and Piedmont* (London: John Murray, 1852), p. 336.

12   Yates, 'Bygone Shows', p. 638.

13   Life expectancy at birth in Britain rose during the nineteenth century from the mid-thirties to the upper forties. Naturally it varied according to gender, region, and socio-economic status, and would have been different for a physician's son from Chertsey and the child of a labourer from Manchester or Glasgow. In 1860, the year of Smith's death, the profession with the highest life expectancy was that of clergyman or priest (46 years) and the lowest was for inn servants and chimney sweeps at just 31 years. A doctor in 1860 had a life expectancy of 39. See R. I. Woods, 'The Population of Britain in the Nineteenth Century', in *British Population History from the Black Death to the Present Day*, ed. by Michael Anderson (Cambridge: Cambridge University Press, 1996), pp. 281-235 (p. 330); Robert Woods, *The Demography of Victorian England and Wales* (Cambridge: Cambridge University Press, 2000), p. 224.

14   Swapni J. Paralikar and Jagdish H. Paralikar, 'High Altitude Medicine', *Indian Journal of Occupational Environmental Medicine*, 14 (Jan-Apr 2010), 6-12.

15   James S. Milledge, John B. West, and Robert B. Schoene, *High Altitude Medicine and Physiology*, 4th edition (Boca Raton, FL: CRC Press, 2007), p. 8.

16   'The First Rotters', p. 546.

17   Hamel had even planned to carry bottled oxygen to test its effect on the body at altitude, although this idea had to be abandoned when he could not find the necessary equipment. Had he done so, it would have been an extraordinarily advanced experiment – mountaineers were still arguing about both the efficacy and the ethics of supplementary oxygen over a century later on various Everest expeditions: 'The First Rotters', p. 547. See also Harriet Tuckey, *Everest: The First Ascent* (London: Rider Books, 2013), and Wade Davis, *Into the Silence: The Great War, Mallory and the Conquest of Everest* (London: Bodley Head, 2011).

18   See, for example, C. G. Monro, 'Mountain Sickness', *Alpine Journal*, 16 (1892-93), 446-55; Percy W. Thomas, 'Rocky Mountain Sickness', *Alpine Journal*, 17 (1894-95), 140-141.

19   Andrew J. Pollard and David R. Murdoch, *The High Altitude Medicine Handbook* (Oxford: Radcliffe Publishing, 2003), p. 3. Partial pressure is simply the pressure that one gas in a mix of gases – for example, oxygen in air – would exert if it were the only gas in the same volume and at the same temperature. So the proportion of oxygen in air declines

as barometric pressure drops.

20 When the author climbed Mont Blanc in the summer of 2014, for example, he first spent two days climbing in the mountains above the Torino mountain hut, and one night sleeping in the hut at 3,375 metres, before returning to Chamonix. He then spent another day walking from Italy's Val Veni to the Gonella hut at 3,071 metres, before continuing to the summit of Mont Blanc the following day. This would generally be regarded as the minimum appropriate period of acclimatization for someone not already conditioned to altitude.

21 See, for example F. Craufurd Grove, 'The Comparative Skill of Travellers and Guides', *Alpine Journal*, 5 (1870-72), 87-96.

22 Francis Philips, *A Reading Party in Switzerland, with an account of the ascent of Mont Blanc, on the 12th and 13th August, 1851* (Manchester: privately printed, 1851), p. 14.

23 Philips, *Reading Party*, p. 47.

24 'Review of *A Reading Party in Switzerland*', *Alpine Journal*, 15 (1890-91), 371-2 (p. 372).

25 Smith's full list of guides is rather confusing since two names appear twice, and one is omitted. He copied the list from the certificate he was given after the ascent, and explained that one guide (whose name he had forgotten) was too poorly to sign. The two names that are repeated twice are Jean Tairraz and Michel Couttet; both are the surnames of well-known dynasties of Chamoniard guides. The two Tairraz men were cousins, and it is likely that the Couttets were cousins or uncle and nephew. The other guides listed by Smith are Jean Carrier; Gedeon Balmat; Frederic Tairraz; Pierre Cachat; Francois Cachat; Joseph Tiarraz; Joseph Tissay; Edouard Carrier; Michel Devouassoud; Auguste Devouassoud; and Pierre Francois Favret. Most of these men belonged to dynasties of mountain guides; Balmat was a descendant of one of the two men who first climbed the mountain, and of another guide who died in the Hamel expedition. Another guide killed in the 1820 avalanche was Auguste Tairraz – brother of the elder Jean Tairraz who guided Smith's party. Even today, the list of guides registered with the Compagnie des Guides de Chamonix includes the names Favret, Balmat, Couttet, and Devouassoud, and one of Chamonix's main museums is the Espace Tairraz.

26 The writer C. Douglas Milner once estimated that the cost of hiring guides on Smith's expedition would have worked out at the equivalent of about £13 for each of the five climbers: C. Douglas Milner, *Mont Blanc and the Aiguilles* (London: Robert Hale, 1955), p. 58.

27 Auldjo, p. 7.

28 Claire Eliane Engel, *A History of Mountaineering in the Alps* (London: George Allen & Unwin, 1950), p. 69.

CHAPTER 12

1   Philips, *Reading Party*, p. 17.

2   Arnold Lunn, *A Century of Mountaineering, 1857-1957* (London: George Allen & Unwin, 1957), p. 49.

3   Whymper, *Chamonix*, p. 43.

4   Philips and his friends had used rudimentary crampons on an earlier day trip to the glacier, but they were not being used on their Mont Blanc ascent, possibly because these early versions were too heavy and cumbersome. Philips, *Reading Party*, p. 12. Crampons,

or 'grappettes', usually consisting of four spikes fitted under the heels of a shoe, had been in use for centuries, but the first complete crampons that would be recognizable to a modern climber were not developed until the 1870s: Ed Douglas, *Mountaineers: Great Tales of Bravery and Conquest* (London: Royal Geographical Society/Alpine Club, 2011), p. 98.

5   Philips, *Reading Party*, p. 25.

6   Another climber, by the name of G. N. Vansittart, also made a successful ascent the same day.

7   The song 'Nina la Mariniere' appeared in the August, 1851 issue of *The Month*, so presumably Smith had already composed it and filed the copy before setting off for the Alps: *The Month*, August 1851, 124-25.

8   This latter activity would be frowned on today, to say the least, but few visitors to the Alps at this stage had any concept of the need for conservation, and Smith's party would have assumed that few if any people would be following in their footsteps. Leaving litter behind soon became socially unacceptable among mountain climbers, although mountaineering literature of the late nineteenth century contains frequent complaints about litter louts, and it was evidently not uncommon for people to leave bottles, sandwich wrappers, and other detritus in the mountains.

9   Some of their remains would eventually reappear at the foot of the glacier between 1861 and 1865, carried down by the movement of the glacier: Mathews, *Annals*, p. 228.

10   Milner, p. 29.

11   Philips, *Reading Party*, p. 38.

12   Philips, *Reading Party*, p. 39.

13   Mathews, p. 189.

14   Smith's party would have been using alpenstocks – walking poles about six feet in length with a metal spike on top. The ice axe, with its pick for gaining purchase on steep snow and ice and adze for cutting steps, did not come into use until well into the 1860s, and even then it was some time before it was widely accepted as a superior tool to the alpenstock. As late as 1868 there was still debate over which was the most useful for Alpine climbing: see H. B. George, 'Axe versus Alpenstock', *Alpine Journal*, 4 (1868-70), 126-29 (p. 126).

15   W. F. Donkin, 'Photography in the High Alps', *Alpine Journal*, 11 (1882-84), 63-71 (p. 65).

16   See Vizetelly, p. 321; Yates, 'Bygone Shows', p. 638.

CHAPTER 13

1   Quoted in Fleming, p. 58.

2   Edward Whymper, *Scrambles Amongst the Alps in the Years 1860-1869* (London: John Murray, 1871), p. 362.

3   Quoted in Joe Kember, 'The View from the Top of Mont Blanc: The Alpine Entertainment in Victorian Britain', *Living Pictures (The Journal of the Popular and Projected Image before 1914)*, 2 (2003), 21-45 (p. 22). Kember, an academic who specializes in film studies and visual culture, has an interesting slant on the disappointment felt by many Mont Blanc climbers, arguing that 'the view from the summit proved disappointing for the Alpinists because it could not deliver the forms of knowledge and authority that were already associated with the panoramic view of the exhibition space' – it was, of course, just such an authoritative and supposedly omniscient view that Smith seemed to offer the

many visitors to 'The Ascent of Mont Blanc' during the 1850s. For another perspective on 'the summit position', see Hansen, *Summits of Modern Man*.

4   Gavin de Beer, *Early Travellers in the Alps* (1930; New York: October House, 1967), p. 182.

5   Perhaps the most prominent were those of the Scottish glaciologist James David Forbes, whose *Travels Through the Alps of Savoy* had been popular and influential when it was published in 1843.

6   Stephen's book was called *The Playground of Europe*. Tellingly even the scientist John Tyndall called his book, published the same year, *Hours of Exercise in the Alps*.

7   Hansen, 'Albert Smith, the Alpine Club, and the Invention of Mountaineering', p. 307.

8   Philips, *Reading Party*, p. 43.

9   Philips, *Reading Party*, p. 43.

10   A copy of the book is held in the Alpine Club Archive in London: 'Copy of the Fuhrerbuchen of Pierre Francois and Edouard Favret', Alpine Club Archive K. 47. Smith retained Favret as a guide again when he visited the newly-opened Grands Mulets hut in 1853, writing in his book that 'nothing could exceed his attention and courage. The glacier was in a very bad state, but his courageous intelligence overcame everything'. William Howard Russell, who was on the same trip, added that Favret was 'one of the most excellent guides in Chamonix'.

11   Quoted in Milner, p. 32. John Forster had succeeded Dickens as editor of the *Daily News* by this stage, but Dickens himself was also a trenchant critic of mountaineering. After the Matterhorn disaster of 1865, in which four of Edward Whymper's companions were killed on the descent, he wrote in *All The Year Round* about the 'foolhardihood' and 'contempt for human life' that he believed Alpine mountaineering entailed: Charles Dickens, 'Hardihood and Foolhardihood', *All The Year Round*, 14 (August 1865), p. 86.

12   Albert Smith, 'The Ascent of Mont Blanc', *The Times*, 20 August, 1851, p. 6.

13   John Ruskin, *Complete Works*, ed. by E. T. Cook and Alexander Wedderburn, 39 vols (London: George Allen, 1903-12), XXXVI, 117.

14   Philips, *Reading Party*, p. 49.

15   NLS, Blackwood papers, Vol. II, MS 4095.

16   NLS, Blackwood papers, Vol. II, MS 4095. The *OED* has no entry for the word 'todge' which was presumably obscure slang for sludge or slush.

17   NLS, Blackwood papers, Vol. II, MS 4107.

18   Denon became the first director of the Louvre, and his book was a founding work of modern Egyptology. See Stephan Oettermann, *The Panorama: History of a Mass Medium* (New York: Zone Books, 1997). Napoleon's Egyptian and Syrian campaign took place from 1798 to 1801.

19   See Hugh Honour, 'Curiosities of the Egyptian Hall', *Country Life*, 115 (January 1954), 38-39.

20   John Timbs, *Curiosities of London* (London: Virtue & Co., 1855), p. 319.

21   Honour, p. 38.

22   Oettermann, p. 129.

23   Honour, p. 39; Huhtamo, p. 136.

24 Except where otherwise stated, this list of Egyptian Hall exhibits is taken from Timbs, *Curiosities of London*.

25 Felix Barker and Peter Jackson, *London: 200 Years of a City and Its People* (London: Macmillan, 1983), p. 251: V&A Theatre Museum, untitled clipping in 'Theatre Buildings: Egyptian Hall' file.

26 Haydon was a painter in Joshua Reynolds' 'Grand Manner', with close ties to the Romantic poets, and in particular to Wordsworth, who dedicated his 1815 sonnet beginning 'High is our calling, Friend' to him. He painted the portrait of *Wordsworth on Helvellyn*, celebrating the poet's ascent of the Lakeland mountain at the age of seventy, in 1842: See Paul O'Keefe, *A Genius for Failure: The Life of Benjamin Robert Haydon* (London: Random House, 2011), p. 154; Lambourne, p. 17.

27 'Theatre Buildings: Egyptian Hall' file, V&A Theatre Museum; Peter Friedrich Monahan, *The American Wild Man: The Science and Theatricality of Nondescription in the Works of Edgar Allan Poe, Jack London, and Djuna Barnes* (unpublished doctoral dissertation, Washington University in St. Louis, 2008), p. 88.

28 Altick, p. 207.

29 'Egyptian Hall, 1845-1873', V&A Theatre Museum.

30 Flanders, p. 273; Hyde, p. 133.

CHAPTER 14

1   Goodman, p. 227. Huhtamo points out that although Smith eschewed dressing up in character on stage, sticking to respectable evening dress, he did pose as some of his characters – for example Edwards the Engineer – in carte-de-visite photographs and stereocards: Huhtamo, p. 225.

2   Tin fiddles were cheap versions of traditional fiddles, made with sheet metal. 'Patter' songs are fast-paced comic songs with alliterative or tongue-twisting lyrics. Among the most famous examples are the works of Gilbert and Sullivan, but they were also a staple of comic opera and at this stage were perhaps most closely associated with John Parry, for whom Smith had written material.

3   'Mont Blanc Gazette and Illustrated Egyptian Hall Advertiser', 1858, BL 1252 f.29.

4   There has been some confusion over how many seasons Smith's show continued for, with some historians equating the six years from 1852 to 1858 with six seasons. However, his first season only lasted from March to September 1852, and each subsequent season began in the autumn and ended the following summer. Analysis of handbills, programmes, newspaper reviews, and other material shows that the seasons ran as follows: Season 1, March 1852 to September 1852; Season 2, November 1852 to August 1853; Season 3, December 1853 to August 1854; Season 4, December 1854 to September 1855; Season 5, December 1855 to September 1856; Season 6, November 1856 to August 1857 (with a brief closure February 1857); Season 7, November 1857 to July 1858. He performed every evening apart from Saturday, when he gave a 2pm or 3pm. He also performed matinees on Tuesdays and Thursdays.

5   The description of Martigny is from 'A Handbook of Mr. Albert Smith's Ascent of Mont Blanc', 1852, Alpine Club Archive, C79.

6   Smith was particularly fond of dogs, and after his 1852 visit to the Alps (at the end of the first season at the Egyptian Hall) he brought back a St. Bernard puppy for Dickens, which the novelist named Linda: Richard Renton, *John Forster and his Friendships*

(London: Chapman and Hall, 1912), p. 236.

7 'Mr. Albert Smith's Ascent of Mont Blanc', *The Morning Post*, 17 March 1852, p. 5.

8 The main paintings in the show were by Beverley, but over the years, as the content of the programme varied, Smith added illustrations by other artists. Edmund Yates recalled travelling to 'a third-rate lecture hall' in Birmingham with Smith's brother Arthur to buy a panorama of the Rhine painted by the German theatrical artist Carl Wilhelm Gropius, which was then incorporated into the show: Yates, 'Bygone Shows', p. 641.

9 Arriving at his guesthouse after visiting the Slave Market in Constantinople, for example, Smith discovered that a batch of *Galignani's Messenger* had arrived, bearing the story of the 'Bermondsey Murder' – the slaying of Patrick O'Connor by the Swiss domestic servant Marie Manning, who was hanged for the crime and later became the model for Hortense in *Bleak House*. 'All the circumstances had to be translated and explained to the foreigners at the *table d'hôte*; and for the next day or two as much proportionate noise was made about the affair in Pera as in London': *Month at Constantinople*, p. 132. Another comic song, *The Young England Traveller*, was also a regular feature of Smith's show. For more on the publication *Galignani's Messenger*, see James Munson and Richard Mullen, *The Smell of the Continent: The British Discover Europe, 1814-1914* (London: Macmillan, 2009), Chapter 11.

10 Yates, 'Bygone Shows', p. 640.

11 Goodman, p. 225.

12 'Mr. Albert Smith's Ascent of Mont Blanc', *Illustrated London News*, 20 March 1852, p. 243.

13 Vizetelly, p. 321.

14 Vizetelly was, predictably enough, among those who passed on this rumour. In an 1853 book on mountain climbing the author Robert Ferguson also appeared to cast doubt on the veracity of Smith's claim to have been to the summit: Robert Ferguson, *Swiss Men and Swiss Mountains* (London: Longman, Brown, Green, and Longmans, 1853), p. 136. Since Francis Philips' account of the ascent accords in most significant points with Smith's, and since Smith himself was frank about the assistance he had required on the final push to the summit, these doubts can safely be dismissed.

15 'Mr. Albert Smith', *The Times*, 18 September 1854, p. 10. 'Ojibbeways' is presumably a reference to the Ojibwe, one of the largest native American groups.

16 Goodman, p. 225.

17 'Mr. Albert Smith's Ascent of Mont Blanc', *Daily News*, 17 March 1852.

18 'Mr. Albert Smith's Ascent of Mont Blanc', *Morning Post*, 17 March, 1852, p. 5.

19 'Our London Commissioner', *Blackwood's Edinburgh Magazine*, 71 (Jan-June 1852), 596-606 (p. 603).

20 'Mr. Albert Smith's Ascent of Mont Blanc', *Illustrated London News*, 10 April 1852, p. 291; 'Mr. Albert Smith's Entertainment', *The Times*, 19 March 1852, p. 8.

21 'Letter to Albert Smith', 10 March 1852; 'Letter to Anne and Harriet Thackeray', 28 August 1852, *Letters and Private Papers*, III.

22 'Letter to Mrs. T. F. Eliot and Kate Perry', 3 March 1853, *Letters and Private Papers*, IV.

23 'Letter to Anne and Harriet Thackeray', 6 August 1852, in *Letters and Private Papers*, III.

24 James Redfoord Bulwer, *Extracts from my Journal* (Norwich: privately printed, 1853), p. 36.

25 Spielmann, p. 304.

26 *Journal of Gideon Mantell, Surgeon and Geologist*, 1818-1852, ed. by E. Cecil Curwen (London, New York, Toronto: Oxford University Press, 1940), p. 290.

27 Goodman, p. 229.

28 A list of these visitors exists in Mike Simkin's private collection of Smith material.

29 The prices do not appear to have varied much throughout the seven seasons that the 'Ascent of Mont Blanc' continued, although the stalls prices did rise to three shillings from 1855. See 'Egyptian Hall, Piccadilly: Mr. Albert Smith's Ascent of Mont Blanc', 1855 British Library, BL.74/1881.c.16.

30 Nathaniel Woodard, *A Plea for the Middle Classes* (London: Joseph Masters, 1848), p. 4. I should acknowledge that my attention was first drawn to this text by A. N. Wilson's discussion of it in *The Victorians* (London: Arrow Books, 2003), p. 281.

31 Jerry White, p. 41.

32 Edmund Yates, *The Business of Pleasure* (London: Chapman and Hall, 1865), p. 101.

33 'Mr. Albert Smith's Mont Blanc', *The Times*, 6 December 1853, p. 10.

34 Thorington, p. 178.

35 Hankinson, *Man of Wars*, p. 42.

36 'Mr. Albert Smith's Ascent of Mont Blanc', *Athenaeum*, 1310 (4 December 1852), 1334-35 (p. 1334).

37 'Albert Smith's Ascent', *Athenaeum*, 1310, (p. 1334).

38 'Mr. Albert Smith's Mont Blanc', *The Era*, 5 December 1852.

39 'The Ascent of Mont Blanc', *Illustrated London News*, 8 December 1852, p. 663.

40 Hollingshead, p. 143.

41 Yates, *Fifty Years*, p. 150.

42 'A Handbook of Mr. Albert Smith's Ascent of Mont Blanc', 1852, British Library, BL10107.cc,4 (1), p. 11.

43 'The Mont Blanc Gazette and Illustrated Egyptian Hall Advertiser', 1858, British Library, BL 1252.f.29.

44 Goodman, p. 229.

45 'A Handbook of Mr. Albert Smith's Ascent of Mont Blanc', 1858, Guildhall Library, PAM 8473.

46 Ralph Hyde, p. 148.

47 'Male and Female Chamois, and St. Bernard Dogs, Belonging to Mr. Albert Smith', *Illustrated London News*, 3 February 1855, p. 147. The 'Bernese girl', who came from the well-known Kehrli family of Swiss wood-turners, normally spent the winter and spring with her family in Switzerland's Bernese Oberland, working in Chamonix during the summer, but came to Britain for a season to learn English. Smith presented her to Victoria at Windsor in January 1855.

48 Altick, p. 477.

49 'Fine Art Gossip', *Athenaeum*, 1329 (16 April 1853), p. 482. The Royal Marionette Theatre, on Adelaide Street off the Strand, had been the Adelaide Gallery, or National

Gallery of Practical Science, Blending Instruction with Amusement, until 1852.

50 Albert Smith, 'The Cabin on the Grands Mulets, Mont Blanc', *Illustrated London News*, 12 November 1853, p. 409.

51 John Macgregor, 'An Ascent of Mont Blanc', letter, *The Times*, 30 September 1853, p. 6.

52 Cross, *The Common Writer*, p. 108.

53 Yates, *Recollections*, I, 241.

54 Walter Jerrold, p. 36.

55 Pitt Lennox, II, p. 8.

56 Alpine Club Archive C.79a.

57 George Augustus Sala, 'Shows', *Temple Bar*, 8 (1863), 125-30 (p. 126).

58 Sala, 'Shows', p. 126.

59 Sala, 'Shows', p. 126.

60 'Pictures of Life at Home and Abroad', *Athenaeum*, 1294 (14 August 1851), p. 870.

61 'The Story of Mont Blanc', *Athenaeum*, 1345 (6 August 1853), p. 937.

62 Jill Neate, *Mountaineering Literature: A Bibliography of Material Published in English* (Milnthorpe, Cumbria: Cicerone Press, 1998), p. 145.

CHAPTER 15

1 'Advertisements and Notices', *Daily News*, 15 March 1852.

2 'Easter Amusements', *Daily News*, 13 April, 1852.

3 'Easter Amusements'.

4 *Morning Chronicle*, 19 March 1852.

5 'The Exhibitions', *The Era*, 18 April 1852.

6 'Easter Amusements'.

7 'Death of Mr. Albert Smith', *Daily Telegraph*, 24 May 1860, p. 2.

8 Guildhall Library, PAM8473.

9 Yates, *Fifty Years*, p. 160.

10 Altick, p. 475.

11 'Mr. Albert Smith's Mont Blanc', *Daily News*, 18 September 1855.

12 Yates, 'Bygone Shows', p. 639.

13 Sala, 'Shows', p. 125.

14 Thorington, p. 153. Freshfield served as President of both the Alpine Club and the Royal Geographical Society and was an editor of the *Alpine Journal*.

15 Quoted in Simkin 'Nineteenth-Century Showman', p. 69.

16 James, p. 165.

17 'Metropolitan Improvements', *The Times*, 13 July 1855, p. 5.

18 The letter is in Jerry White's private collection.

19 Sala, 'Shows', p. 125. An ell was a traditional measurement, based on the distance from the elbow to the tip of the middle finger, typically about 18 inches.

20 Albert Smith, ed., *'Press Orders': The Opinions of the Leading Journals on the Abolition*

of Newspaper Privileges (London: W. Kent, 1853).

21 'Albert Smith's Mont Blanc', *The Morning Chronicle*, 24 August 1857.

22 'Mr. Albert Smith's Mont Blanc', *Morning Chronicle*, 6 December 1853.

23 This was probably the panorama that Edmund Yates and Arthur Smith bought in Birmingham; see footnote 8 to Chapter 14.

24 'Mr. Albert Smith's Ascent of Mont Blanc', 1856, V&A Theatre and Performance Archive, Egyptian Hall file, 1845-1873.

25 'Mont Blanc has become a positive nuisance', *The Times*, 6 October 1856, p. 8.

26 'Another Ascent of Mont Blanc', *The Times*, 6 October 1856, p. 9.

27 'The Final Ascent of Mont Blanc', *Bentley's Miscellany*, 40 (July 1856), 441-56.

28 Ferguson, p. 136.

29 'Good News for Cockney Travellers', *Punch*, 27 (July-December 1854), 110. Smith had given a royal performance at Osborne that same year.

30 'Good News', 110.

31 Bevin, *Cultural Climbs*, p. 122.

32 'Mr. Albert Smith's Mont Blanc, Naples, Pompeii, and Vesuvius'. This copy was found wrapped inside a letter to Mrs. John Leech, LUL MS.45/13, Liverpool University Sydney Jones Library.

33 'Mr. Albert Smith's Mont Blanc, Naples', etc. The House of the Tragic Poet, or Homeric House, had been excavated at Pompei in 1824. Pausanias and Strabo were both ancient Greek geographers. The Atrio del Cavallo is part of the Valle del Gigante, an ancient caldera which separates the smaller volcanic cone of Vesuvius from the larger outer cone of Monte Somma.

34 LUL MS.45/13, Sydney Jones Library.

35 'Mr. Albert Smith's Mont Blanc', *Jackson's Oxford Journal*, 6 September, 1856.

36 Queen Victoria's diary, 25 March 1856, Windsor (Princess Beatrice's copies). This version is an abridged transcript written by Beatrice, Victoria's youngest daughter. Accessed online at: www.queenvictoriasjournals.org

37 'Selections from Mr. Albert Smith's Ascent of Mont Blanc, chiefly pertaining to the "Travelling English" and their autumnal peculiarities', Osborne, 26 August 1854, programme in file M18, Chertsey Museum.

38 Robert B. Brough, *Marston Lynch* (London: Ward and Lock, 1860), p. 219.

39 The 'series of minute PHOTOGRAPHIC PORTRAITS of living celebrites, as microscopic objects' were mounted on small slides, and evidently required a microscope to be viewed. They were produced by a J. Amadio of Throgmorton Street, who also sold microscopes: 'Miniature photographic novelty', EXEBD2694412, Bill Douglas Cinema Museum.

40 'Mont Blanc', *Morning Chronicle*, 24 August 1857.

41 The figures are from the show's UK website.

42 'Can You Keep a Secret', *The Economist*, 23 November 2012.

43 Albert Smith, *The English Hotel Nuisance* (London: David Bryce, 1855), p. 14. The *Athenaeum*, in a generally positive review of the pamphlet, pointed out that as Smith was now so famous he probably received better treatment than most visitors to these European hotels. 'We ourselves should hesitate before consigning a friend to the dingy splendours

and costly economics of the *Univers* at Lyons, and the *Couronne* at Berne', its reviewer warned: 'English Hotel Nuisance', *Athenaeum*, 1746 (9 February 1856), 165-66 (p. 166).

44 'Letter to Albert Smith', 8 August 1855, *Letters of Charles Dickens*, VII, 686.

45 'Letter to Bradbury & Evans', August 1854, *Letters of Charles Dickens*, VII, 389.

46 'Letter to Albert Smith', 12 November 1854, *Letters of Charles Dickens*, VII, 464.

47 'Letter to Catherine Dickens', 21 October 1853, *Letters of Charles Dickens*, VII, 170.

48 'Letter to Timothy Yeats Brown', 19 August 1857, *Letters of Charles Dickens*, VIII, 415.

49 Yates, *Fifty Years*, p. 148.

50 Fitzsimons, p. 137.

51 'Letter to Wilkie Collins', 4 April 1855, *Letters of Charles Dickens*, VII, 585.

52 'Letter to Arthur Smith', 16 April 1855, *Letters of Charles Dickens*, VII, 594.

53 Queen Victoria's diary, Buckingham Palace, 11 May 1855 (Princess Beatrice's copies).

CHAPTER 16

1 Hansen, 'Albert Smith, the Alpine Club', p. 310.

2 In the early stages of the Club's life, members were expected to have climbed an Alpine peak of at least 13,000 feet, although this was soon relaxed to a more general requirement to have 'written about the Alps, performed "mountain exploits" or simply shown an interest in the region': Fleming, p. 172. Smith in fact suggested in his letter to Kennedy (see fn 3 below) that the 13,000 foot rule was 'a little too high', even though he himself qualified for membership under this rule.

3 Mumm, *Alpine Club Register*, p. 295.

4 'Letter from Albert Smith to E. S. Kennedy', 25 November 1857, in B.65, 'Letters Relating to Formation of Alpine Club', Alpine Club Archive.

5 Letter from William Mathews to E. S. Kennedy', 27 November 1857, B.65, Alpine Club Archive.

6 'Letter from Isaac Taylor to E. S. Kennedy', 19 December 1857, B.65, Alpine Club Archive.

7 Perhaps his closest rival for the role of most improbable Alpine Clubman was John Ruskin. Art critic, cultural commentator, and first Slade Professor of Fine Art at Oxford, Ruskin was also outraged by what he regarded as the philistinism of mountaineers who 'made racecourses of the cathedrals of the earth' and regarded the Alps as 'soaped poles in bear gardens'. Ruskin nonetheless became a member in 1869, although he resigned from the Club in 1882: Mumm, *Alpine Club Register*, p. 287; John Ruskin, *Sesame and Lilies* (1865: London & New Haven, CT: Yale University Press, 2002), p. 53.

8 4 June 1858, *The Apprenticeship of a Mountaineer: Edward Whymper's London Diary, 1855-59*, ed. by Ian Smith (London: London Record Society Publications, 2008), p. 139.

9 Whymper, *Chamonix and the Range of Mont Blanc*, p. 45.

10 The full title was *Where There's a Will There's a Way: An Ascent of Mont Blanc by a New Route and Without guides* (London: Longman, Brown, Green and Longmans, 1856). Hudson later joined Whymper's 1865 assault on the Matterhorn and was killed on the descent.

11 Mathews, *Annals*, p. 196.

12 'New Publications', *Climbers' Club Journal*, 1 (August 1898), 110-13 (p. 110).

13 William Augustus Brevoort Coolidge, *The Alps in Nature and History* (London: Methuen, 1908), p. 231.

14 Arnold Lunn, *A Century of Mountaineering, 1857-1957* (London: George Allen & Unwin, 1957), p. 29.

15 Unsworth, *Hold the Heights*, p. 384.

16 'The Art of Alpine Travel', *Cornhill Magazine*, July-Dec 1862, pp. 206-16 (p. 206).

17 For studies of the wider history of mountaineering in the period, see Peter Hansen, 'British Mountaineering, 1850-1914' (unpublished doctoral dissertation, Harvard University, 1991); Fleming, *Killing Dragons*, Ring, *How the English Made the Alps*; Ronald Clark, *The Victorian Mountaineers* (London: B. T. Batsford, 1953); Robert Macfarlane, *Mountains of the Mind* (London: Granta, 2008); Simon Thompson, *Unjustifiable Risk: The Story of British Climbing* (Milnthorpe, Cumbria: Cicerone, 2010); Unsworth, *Hold the Heights*. For an interesting perspective on the activities and attitudes of both mountaineers and tourists in the Alps, see Ann C. Colley, *Victorians in the Mountains: Sinking the Sublime* (Farnham, Surrey: Ashgate, 2010).

18 Hansen, 'Albert Smith, the Alpine Club', p. 300.

19 Brown & DeBeer, p. 442.

20 *Murray's Handbook for Travellers in Switzerland, Savoy, and Piedmont* (London: John Murray, 1856), p. 360.

21 *The Knapack Guide for Travellers in Switzerland* (London: John Murray, 1867), p. 403.

22 J. Stogdon, 'The Late Accident on Mont Blanc', *Alpine Journal*, 5 (1870-72), 194-99 (p. 199).

23 Leslie Stephen, 'Alpine Climbing', in *British Sports and Pastimes*, ed. by Anthony Trollope (London: Virtue, Spalding & Co., 1865), pp. 275-89 (p. 265).

24 Andrew Beattie, *The Alps: A Cultural History* (Oxford: Signal Books, 2006), p. 177. Montenvers got its own tourist railway line in 1908.

25 Quoted in Clark, *Victorian Mountaineers*, p. 54.

26 Jim Ring, p. 85; Fleming, p. 296.

27 Ring, p. 93.

28 John Urry, *The Tourist Gaze* (London: Sage Publications, 1990), p. 24.

29 Urry, p. 141.

30 Yates, *Business of Pleasure,* p. 101.

31 William Brockedon, *Journals of Excursions in the Alps: The Pennine, Graian, Cottian, Rhetian, Lepontian, and Bernese* (London: James Duncan, 1833), p. 169.

32 Brockedon, p. 169.

33 Albert Smith, *Pictures of Life at Home and Abroad* (London: Richard Bentley, 1852), p. 3.

34 Hansen, 'British Mountaineering', p. 259-62.

35 Herman Merivale, 'Alpine Travellers', *Edinburgh Review*, 104 (October 1856), 433-453 (p. 446).

36 Henry and Athol Mayhew, *Mont Blanc: A Comedy, in Three Acts* (London: n.p., 1874).

37 Leslie Stephen, 'Alpine Climbing', in *British Sports and Pastimes*, ed. by Anthony

Trollope (London: Virtue, Spalding, 1868), pp. 257-89 (p. 287).

38 Leslie Stephen, 'Round Mont Blanc', *Alpine Journal*, 5 (1870-72), 289-305 (p. 295); Leslie Stephen, *The Playground of Europe* (London: Longmans, Green, 1871), p. 289; Leslie Stephen, 'A New Pass in the Chain of Mont Blanc', *Alpine Journal*, 6 (1872-74), 351-364 (p. 352).

39 Douglas Freshfield, *Italian Alps: Sketches in the Mountains of Ticino, Lombardy, the Trentino, and Venetia* (London: Longmans, Green, & Co., 1875), p. 2.

40 Minnie was, of course, the daughter of William Makepeace Thackeray: *Selected Letters of Leslie Stephen, 1864-1882*, 2 vols, ed. by John W. Bicknell (Basingstoke: Macmillan, 1996), I, 51.

41 John Hill Burton, *The Cairngorm Mountains* (Edinburgh: William Blackwood, 1864), p. 4.

CHAPTER 17

1 Most of the London and national papers carried accounts of Smith's final performance and his speech at the end, although oddly *The Times* did not, despite having followed each season closely up to this point. The quotations here are from 'Mr. Albert Smith', *Morning Post*, 7 July 1858, p. 5; 'Mr. Albert Smith', *Daily News*, 7 July 1858.

2 D. J. Taylor, *Thackeray* (London: Chatto & Windus, 1999) p. 398.

3 Ballantine, p. 136.

4 'Letter to Charles Dickens', 7 December 1857, *Letters and Private Papers*, IV, 59.

5 Barbara Black, *A Room of His Own: A Literary-Cultural Study of Victorian Clubland* (Athens, Ohio: University of Ohio Press, 2012), p. 142-44. Taylor's biography of Thackeray also devotes a chapter to the affair, emphasizing the significance of the rivalry between Thackeray and Dickens in stoking the controversy and the way in which the club split between older, more aristocratic, and younger, more bohemian members.

6 'Letter from Albert Smith to Charles Dickens', October 1855, *Letters and Private Papers*, VII, 718. The letter seems to have put Dickens in an awkward position, since the dinner, at the London Tavern, was being organized not by him but by the writer and civil servant Peter Cunningham. He forwarded Smith's request to Cunningham, telling him he had replied to Smith that the dinner was private and the guest list was closed, 'but that I suppose he would not be excluded – that the arrangements are, however, under your charge'. In the event, Smith did attend, and improvised a comic song. Other attendees included Mark Lemon, Clarkson Stanfield, John Forster and John Leech and the actor William Macready: see *Macready's Reminiscences*, ed. by Sir F. W. Pollock (London: Harper, 1875) p. 657.

7 Appendix XX-B 'Address to the Garrick Club', 23 April 1860, *Letters and Private Papers of W. M. Thackeray*, ed. by Harden, II, 1419.

8 'Letter to William Howard Russell', 7 July 1858, *Letters and Private Papers*, VII, 599.

9 Smith, *To China and Back*, p. 6.

10 Lascars referred to sailors from the Indian subcontinent; 'seedy-boys' were East African Muslim crewmen, usually from Zanzibar or Mombasa; Cingalese is an archaic spelling of Sinhalese (the majority ethnic group on Sri Lanka, then Ceylon); I have been unable to trace the origin of the term 'Simale-boys - it may refer to Somali crewmen, but the word 'Somali' was already in usage by the 1850s.

11 *To China and Back*, p. 49.

12 Reproduced in 'Handbill for Mr. Albert Smith's Mont Blanc to China', EXEBD128882, Bill Douglas Cinema Museum.

13 Anglo-Indian in this context does not refer to people of mixed European and Indian descent, who at this time were usually referred to as 'Eurasians', but to people of British or other European descent born in India. As we will see, Smith regarded them – whether with justification or not – as collectively the most hidebound, conceited, and arrogant people he had come across anywhere.

14 William Howard Russell, *My Diary in India*, 2 vols (London: Routledge, Warne, and Routledge, 1860), II, 255.

15 'Smith, Albert Richard. A.L.S. to 'Billy' [Sir William Howard Russell], London, Feb 1860', in The Henry W. and Albert Berg Collection of English and American Literature, The New York Public Library Astor, Lenox and Tilden Foundations.

16 Yates, *Recollections and Experiences*, II, 49.

17 Yates, *Recollections and Experiences*, II, 50.

18 'Egyptian Hall: Albert Smith's China', *Morning Chronicle*, 23 December 1858.

19 EXEBD128882, Bill Douglas Cinema Museum.

20 Goodman, p. 230.

21 'The China Times', in 'Playhouses, theatres, and other places of public amusement in London and its suburbs from the reign of Queen Elizabeth to William IV, 8 Volumes, VIII, Garrick Club Library.

22 EXEBD128882, Bill Douglas Cinema Museum.

23 'Mr. Albert Smith', *Morning Post*, 23 December 1858, p. 5; 'Mr. Albert Smith', *The Standard*, 23 December 1858, p. 3.

24 'Egyptian Hall – Albert Smith's China and the Celestials', *The Era*, 26 December 1858.

25 *The Amberley Papers: Bertrand Russell's Family Background*, 2 vols, ed. by Bertrand and Patricia Russell (London: George Allen & Unwin, 1937), I, 57.

26 Yates, 'Bygone Shows', p. 642.

27 The phrases are from Goodman, p. 231, and from Smith's *Lancet* obituary: 'The Last Hours of Mr. Albert Smith', *The Lancet*, June 1860, p. 555.

28 'Last Hours', *The Lancet*.

29 There are numerous accounts of the Ellen Ternan affair and its aftermath. I have paraphrased those given by Michael Slater in *The Great Charles Dickens Scandal* (New Haven, CT & London: Yale University Press 2012) and *Dickens and Women* (London: J. M. Dent, 1983) and by Patrick Leary in *The Punch Brotherhood*.

30 'Letter to Albert Smith', 14 February, 1860, *Letters of Charles Dickens*, IX, 214.

31 'Letter to Albert Smith', 15 February, 1860, *Letters of Charles Dickens*, IX, 214.

32 A copy of the will is in Chertsey Museum.

33 Yates, *Recollections and Experiences*, p. 153. Smith introduced Yates to his future wife, Louise Wilkinson, daughter of the founder of the Wilkinson Sword razor blades manufacturer, during a visit to a diorama of the Holy Land at St. George's Gallery, Hyde Park Corner. He was best man at their wedding: *Recollections*, p. 168.

34 Yates, *Recollections*, p. 52.

CONCLUSION

1   Maggie B. B. Gale & Viv Gardner, *Women, Theatre and Performance: New Histories, New Historiographies* (Manchester: Manchester University Press, 2000), p. 32fn.

2   Altick, p 505.

3   Egyptian Hall file, 1845-1873, V&A Theatre Archive.

4   The evidence for precisely when the Hall was demolished is somewhat contradictory. The V&A Theatre Archive has a pencil drawing by Sir Muirhead Bone of its demolition dated 1904, but a handbill dated Christmas 1904 seems to indicate that it was still standing then and was due to be demolished in 1905: Colin Sorensen Collection, THM/197, V&A Theatre Archive.

5   Whymper died in Chamonix in 1911, at the age of 71.

6   Smith, *Story of Mont Blanc*, p. 207.

7   This is not such of a stretch of the imagination as it might seem. As early as 1869 Stephen was referring to 'the whole cockney tribe, whether of English, American or German variety', suggesting that the word's definition had been expanded to include just about anyone, of any nationality, of whom Steven disapproved: Leslie Stephen, Letter to Charles Eliot Norton, 23 June 1869, in Bicknell, I, 70.

8   Bernard Crick, 'Orwell and Biography', *London Review of Books*, 4 (7 October 1982), 22-24.

SELECT BIBLIOGRAPHY

'Mr. Albert Smith', *Athenaeum*, 1700 (26 May, 1860), 719

The Peasants of Chamouni: Containing an Attempt to Reach the Summit of Mont Blanc, and a Delineation of the Scenery Among the Alps (London: Baldwin, Cradock, and Joy, 1823)

à Beckett, Arthur William, *The à Becketts of Punch* (London: Archibald Constable,1903)

Adrian, A. A., *Mark Lemon, The First Editor of Punch* (London: Oxford University Press, 1966)

Altick, Richard D., *The Shows of London* (Cambridge, MA. & London: Belknap Press of Harvard University Press, 1978)

Atkins, John Black, *The Life of Sir William Howard Russell, C.V.O., LL.D., The First Special Correspondent*, 2 vols (London: John Murray, 1911)

Auldjo, John, *Narrative of an Ascent to the Summit of Mont Blanc, on the eighth and ninth of August, 1827* 3rd edition (1828: London: Longman, Green, Brown, and Longmans, 1856)

Band, George, *Summit: 150 Years of the Alpine Club* (London: HarperCollins, 2006)

Beattie, Andrew, *The Alps: A Cultural History* (Oxford: Signal Books, 2006)

Bevin, Darren, *Cultural Climbs: John Ruskin, Albert Smith and the Alpine Aesthetic* (Saarbrucken: DVM, 2010)

Black, Barbara, *A Room of One's Own: A Literary-Cultural Study of Victorian Clubland* (Athens, Ohio: University of Ohio Press, 2012)

Brake, Laurel and Demoor, Marysa, eds, *Dictionary of Nineteenth-Century Journalism in Great Britain and Ireland* (Gent and London: Academia Press & British Library, 2009)

Clark, Ronald, *The Victorian Mountaineers* (London: B. T. Batsford, 1953)

Colley, Ann C.. Victorians in the Mountains: Sinking the Sublime (Farnham, Surrey: Ashgate, 2010)

Comment, Bernard, *The Panorama* (London: Reaktion Books, 1999)

Cross, Nigel, *The Common Writer: Life in Nineteenth-Century Grub Street* (Cambridge: Cambridge University Press, 1985)

DeBeer, Gavin, *Early Travellers in the Alps* (1930; New York: October House, 1967)

DeBeer, Gavin and Brown, Thomas Graham, *The First Ascent of Mont Blanc* (London: Oxford University Press, 1957)

Dickens, Charles, *The Speeches of Charles Dickens* (London: Michael Joseph, 1937)

Edwards, P.D., *Dickens' 'Young Men': George Augustus Sala, Edmund Yates and the World of Victorian Journalism* (Aldershot: Ashgate, 1977)

Engel, Claire Eliane, *A History of Mountaineering in the Alps* (London: George Allen & Unwin, 1950)

Ferguson, Robert, *Swiss Men and Swiss Mountains* (London: Longman, Brown, Green, and Longmans, 1853)

Fitzsimons, Raymund, *The Baron of Piccadilly: The Travels and Entertainments of Albert Smith, 1816-1860* (London: Geoffrey Bles, 1967)

Fleming, Fergus, *Killing Dragons: The Conquest of the Alps* (London: Granta, 2000)

Gernsheim, Alison and Helmut, *L. J. M. Daguerre: The History of the Diorama and the Daguerrotype* (New York: Dover Publications, 1968)

Goodman, Walter, *The Keeleys, On the Stage and at Home* (London: Richard Bentley, 1895)

Hankinson, Alan, *Man of Wars: William Howard Russell of* The Times (London: Heinemann, 1982)

Hansen, Peter, 'British Mountaineering, 1850-1914' (unpublished doctoral dissertation, Harvard University, 1991)

————, 'Albert Smith, the Alpine Club, and the Invention of Mountaineering in Mid-Victorian Britain', *Journal of British Studies*, 34 (1995), 300-24

————, *The Summits of Modern Man: Mountaineering after the Enlightenment* (Cambridge MA & London: Harvard University Press, 2013)

Hodder, Edwin, *John Macgregor, 'Rob Roy'* (London: Hodder Brothers, 1894)

Hodder, George, *Memories of my Time* (London: Tinsley Brothers, 1870)

Honour, Hugh, 'Curiosities of the Egyptian Hall', *Country Life*, 115 (January 1954), 38-9

House, Madeline, Storey, Graham, Tillotson, Kathleen, eds, *The Letters of Charles Dickens*, The Pilgrim Edition, 12 vols (Oxford: Clarendon Press, 1965-2002)

Huhtamo, Erkki, *Illusions in Motion: Media Archaeology of the Moving Panorama and Related Spectacles* (Cambridge, MA: M.I.T. Books, 2013)

Hyde, Ralph, *Panoramania: The Art and Entertainment of the 'All-Embracing' View* (London: Trefoil Publications/Barbican Art Gallery, 1998)

Irving, R. L. G., *A History of British Mountaineering* (London: B. T. Batsford, 1955)

Jerrold, Walter, *Douglas Jerrold and 'Punch'* (London: Macmillan, 1910)

Kember, Joe, 'The View from the Top of Mont Blanc: The Alpine Entertainment in Victorian Britain', *Living Pictures (The Journal of the Popular and Projected Image before 1914)*, 2 (2003), 21-45

Kinglake, Alexander William, *Eothen, or Traces of Travel Brought Home from the East* (London: John Ollivier, 1844)

Lambourne, Lionel, *Victorian Painting* (London: Phaidon, 1991)

Leary, Patrick, *The Punch Brotherhood: Table Talk and Print Culture in Mid-Victorian London* (London: British Library, 2010)

Lennox, Lord William Pitt, *Celebrities I Have Known*, 2 vols (London: Hurst and Blackett, 1877)

Lunn, Arnold, *A Century of Mountaineering, 1857-1957* (London: George Allen & Unwin, 1957)

Macfarlane, Robert, *Mountains of the Mind* (London: Granta, 2008)

Mathews, Charles Edward, *The Annals of Mont Blanc* (London: T. Fisher Unwin, 1898)

Mayhew, Athol, *A Jorum of 'Punch'* (London: Downey & Co., 1895)

Milner, C. Douglas, *Mont Blanc and the Aiguilles* (London: Robert Hale, 1955)

Mullen, Richard and Munson, James, *The Smell of the Continent: The British Discover Europe, 1814-1914* (London: Macmillan, 2009)

Mumm, A. L., *The Alpine Club Register, 1857-1863* (London: Edward Arnold, 1923)

Neate, Jill, *Mountaineering Literature: A Bibliography of Material Published in English* (Milnthorpe, Cumbria: Cicerone Press, 1998)

Oettermann, Stephen, *The Panorama: History of a Mass Medium* (New York: Zone Books, 1997)

Philips, Francis, *A Reading Party in Switzerland, with an account of the ascent of Mont Blanc, on the 12th and 13th August, 1851* (Manchester: privately printed, 1851)

Ray, Gordon N., ed, *The Letters and Private Papers of William Makepeace Thackeray*, 4 vols (London: Oxford University Press, 1945-6)

————, *Thackeray: The Age of Wisdom, 1847-1863* (London: Oxford University Press, 1958)

Ring, Jim, *How the English Made the Alps* (London: John Murray, 2000)

Sala, George Augustus, *The Life and Adventures of George Augustus Sala, Written by Himself*, 2 vols (London: Cassell, 1895)

Schama, Simon, *Landscape and Memory* (New York: Alfred A. Knopf, 1995)

Simkin, Mike, 'Albert Smith: A Nineteenth-Century Showman', *New Magic Lantern Journal*, 4 (1986), 68-71

Spielmann, *The History of Punch* (London: Cassell & Company, 1895)

Stedman Jones, Gareth, 'The "cockney" and the nation, 1780-1988', in *Metropolis London: Histories and Representations since 1800*, ed. by David Feldman and Gareth Stedman Jones (London and New York: Routledge, 1989), pp. 271-324

Sutherland Edwards, H., *Personal Recollections* (London: Cassell, 1900)

Taylor, D. J., *Thackeray* (London: Chatto & Windus, 1999)

Thompson, Simon, *Unjustifiable Risk: The Story of British Climbing* (Milnthorpe, Cumbria: Cicerone, 2010)

Thorington, J. Monroe, *Mont Blanc Sideshow: The Life and Times of Albert Smith* (Philadelphia: John C. Winston Company, 1934)

Timbs, John, *Curiosities of London* (London: Virtue & Co., 1855)

————, *Anecdote Lives of the Later Wits and Humourists*, 2 vols (London: Richard Bentley, 1874), II

Titmarsh, A. M. (W. M. Thackeray), *Notes of Journey from Cornhill to Grand Cairo* (London: Chapman and Hall, 1846)

Unsworth, Walt, *Savage Snows: The Story of Mont Blanc* (London: Hodder & Stoughton, 1986)

————, *Hold the Heights: The Foundations of Mountaineering* (London: Hodder & Stoughton, 1993)

Vizetelly, Henry, *Glances Back Through Seventy Years*, 2 vols (London: Kegan Paul, 1893), I

Warburton, Eliot, *The Crescent and the Cross: or, Romance and Realities of Eastern Travel* (London: Henry Colburn, 1845)

Whymper, Edward, *Chamonix and the Range of Mont Blanc* (London: John Murray, 1896)

White, Jerry, 'Unsentimental Traveller: The London Novels of Albert Smith', *The London Journal*, Vol. 32, Number 1 (March 2007), 29-51

Williams, Montagu, *Leaves of a Life*, 2 vols (London: Macmillan, 1890)

Yates, Edmund, *The Business of Pleasure* (London: Chapman and Hall, 1865)

——————, *His Recollections and Experiences*, 2 vols (London: Richard Bentley, 1885)

——————, *Fifty Years of London Life* (New York: Harper & Brothers, 1885)

——————, 'Bygone Shows', *Fortnightly Review*, 39 (Jan-June, 1886), 633-47

Selected Works by Albert Smith

Articles, serializations, and books

'A Rencontre with the Brigands', *Bentley's Miscellany*, 9 (1841), 375-81

'The Armourer of Paris: A Romance of the Fifteenth Century', *London Saturday Journal*, 2 (1842)

'Curiosities of Medical Experience', *Punch, or The London Charivari*, 2 (Jan-June, 1842), 145-46

'Physiology of the London Idler', *Punch, or The London Charivari*, 3 (July-Dec, 1842), 5

Adventures of Jack Holyday, With Something About his Sister (London: William S. Orr, 1844)

The Adventures of Mr. Ledbury and His Friend Jack Johnson (London: Richard Bentley, 1844)

The London Medical Student and Curiosities of Medical Experience (London: Carey and Hart, 1845)

The Fortunes of the Scattergood Family (London: Richard Bentley, 1845)

The Marchioness of Brinvilliers: The Poisoner of the Seventeenth Century. A Romance of Old Paris (London: Richard Bentley, 1846)

The Natural History of Stuck-Up People (London: David Bogue, 1847)

The Natural History of the Gent (London: David Bogue, 1847)

The Natural History of the Ballet-Girl (London: David Bogue, 1847)

'A Go-Ahead Day with Barnum', *Bentley's Miscellany*, 21 (1847), 522-27 and 623-28

'Ascent of Mr. Green's Balloon from Cremorne Gardens', *Illustrated London News*, 12 June 1847, p. 379

'Lord Mayor's Day', *Bentley's Miscellany*, 24 (1848), 603-08

The Man in the Moon (co-edited with Angus Reach, 1847-49)

The Social Parliament: Act the First (London: David Bogue, 1848)

Comic Sketches from the Wassail-Bowl (London: Richard Bentley, 1848)

Why Our Theatres are Not Supported (London: Kent and Richards, 1848)

A Bowl of Punch (London: Richard Bentley, 1848)

A Pottle of Strawberries, to Beguile a Short Journey, or a Long Half Hour (London: David Bogue, 1848)

The Struggles and Adventures of Christopher Tadpole (London: Richard Bentley, 1848)

Natural History of the Idler upon the Town (London: David Bogue, 1848)

The Natural History of the Flirt (London: David Bogue, 1848)

'Recollections of a Cheap Tour', *Bentley's Miscellany*, 24 (1848), 408-16 and 484-91

'Lord Mayor's Day', *Bentley's Miscellany*, 24 (1848), 603-8

'How I got away from Paris after the Rebellion in June', *Bentley's Miscellany*, 24 (1848), 210-16

Natural History of Evening Parties (London: David Bogue, 1849)

Gavarni in London: Sketches of Life and Character (London: David Bogue, 1849)

The Pottleton Legacy: A Story of Town and Country Life (London: David Bogue, 1849)

'The Panoramania', *Illustrated London News*, 25 May, 1850, p. 363.

The Town and Country Miscellany (London, 1850)

A Month at Constantinople (London: David Bogue, 1850)

The Month: A View of Passing Subjects and Manners, Home and Foreign, Social and General (1851)

Pictures of Life at Home and Abroad (London: Richard Bentley, 1852)

The Story of Mont Blanc (London: David Bogue, 1853)

Press Orders: The Opinions of The Leading Journals on the Abolition of Newspaper Privileges (London: W. Kent, 1853)

The English Hotel Nuisance (London: David Bryce, 1855)

'Theatrical Ashes', *Household Words*, 13 (1856), 217-20

To China and Back: Being a Diary Kept, Out and Home (London: Chapman and Hall, 1859)

Wild Oats and Dead Leaves (London: Chapman and Hall, 1860)

Plays (some of these were jointly written or adapted from existing plays)

Blanche Heriot, or The Chertsey Curfew (1842)

The Revolt of Bruges (1842)

The Pearl of Chamouni (1843)

Cherry and Fairstar (1844)

Valentine and Orson (1844)

Whittington and his Cat (1845)

The Cricket on the Hearth (1845)

The Enchanted Horse (1845)

Hop-O'-My Thumb, or The Seven League Boots: A Romance of Nursery History (1846)

The Battle of Life (1846)

The Headsman (1849)

Esmerelda (1850)

Alhambra (1851)

Novelty Fair (1851)

Harlequin Guy Fawkes (1855)

ACKNOWLEDGEMENTS

As the following list suggests, the kindness and helpfulness I have met with from so many busy people in the course of writing this book has been humbling. If I have inadvertently left anyone out, I sincerely apologise.

This project began life in 2009 as a dissertation at Birkbeck, University of London. Dr. Ana Parejo Vadillo's advice on and supervision of the dissertation were invaluable, and I would like to pay tribute to all the staff on Birkbeck's wonderful Victorian Studies M.A. course. I would also like to thank Dr. Tanya Izzard for her work on indexing the book, and my publisher, Dr. Catherine Pope, for her encouragement, advice, and patience with a much-delayed manuscript.

While carrying out further research I have been greatly assisted by the staff of the British Library, the London Library, the National Library of Scotland in Edinburgh, the Bodleian Library, Oxford, the Sydney Jones Library at the University of Liverpool (particularly Lorna Goudie of the Special Collections and Archives section), and the staff of the V&A Performance Reading Room, particularly Simon Sladen; by Dr. Phil Wickham and his staff at the Bill Douglas Cinema Museum at the University of Exeter; and by Dr. Isaac Gewirtz and Lyndsi Barnes of the Berg Collection of the New York Public Library.

As well as two previous biographies of Albert Smith, written by J. Monroe Thorington and Raymund Fitzsimons in the 1930s and 1960s respectively, more recent work on Smith has been published by Simon Schama, Peter Hansen, Darren Bevin, Mike Simkin, Jerry White, Ralph Hyde, Ann C. Colley, and Erkki Huhtamo. Each of these sources has been valuable, and I hope I have given adequate credit in the text or footnotes whenever they have been cited. I contacted several of these writers during my own research, and they invariably responded with great kindness and generosity. Professor Hansen, of Worcester Polytechnic Institute, Massachusetts, provided me with a number of contacts and helpful suggestions for tracking down material relating to Smith, particularly in the United States. Jerry White, Visiting Professor at Birkbeck, generously invited me to his home and allowed me to browse and quote from his extensive collection of material on Smith, not to mention driving me to and from his local train station and providing me with lunch. I was received with the same hospitality by Mike and Theresa Simkin when I visited their home to view Mike's collection of Smith material and memorabilia, as well as his renowned Phantasmagoria Museum.

Sally Gilbert, Archivist of Merchant Taylors' School, and Annie Lindsay, Trust Archivist and Records Manager, UCLH NHS Foundation Trust, were both very helpful in responding to queries about Albert Smith's school days and his time as a medical student at Middlesex Hospital respectively.

Many thanks are due to Glyn Hughes, Hon. Archivist of the Alpine Club, and Tadeusz Hudowski, Librarian of the Alpine Club. I would also like to pay tribute to the collective knowledge of the Victoria online discussion list, founded and managed by Patrick Leary. Over the years I have submitted a number of queries to this invaluable forum, including several relating to this book, and have always been struck by the helpfulness and erudition of its members.

I would also like to thank Russ Taylor of the Harold B. Lee Library at Brigham Young University, Utah; Marcus Risdell, Curator of the Garrick Club Library & Collections; Margaret Hunt and Doris Neville-Davies of Chertsey Museum; Bernadette Tsuda of the Office de Tourisme de Chamonix; Alexia Lazou of the Magic Lantern Society; and Lucinda Moore of the Mary Evans Picture Library.

Thanks also to Dr. John Cooper of Exeter University for his help with the illustrations; to Robin Healey for kindly contacting me and inviting me to visit his home and view letters by Albert Smith in his possession; and to Al Murray (one of the incidental joys of researching this book has been the discovery that the man best known in Britain as 'The Pub Landlord' also happens to be the executor of the Thackeray literary estate).

Leslie Stephen wrote in 1871 that the best way to describe his own Alpine ascents would be to say that his guides had 'succeeded in performing a feat requiring skill, strength, and courage, the difficulty of which was much increased by the difficulty of taking with him his knapsack and his employer'. Stephen, an accomplished mountaineer in his own right, was being modest. I am not when I echo his words by saying that my own ascent of Mont Blanc over 160 years after Smith's would have been unthinkable without the skill, experience, and guidance of Chamonix mountain guide Stuart Macdonald. The same applies to our climbs on the Tour Ronde and the Arête de Rochefort, and equally to my time with Mark Thomas on the Aiguille du Midi later that same week.

Finally, thanks as always to Sally for her support, encouragement, and love.

ABOUT THE AUTHOR

Alan McNee is a former journalist. He has a Master's degree in Victorian Studies and a PhD from Birkbeck, University of London. *The Cockney Who Sold the Alps* is his first book. He lives in London.

INDEX

Page references in bold indicate an illustration; page references in italics indicate a note.

Victorian Secrets

The Perfect Man: The Muscular Life and Times of Eugen Sandow, Victorian Strongman by David Waller

Eugen Sandow (1867-1925) was the Victorian Arnold Schwarzenegger – a world-famous celebrity, and possessor of what was then considered to be the most perfect male body. He rose from obscurity in Prussia to become a music-hall sensation in late-Victorian London, going on to great success as a performer in North America and throughout the British Empire.

Written with humour and insight into the popular culture of late-Victorian England, Waller's book argues that Sandow deserves to be resurrected as a significant cultural figure whose life, like that of Oscar Wilde, tells us a great deal about sexuality and celebrity at the *fin de siècle*.

"Hugely entertaining ... Waller skillfully places Sandow within the context of the age." Juliet Nicolson, *The Evening Standard*

"Waller...furnishes a narrative rich in stories reflecting Victorian life." Valerie Grove, *The Times*

"Waller's lively, colourful and fascinating book should help restore interest in an unjustly forgotten icon." Miranda Seymour - *The Daily Telegraph*

ISBN: 978-1-906469-25-2 (also available in a Kindle edition)

www.victoriansecrets.co.uk

Victorian Secrets

Hope and Glory: A Life of Dame Clara Butt
by Maurice Leonard

"Maurice Leonard has a gift for creating character and embroidering it with the most wonderful anecdotes and perceptions." *Jilly Cooper*

Dame Clara Butt (1872-1936) was one of the most celebrated singers of the Victorian and Edwardian eras, a symbol of the glory of a Britain on whose Empire the sun never set. Standing an Amazonian 6'2" tall, Clara had a glorious contralto voice of such power that when she sang in Dover, Sir Thomas Beecham swore she could be heard in Calais. A friend of the royal family, Clara was made a Dame in recognition of her sterling work during the First World War. Her rousing performances of *Land of Hope and Glory* brought the nation together and raised thousands of pounds for charity.

Filling concert halls throughout the world, Clara was one of the first singers to undertake international tours, visiting Canada, Australia, New Zealand, South Africa, and Japan. She travelled with an entourage of over twenty people who fulfilled her every need. Her demands were many, but Clara never failed to delight her adoring audiences. At the height of her career, Clara was locked in rivalry with the celebrated soprano Nellie Melba, almost ending in a libel case when Clara wrote her memoirs.

In the first biography since her death, Maurice Leonard tells Dame Clara Butt's remarkable story, from humble beginnings in Sussex, to her dazzling apotheosis by an adoring nation. With humour and insight, Leonard reveals the woman behind the cultural icon.

ISBN: 978-1-906469-25-2 (also available in a Kindle edition)

www.victoriansecrets.co.uk

Lightning Source UK Ltd.
Milton Keynes UK
UKOW06f1819190515

251889UK00014B/546/P